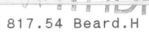

Also by Henry Beard
(*as author or coauthor*)

THE OFFICIAL POLITICALLY CORRECT DICTIONARY AND HANDBOOK
FRENCH FOR CATS
ADVANCED FRENCH FOR EXCEPTIONAL CATS
LATIN FOR ALL OCCASIONS
LATIN FOR EVEN MORE OCCASIONS
THE BOOK OF SEQUELS
MULLIGAN'S LAWS
THE OFFICIAL EXCEPTIONS TO THE RULES OF GOLF
MISS PIGGY'S GUIDE TO LIFE
SAILING:
A Sailor's Dictionary
FISHING:
An Angler's Dictionary
GOLFING:
A Duffer's Dictionary
SKIING:
A Skier's Dictionary
THE PENTAGON CATALOG

•

Also by Christopher Cerf
(*as author or coauthor*)

THE OFFICIAL POLITICALLY CORRECT DICTIONARY AND HANDBOOK
THE GULF WAR READER
THE BOOK OF SEQUELS
THE EXPERTS SPEAK
THE PENTAGON CATALOG
SMALL FIRES
THE 80s: A LOOK BACK
(published in 1979)
THE WORLD'S LARGEST CHEESE

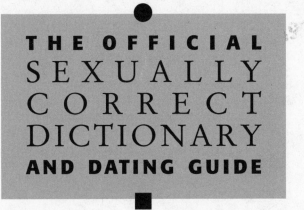

# THE OFFICIAL
# SEXUALLY
# CORRECT
# DICTIONARY
# AND DATING GUIDE

# THE OFFICIAL SEXUALLY CORRECT DICTIONARY AND DATING GUIDE

HENRY BEARD AND CHRISTOPHER CERF

*Produced in Conjunction with The American Gender Society*

Designed by ROBERT BULL DESIGN

Contributing Illustrators:
LAUREN ATTINELLO AND RUSS HEATH

VILLARD BOOKS | NEW YORK
1995

VILLARD BOOKS is a registered trademark of Random House, Inc.

Grateful acknowledgment is made to the following for permission to
reprint previously published material:

ALAN HAMILTON: Excerpts from an essay by Alan Hamilton that appeared
on the Internet. For further information, please contact the Bisexual
Resource Center, P.O. Box 639, Cambridge, MA 02140. Reprinted by
permission.

INTERNATIONAL CREATIVE MANAGEMENT: Excerpt from "Inward, Ho!" by
Doug Stanton, from the October 1991 issue of *Esquire*. Copyright © 1991
by Doug Stanton. Reprinted by permission of International Creative
Management.

Library of Congress Cataloging-in-Publication Data
Beard, Henry.
      The official sexually correct dictionary and dating guide / Henry
   Beard and Christopher Cerf.—1st ed.
          p.      cm.
      ISBN 0-679-75641-8
      1. Wit and humor, American.   2. Euphemism—Humor.   3. Language
and culture—Humor.   4. Dating (Social customs)—Humor.   I. Cerf,
Christopher.   II. Title.
PN6162.B373     1995
818'.5402—dc20    94-36542

Manufactured in the United States of America
98765432
First Edition

For Catharine and Jeffrey and Andrea and John,
who showed us that
"the mythic celebration of female negation"
conquers all,
and
Dr. Shepherd Bliss,
who taught us to root our bodies to the ground
with our proud serpents' tails

"Romance . . . is rape embellished with meaningful looks."
—ANDREA DWORKIN, *"The Night and Danger"*

# Everything You Always Wanted to Know About Sex*
## (*but were afraid you'd be arrested for asking)

If you're a man, and a beautiful woman made a pass at you, would you respond? If you're a woman, and a man invited you to a candle-light dinner or told you he "likes your outfit," would you think twice before reporting him to the police? If you're a male professor, would you consider making eye contact with your female students, or, for that matter, *not* making eye contact with them? Do you think it's permissible to use the words "man" or "woman" or "male" or "female" at all?

If you answered "yes" to even one of these questions, then frankly there's no way you can survive in the be-sensitive-or-else nineties without reading—and committing to memory—the advice we've gathered for you in *The Official Sexually Correct Dictionary*. Indeed, this handy encyclopedia of dating don'ts and don'ts may be all that stands between you and the unwitting perpetration of a serious crime, the unconscious betrayal of your own gender, or both.

Plainly, in an age in which lip licking, hand holding in public, and leaving one's newspaper open to a page on which a bra advertisement appears have been outlawed as harassment, and the very act of *asking* for sexual consent is considered a sex crime, once-celebrated gurus such as Kinsey, Masters and Johnson, and Shere Hite are pitifully out-of-date. What's needed are *new* authorities who have painstakingly read the sexual harassment policies of hundreds of educational institutions and corporations; who have patiently consulted the world's leading gender reconciliation facilitators, less-dangerous sex specialists, designated sober monitors, and sexual offense advocates; and who have sifted through all the latest academic works on sex and gender.

Pardon our immodesty, but we are those new authorities. And, in *The Official Sexually Correct Dictionary,* we'll tell you precisely what you can do, where you can do it, what to call it, whom you can do it with, and what they'll do to you if you try.

If you get the idea that your sexual options are somewhat more limited than they might have been just a few years back, you're right. But all is not lost. Intercourse, and even dating, may be out of the question, but the visionaries quoted in our book have come up with some truly wonderful activities to replace them. In *The Official Sexually Correct Dictionary,* you'll learn how to (and why you should):

- tie yourself to the top of a tree
- make contact with the Cro-Magnon man within your psyche
- regain your lost virginity
- participate in a condom relay race
- dress up like a gorilla or pretend to be a dolphin

And much, much more!

So please accept our best wishes for happy and instructive reading. In the meantime, don't eat provocatively. Don't read Shakespeare or Byron. Don't use male pronouns. Don't wear an obscene hat.

And, wherever you are, whatever you do, never, never take "yes" for an answer. "Yes" means "no."

HENRY BEARD and CHRISTOPHER CERF

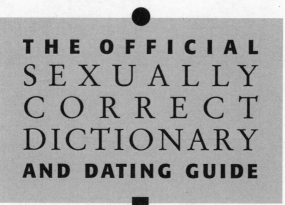

# THE OFFICIAL
# SEXUALLY
# CORRECT
# DICTIONARY
# AND DATING GUIDE

# A

**acquaintance rape.** Andrea Parrot and Laurie Bechhofer, editors of an influential book on acquaintance rape, define it as "nonconsensual sex between adults who know each other"—a category which, according to a training manual distributed at Swarthmore College, spans "a spectrum of incidents and behaviors ranging from crimes legally defined as rape to verbal harassment and inappropriate innuendo."[1] Parrot and Bechhofer call acquaintance rape "the hidden crime" because a woman who survives it frequently does not "label her experience as such." The extent of this "hiddenness" is illustrated by the fact that in the four years after Ellen Doherty, a rape counselor at St. Luke's–Roosevelt Hospital near Columbia University in New York City, identified acquaintance rape as "the single largest problem on college campuses today," not one single rape appeared on the logs of the Columbia security department.[2]

**aesthetic appreciation.** A form of workplace sexual harassment that Kenneth C. Cooper, a widely quoted authority on the subject, defines as the "nonaggressive" expression, by a male manager, of his appreciation for a female employee's "physical or sexual features." As an example of this all-too-infrequently punished offense, Cooper cites the case of an alleged perpetrator's saying to a coworker: "Gee..." sigh "...You're looking better every day!"[3] See also: **lookism; mental groping**.

*Princess Grace of Monaco, an* **aesthetic appreciation** *survivor.*

**affection, public displays of.** A couple contemplating kissing or holding hands in public should be advised that the Minnesota Department of Education has issued guidelines warning the state's public school students not to engage in "displays of affection in hallways," on the grounds that such displays "may offend others" and are "heterosexist."[4] See also: **heterosexism.**

**ageism.** Discrimination by the white-male-dominated culture against the longer-living, typified, for example, by men's tendency to favor younger women over older ones as their sexual partners.[5] See also: **aging; beauty myth.**

**aging.** The reason men have proclaimed aging in women to be "unbeautiful," Naomi Wolf informs us in *The Beauty Myth,* is that "women grow more powerful with time," and would therefore pose a greater threat to masculine institutional dominance if their influence were not artificially diminished.[6] See also: **beauty myth.**

**alcohol.** Alcohol, psychologists Barry R. Burkhart and Mary Ellen Fromuth warn us, increases the frequency of "sexually coercive misbehavior" in two important ways: (1) It is "used by men to compromise women's ability to resist"; and (2) It is a "disinhibiting cue for males' aggressive conduct."[7] With this in mind, women may be wise to heed the following advice on the subject of intoxicating beverages from Josh McDowell, author of *It Can Happen to You: What You Need to Know About Preventing and Recovering from Date Rape:* "Stay away from these substances yourself, and stay away from the men who use them."[8] See also: **drinking and penile driving; offering a woman a drink.**

**allowing oneself to be seduced.** See: **receptive noninitiation.**

**alternative body image.** A nonlookist, nonsizeist term useful for describing the appearance presented by individuals who, to quote *The Feminist Dictionary,* "weigh more than the fashion, entertainment, and health industries say is appropriate."[9] Example: *Vanessa's favorite sexually correct Bill Cosby character was* **Alternative-Body-Imaged** *Albert.*

**androcide.** Valerie Solanas, legendary founder of the Society for Cutting Up Men (SCUM), argued persuasively in her classic *SCUM Manifesto* that the most efficient way of ridding the world of male domination would be to eliminate the men themselves. In what is now hailed as a landmark moment in political theater, she dramatically began the process of translating her words into deeds by shooting (but failing to kill) pop artist Andy Warhol.[10] See also: **gynocide; murder.**

**androgynous love.** People who play the role of a "man" or "woman" when they relate to a sex partner, or who insist that gender is an important criterion when deciding whom to date, will never find "ideal" love, according to University of Massachusetts philosopher Ann Ferguson. The problem, Ferguson explains in her groundbreaking essay "Androgyny as an Ideal for Human Development," is that ideal love would be "love between equals," but, because the feminine role "taught in our society" makes women "less powerful and less free than the masculine role makes men," such equality, and therefore such love, is by definition unattainable. But Ferguson foresees a more cheerful future: "[With the] disappearance, in an overpopulated world, of any biological need for sex to be associated with procreation," she writes, "it would no longer matter what biological sex individuals had. Love relationships, and the sexual relationships developing out of them, would be based on the individual meshing-together of androgynous human beings."[11] (Note: After "Androgyny as an Ideal for Human Development" was published, Jan Raymond pointed out that "androgyny" was an unacceptable term because it "puts the male aspect of human nature first, making it primary, and sees the female aspect welded to that as a secondary attribute." In her recent book *Blood at the Root,* Ann Ferguson praises Raymond for this critique. "I now use the term **gynandry** to refer to the type of personal development I earlier called androgyny," Ferguson writes.[12])

**androgyny.** See: **gynandry.**

**anorexia nervosa.** An eating disorder that, to quote Dr. Michael Blumenfield of the New York Medical College, is "characterized by severe and prolonged refusal to eat, extreme weight loss, distorted body image, [and] termination of the menstrual cycle or impotence."[13] Joan Jacobs Brumberg, former director of women's studies at Cornell University, offers the horrifying statistic that 150,000 American women and girls die of anorexia each year—more than three times the annual U.S. death toll from auto accidents. Brumberg places the blame for this epidemic squarely on "a misogynistic society that demeans women . . . by objectifying their bodies,"[14] and Naomi Wolf, who quotes the same 150,000 figure in her book, *The Beauty Myth*, agrees. These multitudes of anonymous young women were "starved not by nature, but by men," Wolf points out. "How," she wonders, "might America react" to a similar "mass self-immolation by hunger" of its favorite *sons*?[15] (Note: After Wolf's book was published, it was revealed that the 150,000-per-year estimate was somewhat exaggerated: According to the National Center for Health Statistics, the actual number of Americans who died of anorexia *and* bulimia in 1991 was 54.[16] But, as any size-acceptance activist will attest, even 54 deaths attributable to the "oppressive gender system" are 54 too many.) See also: **bulimia; size acceptance movement.**

**Antioch Rules.** A landmark collection of regulations governing sexual conduct named after Antioch College, in Yellow Springs, Ohio, where they were first instituted. The basic premise underlying the Antioch Rules—or, more properly, "The Antioch College Sexual Offense Policy"—is that no sexual act is permissible unless and until any party who might be called upon to participate has given her or his "willing and verbal consent." Merely "asking 'do you want to have sex' is not enough," Karen Hall, Antioch's "sexual offense advocate," explained at a consent workshop for first-year male students attended by *The New York Times.* "Each step of the way, you have to ask. If you want to take her blouse off, you have to ask. If you want to touch her breast, you have to ask. If you want to move your hand down to her genitals, you have to ask. If you want to put your hand inside her, you have to ask." Furthermore, Hall told her listeners, "consent is not meaningful" if the woman who gives it is under the influence of drugs (prescription or recreational) or alcohol. Or, as *Newsweek* correspondent Sarah Crichton puts it: "If she's drunk, she's not mentally there, and her consent counts for zip."[17] See also: **continuum theories; sexual consent forms; verbal rape.**

**Antioch Rules, uselessness of.** Well intentioned though they may be, the Antioch Rules "don't get rid of the problem of unwanted sex at all," lamented *The New Yorker* in a November 1993 "Comment" piece. "By not merely recommending but actually mandating chatter during foreplay," the magazine argued, the rules simply shift the advantage in obtaining nonvoluntary sexual compliance "from the muscle-bound frat boy to the honey-tongued French major."[18]

Remembrance of Things Past, *a potential tool for obtaining nonvoluntary sexual compliance under the* **Antioch Rules.**

**antirape activism, male.** Because "each individual man represents a system in which women and other 'un-men' are exploited, oppressed, dominated, and even killed because they do not belong to the class 'man,'" Rus Ervin Funk tells us in *Stopping Rape: A Challenge for Men*, it's the duty of all men to work tirelessly toward a world where "gender justice" reigns and rape no longer exists. But, Funk cautions, men mustn't count on women to praise them for their efforts. "As one feminist told me when I was first starting [my antirape work]," he recounts, " 'Don't expect applause for taking out the trash. Rape is your trash. I'm not going to pat you on the back for doing what you should have been doing all along.' "[19]

**ape within.** Douglas Gillette, a mythologist and a well-known leader of men's therapy groups, has shown a remarkable ability to convince men that there is "a great male ape" within their psyches in whose animal spirit they must participate if they are to find the "empowerment" necessary to sustain "intimate relationships." Gillette's efforts to persuade women that they should participate in the spirit of the "provocatively yielding female ape" within *their* psyches appear, as of this writing, to be encountering somewhat more resistance.[20] (Note: Acceptance of Gillette's suggestion that women must learn to cooperate with the "instinctual man-woman 'Me Tarzan–You Jane' push" from humankind's "primate past" has also come a bit more slowly than he might have wished.) See also: **Cro-Magnon man within; gorilla, dressing up as a.**

**armpit sex.** The Terrence Higgins Trust, a British AIDS support group, preaches the virtues of "armpit sex" as a "safe and exciting" alternative to the more dangerous "penetrative" varieties of erotic contact.[21]

*An* **armpit.**

**arm touching.** Susan Strauss and Pamela Espeland, authors of *Sexual Harassment and Teens: A Program for Positive Change,* observe ominously that "arm touching" is one of a long list of specific "sexually harassing behaviors" that have been "reported in U.S. high schools."[22]

**art "masterpieces" featuring nude women.** It is no longer appropriate to display in public places art "masterpieces"—perhaps it's no coincidence that the male-dominated art community insists on calling them that!—featuring naked women. Indeed,

Nancy Stumhofer, an English instructor at Penn State University, won an important battle in the war against patriarchy when she convinced university officials that a reproduction of Goya's "The Naked Maja" hanging in her classroom was harassing her and her

students by creating a hostile acade-mic environment. "Any nude pic-ture of a female," Stumhofer argued, "encourages males to make remarks about body parts." The officials removed the offending painting.[23] See also: **nude slides in class presen-tations.**

*"Nude Descending a Staircase":*
*An **art "masterpiece"** that*
*encourages men to make remarks*
*about body parts.*

**asking for a date.** See: dates, asking for.

**autononeroticism.** Male readers who are opposed to masturbation on political or moral grounds, but who are anxious to donate sperm for medical use, will be thrilled to learn of the development of a Vatican-approved vibrating machine that attaches to the testi-cles and, according to the University of the Sacred Heart in Rome, successfully gathers semen in such a way that "components that constitute the masturbation act"—"direct stimulation of the geni-tal organ" and "erotic feelings"—"would seem to be absent."[24]

**backlash.** Susan Faludi describes this phenomenon, in her best-selling book of the same name, as "a powerful counterassault on women's rights . . . an attempt to retract the handful of small and hard-won victories that the feminist movement did manage to win for women." Reminding her readers that *Backlash* was the title of a 1947 movie "in which a man frames his wife for a murder he's committed," Faludi observes that the modern backlash against women's rights works in "much the same way"—"it stands the truth boldly on its head" and "charges feminists with all the crimes" that patriarchal society itself has perpetrated. The backlash is all the more insidious, Faludi points out, because, when "cornered," it simply "denies its own existence." Sadly, Faludi concludes, even such self-professed feminists as Susan Brownmiller, Betty Friedan, and Germaine Greer have been deluded—perhaps through a process of internalized oppression—into becoming agents of the backlash.[25] See also: **internalized oppression**.

**backlash backlash.** A term coined by *The Atlanta Journal and Constitution* to describe what is perhaps the most ingenious aspect of Susan Faludi's backlash theory: that any criticism of it, no matter how mild, can be—and usually is—summarily dismissed as "just another example of backlash."[26]

**bananas.** See: **fructal objectification**.

**baster babies.** A colloquial term for children whose mothers conceived them by artificially inseminating themselves with a turkey baster. Turkey-baster insemination has become particularly popular among prospective mothers who, for personal or political reasons, prefer to remain heterosexually celibate, and who regard reproductive matters as far too private to be shared with the bureaucratic and patriarchal medical establishment.[27] See also: **sperm-egg mixers; turkey-baster insemination; heterosexual celibacy; standing on one's head**.

**beauty.** Although "the West pretends that all ideals of female beauty stem from one Platonic Ideal Woman," Naomi Wolf tells us, the concept of feminine beauty is actually a "social fiction" created to keep women from usurping men's institutional power. Reinforced by powerful, male-controlled institutions such as "the $33-billion-a-year diet industry," the "$20-billion cosmetics industry," "the $300-million cosmetic surgery industry," and "the $7-billion pornography industry," the marketplace is flooded with "hallucinatory" images of "how women should look," Wolf writes. These "formulaic and endlessly reproduced 'beautiful' images" enable the dominant male culture to defend itself by "evading the fact of real women, our faces and voices and bodies." By premising women's identity upon their "beauty," Wolf adds, men insure that "we will remain vulnerable to outside approval, carrying the vital sensitive organ of self-esteem exposed to the air."[28] See also: **cosmetic subjugation; fashion profiteers**.

**beauty myth.** A term coined by Naomi Wolf to describe the "vital lie" that "the quality called 'beauty' objectively and universally exists," that "women must want to embody it and men must want to possess women," that "this embodiment is an imperative for women and not for men," and that this situation is "necessary and natural because it is biological, sexual and evolutionary." "None of this is true," Wolf writes. In actuality, beauty is "a culturally imposed physical standard" that the male-dominated culture uses to force women into an "unnatural" competition for "resources that men have appropriated for themselves."[29]

**Beethoven's Ninth Symphony.** Music lovers who want to demonstrate their solidarity with the

*A woman exercising proper caution while playing* **Beethoven's Ninth Symphony.**

antirape movement should avoid all performances—recorded or live—of Beethoven's Ninth Symphony, the first movement of which, feminist musicologist Susan McClary of the University of Minnesota informs us, contains "one of the most horrifying moments in music." The offending passage is the recapitulation of the principal theme, during which, McClary writes, "the carefully prepared cadence is frustrated, damming up energy which finally explodes in the throttling murderous rage of a rapist incapable of attaining release."[30]

**believing that one is male.** Men may be a bit taken aback to learn from essayist John Stoltenberg that "the belief that one is male, the belief that there is a male sex, the belief that one belongs to it" is merely a "politically constructed idea" designed to allow "people born with penises" to dominate those who weren't. If you're among those who "happen to be penised," however, don't despair: Stoltenberg's books, *Refusing to Be a Man* and *The End of Manhood,* can start you on the road to "gender justice."[31] See also: **essentialism.**

**belly dancing.**  See: **metaphorical harassment.**

**bergamot oil.**  Zsuzsanna Emese Budapest, the first genetic witch in the United States to embrace feminism and the founder of the Susan B. Anthony Coven #1, suggests that wearing bergamot oil on the job can be a good protection against sexual harassment. "When you put on the oil," she advises in her book *The Goddess in the Office,* "visualize a peaceful interaction with your would-be harassers. If they inquire what you are wearing, say it's called 'Strike Back' perfume, the newest thing on the market."[32] See also: **Hot Foot powder; pig's tongue.**

**Big Bang Theory.**  One reason more young women don't choose astronomy as a career, Meg Urry of the Space Telescope and Science Institute told CNN in 1993, is that they are put off by the sexist terminology, such as "Big Bang Theory," used by the males who dominate the field.[33]

**Bill of Rights.** Pornography is such a significant cause of violence to women, Karen Santoriello explained during a "Pornography on Campus" forum sponsored by the University of Massachusetts, that the Bill of Rights, by protecting it, is causing half the U.S. population to "live in danger." "Does the society consider the safety of the First Amendment to be of greater importance than the safety of its people?" she wondered.[34] See also: **Dworkin-MacKinnon Law; First Amendment.**

The **Bill of Rights,** a causative factor in the spread of rape.

**Billy the Kid Sex Workshops.** See: **Cherokee Sex Workshops.**

**binge-purge syndrome.** See: bulimia.

**biophilic energy.** The "life-loving energy" which, according to Boston College **thealogian** Mary Daly, is specific only to women. Men, on the contrary, are characterized by "necrophilic," or death-loving, energy and, as philosopher Marilyn Frye has explained, they need to siphon off women's biophilic energy in order to "go on with what they call living."[35] See: **male parasitism; necrophilic energy; Patriarchal Imperative.**

**biphobia.** Alan Hamilton, author of the *Sexual Identity and Gender Identity Glossary,* defines this as "the oppression or mistreatment of bisexuals, especially by lesbians and gay men."[36]

**bleating.** See: ram, behaving like a.

**blind dates.** When it comes to the subject of blind dates, the advice offered by Josh McDowell, author of *It Can Happen to You: What*

*You Need to Know About Preventing and Recovering from Date Rape,* is unambiguous and uncompromising. "Avoid blind dates," he tells women. "Date only persons you know."[37]

**blowing kisses.** Though experts hail "blowing kisses" as a safer-sex method of expressing affection for one's date or partner, anyone tempted to employ it should be advised that, according to gender-equity authority Susan Strauss, "making kissing sounds or smacking sounds" constitutes sexual harassment.[38]

**blow-up-the-condom-until-it-bursts contests.** See: Condom Olympics.

**blue balls.** If a woman has been engaging in heavy petting with a man and then abruptly stops, warn Charlene Muelenhard and Jennifer Schrag, the man may beg her to continue on the grounds that he'll be left with "blue balls," which they define as "an uncomfortable condition involving testicular congestion resulting from sexual arousal without orgasm." But such entreaties, they point out, are "sexually coercive," and the woman has absolutely no obligation to heed them.[39] Indeed, an increasing number of sexual harassment codes (including the Antioch Sexual Offense Policy) specifically list "sexual coercion" as a punishable offense,[40] and Muelenhard's and Schrag's anthologist, Andrea Parrot, characterizes it as **soft rape.**[41]

**bobbitt.** To sever, "by a less than surgical method," the private parts of a male sexual offender. The term, suggested and defined by Stephen A. All III in a letter reprinted in *Time* magazine, celebrates Lorena Bobbitt's creative response to the abuse inflicted upon her by her husband, John Wayne Bobbitt. (M. Robert Paglee, also quoted in *Time,* prefers the word **bobbittize.**)[42] See also: **bobbittectomy; castration; sociosexual vigilantism.**

**bobbittectomy.** The "swift disarmament"—to use columnist Barbara Ehrenreich's felicitous phrase—of a man who "uses his penis as a weapon."[43] See also: **bobbitt; castration; sociosexual vigilantism.**

**bobbittize.** See: **bobbitt.**

**body development, teasing about.** The Minnesota Department of Education officially lists "teasing other students about body development (either overdevelopment or underdevelopment)" as an example of "hostile environment sexual harassment." As such, it is actionable under the state's anti–sexual harassment law, which covers all public school children, from kindergarten through high school.[44] See also: **breastism.**

**body-image-inclusive dating.** See: size-affirmative dating.

**bottom patting.** See: friendly pats.

**bra advertisements.** Thanks to the courageous ruling of U.S. judge Howell Melton in the case of *Robinson* v. *Jacksonville Shipyards,* it is now officially considered an act of **hostile environment sexual harassment** to leave open on one's desk a newspaper displaying an advertisement in which a woman is seen modeling a bra or panties.[45]

**bra dancing.** As Rus Ervin Funk points out in *Stopping Rape: A Challenge for Men,* one of the great societal injustices created by patriarchy is that "men have the choice of taking off our shirts when we are hot" and women do not.[46] To protest this inequity, a growing cadre of college women are defiantly stripping down to their bras before dancing at campus parties. Some women, however, worry that this is playing into the hands of potential harassers and abusers. "Now tell me, is it not the dead white man's *dream* to go to a party and 'get a free look' at countless women dancing in their bras?" a Hampshire College student named Jenny remarked in an electronic message posted on the Internet. "I just don't see the feminism here."[47] But perhaps Jenny might find comfort in the words of "Lauren" and "Cordelia," two undergraduate feminists who, when classmates accused them of "hypocrisy" for appearing at a costume party dressed as prostitutes, offered the following defense to writer Katie Roiphe:

> Fashion is an ideological statement. We dress this way because we want to. We are exhibiting our control over our own sexuality. We are empowering ourselves.[48]

"Seth," a "living" white male participant in Jenny's Internet discussion group, also offered a reassuring—if not exactly gender-sensitive—response to Jenny's concerns:

> Considering the physical attractiveness of most of the . . . man-bashers . . . I know personally, I'd probably look the other way if they removed any of their clothing.[49]

**bra holsters.** *Women & Guns* magazine suggests that members of "the armed sisterhood" may find that bra holsters are "not a bad idea" as long as they don't "get in the way when you reach for the MC-10 submachine gun in your shoulder sling." Before investing in a bra holster, however, the thoughtful women's self-defense advocate may want to consider two frequently raised objections posed by the publication: (1) Bra holsters represent "an obscene juxtaposition of the icon of death with the symbol of nurturing"; and (2) Like far too many other products in this patriarchal society, bra holsters were invented "by males for females."[50] See also: **Women's Empowerment in the '90s.**

**"brainwashed by patriarchy."** A popular phrase useful for describing individuals who, even after being presented with all the available evidence, continue to insist, for example, that the First Amendment does not pose a dire threat to women; that women who agree to sleep with men are not necessarily collaborating in the erasure of their own gender; or that, although rape is one of the most serious issues confronting our society today, Catharine A. MacKinnon's assertion that "almost half of all women are raped or victims of attempted rape at least once in their lives"[51] may be something of an exaggeration.[52]

**breastism.** Discrimination in favor of or against women based on the size or perceived attractiveness of their breasts, and the related tendency of men in heteropatriarchal society to

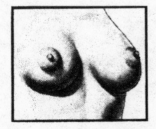

*A pair of* **breastism** *cues.*

objectify and/or stereotype women whose breasts are larger, or smaller, than the norm.[53]

**breastist mascots.** "Hooter," the mascot of Kennesaw State College's "State Owls" athletic teams, was renamed "KaSCey" because "hooters" is a vulgar term for a woman's breasts. The change came none too soon for *The Atlanta Journal and Constitution.* "The need for sensitivity is the price we pay for becoming a more inclusive society," the newspaper editorialized. "Beyond the name 'Hooters' is the offensive behavior it may encourage."[54]

**breeder.** A fashionably condescending term for an individual who, to quote Alan Hamilton's *Sexual Identity and Gender Identity Glossary,* "has significant sexual and romantic attractions primarily to members of the other sex (than oneself)."[55]

*Tipper Gore, a* **breeder.**

**brushing up against women during coed soccer games.** Any man participating in a mixed-gender soccer game must take special care not to brush up against any of his female teammates or opponents. A student who did so was one of the first perpetrators to be reported under the Antioch College Sexual Offense Policy. (Happily, *The New York Times* reports, all it took to set the offender straight was a heart-to-heart chat with Antioch's dean of students, Marian Jensen.)[56] See also: **Antioch Rules.**

**BUFF.** An acronym for "Brothers United for Future Foreskins," a California-based organization that has brought to the foreskin restoration movement a commitment to honor the spiritual debt modern uncircumcising techniques, such as the adhesive-tape-cum-fishing-weight method advocated by Dr. Jim Bigelow, owe to the "primitive peoples" who successfully distended such other body parts as earlobes and lips.[57] See also: **circumcision survivors; foreskin restoration movement; NOHARMM; RECAP; UNCIRC; uncircumcising.**

**bulimia.** Dr. Michael Blumenfield of the New York Medical School defines bulimia as "a disorder characterized by compulsive eating binges followed by some effort to counteract the weight gain that would result from these binges, usually vomiting, but often excessive exercising, fasting or use of diet pills, laxatives or diuretics."[58] Citing a study (which, despite their diligence, the compilers of this dictionary have been unable to locate) claiming that over 50 percent of American girls and women between the age of ten and thirty "suffer with eating disorders" such as bulimia, body-image authority Demetria Iazzetto places the blame squarely on women's having "internalized" the male culture's "misogynistic message . . . that we cannot trust our bodies, and that they are to be feared and hated."[59] Also called **binge-purge syndrome.** See also: **anorexia nervosa; beauty myth; size-acceptance movement.**

**camps, keeping women in.** See: couples.

**candlelight dinners.** Since a man who treats his date to a candle-light dinner is, more often than not, offering to exchange an economic reward for sexual favors, University of Colorado professor Alison Jaggar categorizes such dinners as **prostitution.**[60] See also: **tables for two.**

**candy.** Presenting a woman with a small gift or favor, such as candy or flowers, seems to suggest "fondness" on the part of a man, but the woman should beware: Such a gift or favor, notes Hunter College sexual harassment expert Sue Rosenberg Zalk, may well be "a vehicle for rendering the woman submissive, dependent and obliged."[61] See: **sexual bribery.**

*A man presenting a woman with a box of **candy,** a vehicle for rendering her submissive, dependent, and obliged.*

**castration.** Kristen Asmus, writing in the *Colorado Daily,* looks forward to a bright new day when women who feel sexually harassed "will stop talking about castration, and make it a reality."[62] (For another of Kristen Asmus's creative solutions to the abuse problem, see: **murder.**)

**castration, virtual.** See: virtual rape.

**celibacy.** "As a revolt against a set of male definitions about women's sexuality, all women should forego intercourse," insists Sally Cline, author of *Women, Celibacy and Passion.*[63] The rewards of "celebrating celibacy" will be manifold, she promises. Not only will one be avoiding "genital penetration" (an act, Cline notes, that women "have little regard for"); one will also be opening oneself to unimagined new pleasures. To illustrate her point, the author relates the joyful story of "Geoff" and "Margaret," a married couple who recently gave up coitus. "I go on spiritual retreats to the country with women friends while Geoffrey is involved in his piano practice and gardening," Margaret exults. "I should never have had the time or energy to find any of this out if we had continued in the old way."[64] Julie Burchill, writing in *The Spectator,* couldn't agree more strongly. "In times when lots of concentration is needed," she states, "there can be no doubt that sex is far too effective a muscle relaxant, leaving the mind slack and rosy."[65] See also: **masturbation, female; second virginity**.

**charting.** Here's a great suggestion for college women from Montana Katz and Veronica Vieland, authors of *Get Smart: What You Should Know (but Won't Learn in Class) About Sexual Harassment and Sex Discrimination:* Bring to all your classes charts on which you can note such information as how many times male professors call on female, as opposed to male, students; what kind of body language professors use ("serious" or "offhand") when conversing with women; and how often professors miss the opportunity to use a female or gender-neutral generic pronoun instead of a male one. There also should be a place on your chart, Katz and Vieland recommend, for noting particularly egregious examples of sexist behavior, such as the assignment of a text that "presents a denigrating view of women" or the telling of an "exclusionary" anecdote. "At the end of the term when you are filling out course evaluations," write the authors, "you will be able to comment on the specific problems you experienced as a woman in the class," a process that, they confidently predict, "will assist the professor in taking steps" to modify his improper behavior. "Another thing you might do with the tallies," Katz and Vieland add, "would be to write a letter to the editor of your campus newspaper [or] write an article on the problems you have uncovered." "Ask for responses from readers," they advise.[66]

**chastity belts.** Proclaiming that "Responsibility is the Choice of the 90s," Chastity U.S.A., of Los Angeles, California, is marketing a series of designer chastity belts that women can wear "over jeans or leggings." "Each belt comes with a set of keys that you can lock

*Two individuals demonstrating their choice of responsibility by wearing designer **chastity belts** marketed by Chastity U.S.A.*

or unlock at your own choosing," the company tells prospective customers. And there's no need to worry about actually locking oneself in. "In the event the keys are lost," a company ad explains, "the belt can be removed by unsnapping the back straps."[67] To order your own chastity belt, call toll-free (800) 305-5525, or mail an inquiry to:

Chastity U.S.A.
P.O. Box 471
Burbank, CA 91503

**Cherokee Sex Workshops.** Seminars conducted by a self-proclaimed Cherokee medicine man from Scottsdale, Arizona, who promised—via a widely disseminated TV infomercial—to provide all comers with personalized instruction in ancient Native American sex rituals. An American Indian Movement (AIM) investigation not only exposed the "medicine man" as a fraud, but also revealed that his workshops featured orgies and bestiality. As part of his settlement with AIM, the man agreed to stop calling himself a Cherokee. He now identifies himself as the reincarnation of Billy the Kid, and under the name William Bonney, he was, as of last report, still conducting his sex workshops.[68]

**chick, referring to a woman as**
**a.** See: likening a woman to an animal.

**chivalry.** Nancy Henley, author of *Body Politics,* describes "chivalry" as "an oppressive tool" designed to make women feel incapable of dealing with the world without perpetual assistance.[69]

*Sir Walter Raleigh using* **chivalry** *to oppress Queen Elizabeth I.*

**Christa, Daughter of God.** *Newsweek* reports that, "since Jesus' human sexuality is not part of his divinity as the Christ," an increasing number of Christian women are calling for the replacement of traditional renderings of the Savior on the cross with replicas of "Christa," a crucifix with a nude female body created by sculptor Edwina Sandys.[70] Ironically, however, the campaign to propagate this gender-redeeming image is at spiritual odds with the equally popular movement, spearheaded by Nancy Stumhofer of Penn State University, to prevent the public display of art displaying naked women. Such art, says Stumhofer, "encourages males to make remarks about body parts."[71]

**Christa,** *a gender-redeeming image of the Savior.*

**circumcision survivors.** Those forced as infants to undergo the physical agony and emotional humiliation of foreskin removal. Fortunately, there are several self-help options available to recovering circumcision survivors. For example, Ronald Goldman, of Boston's Circumcision Resource Center, recommends primal therapy, which, by giving a patient the opportunity to relive his own circumcision, helps him come to terms with it. Dr. James Bigelow, author of *The Joy of Uncircumcising,* outlines a do-it-yourself procedure involving adhesive tape and small lead fishing weights that can enable survivors to "re-create" their foreskins.[72] Surgical foreskin reconstruction is another possibility, although its $15,000 cost may place it beyond the means of some survivors. Also valuable is *The Uncut Version,* an informational video available from Katie Cadigan, at P.O. Box 793, Mountain View, CA 94042, (415) 965-7776.[73]

For more information about these and other resources, see: BUFF; foreskin restoration movement; keratinization; NOHARMM; RECAP; UNCIRC; uncircumcising.

**close dancing.**  See: dancing too close.

**clothing, verbal comments about.**  "Verbal comments about clothing" comprise one of the specific categories of "sexually harassing behaviors" that readers of *Sexual Harassment and Teens: A Program for Positive Change,* by Susan Strauss and Pamela Espeland, are warned have been "reported in U.S. high schools."[74]

*A blatant example of a man's making* **verbal comments about clothing.**

**co.** A gender-neutral word coined by writer Mary Orovan to supplant the sexist pronouns "she," "he," "her," and "him." Orovan also recommends that **cos** should be substituted for "his" and "her," and that "herself" and "himself" should be replaced by **coself**.[75] According to feminist linguists Cheris Kramarae and Paula Treichler, all three new terms are now in everyday use at several "alternative-lifestyle communities in Virginia and Missouri."[76] Example: *The handtowels in Mark and Betsy's sexually correct lavatory read* **cos** *and* **cos**, *respectively.*

**coffee, asking a woman student out for.** Professor Alan Charles Kors of the University of Pennsylvania warns that a male faculty member who asks female students "out for coffee or a drink to talk about Wittgenstein, God, death, or, for that matter, liberty" is leaving himself open to accusations of sexual harassment or worse.[77]

**coffee, failing to ask a woman student out for.** *The Barnard/Columbia Women's Handbook* warns that a male faculty member who "shuns female students outside of class . . . for fear of accusation of sexual harassment" is guilty of a subtle but harmful form of sexism that can seriously "impact our performance in the classroom and our plans for future study."[78]

**coitus.** "Coitus," Andrea Dworkin informs us, "is punishment."[79] See also: **intercourse**.

**collaborators.** Andrea Dworkin notes that women who claim to enjoy heterosexual lovemaking are "collaborators, more base in their collaboration than other collaborators have ever been, experiencing pleasure in their own inferiority, calling intercourse freedom."[80]

*Mae West, a notorious* **collaborator,** *experiencing pleasure in her own inferiority.*

**college.** Women planning to attend college or contemplating an academic career may have second thoughts after reading the following gloomy assessment of university life made by Bernice Sandler, director of the catchily named Project on the Status and Education of Women of the Association of American Colleges. "It is increasingly clear," Sandler laments, "that for a large number of students, faculty and staff, the college environment is not one of learning and support but one of stress and exploitation."[81]

**colonization.** Men's use of compulsory heterosexual relations to take over, control, subjugate, and enslave women, and women's bodies, for their own use, pleasure, and economic advantage. As Cheryl Clarke explains, "It is profitable for our colonizers to confine our bodies and alienate us from our own life processes as it was profitable for the European to enslave the African and destroy all memory of a prior freedom and self-determination—Alex Haley notwithstanding."[82] As the concept of "colonization" catches on in common usage, the term is more and more frequently being used as a synonym for "sexual intercourse." Example: *"I'm sorry, Bob,"* said Midge, *"but, exercising my rights under the Antioch Sexual Offense Policy, I hereby deny you permission to colonize me."* See also: **compulsory heterosexuality.**

**compliments.** See: flattery; love notes.

**compulsory heterosexuality.** National Book Award–winning poet Adrienne Rich coined this phrase, defining it, in an oft-quoted essay published in the women's studies journal *Signs* in 1980, as "the enforcement of heterosexuality for women as a means of assuring male right of physical, economical, and emotional access."[83] Rich's article was groundbreaking, to be sure, but it is important to note that it was met with something less than universal acclaim. Ariane Brunet and Louise Turcotte, for example, denounced Rich on the grounds that, by attacking *compulsory* heterosexuality rather than heterosexuality per se, she appeared to be validating *optional* heterosexuality.[84]

**conceptual rape.** The imagined participation in sexual activity with a person whose explicit consent to be included in each and every fantasized act has not been specifically obtained in advance. If the imagined sex occurs while the perpetrator is on a date with the survivor, or if the survivor is someone whom the perpetrator has previously dated or wishes to date in the future, the offense may be classified as **conceptual date rape.**[85]

Sports Illustrated *swimsuit model Christie Brinkley, a* **conceptual rape** *survivor.*

**condom, lambskin.** A contraceptive device—also known as a "natural condom"—that is less likely than a latex condom to trigger a life-threatening anaphylactic-shock reaction in those who come in contact with it, but is generally considered "unsafe" to use because tests have shown it to be too porous to prevent the smallest of the germs and viruses responsible for causing sexually transmitted diseases from getting through.[86] (Note: Those who do choose to wear a lambskin condom should first ascertain whether or not their companion is a member of an animal-rights group, since many such organizations specifically regard the manufacture of "natural" contraceptives as an act of speciesist oppression.)

**condom, latex.** A contraceptive device that tests have shown to be far more reliable than a lambskin condom at blocking the passage of the germs and viruses that cause STDs, but is considered "unsafe" by a growing number of medical specialists because of its underreported propensity for triggering dangerous allergic reactions in those exposed to it.[87] See: **latex-induced shock.**

**condom, natural.** See: condom, lambskin.

**condom layering.** The recent announcement by New York University dermatologist Ronald Brancaccio that allergic reactions to latex have reached "epidemic" proportions, combined with the well-documented evidence that animal-skin condoms are too porous to prevent the spread of sexually transmitted diseases, is leading even those men and women who don't object to sex on political grounds to wonder if penetrative contact of any kind is a practical option. Well, there's new hope for people in this category, and it comes from an innovative new method of protection called "condom layering"—the wearing of two or more condoms at once in order to benefit simultaneously from the impermeability of latex and the hypoallergenic qualities of animal skin. Josephine Bolus, a nurse practitioner at the Kings County Hospital Center in Brooklyn and a champion of condom layering, offers the following instructions: To protect the person being penetrated from having an allergic reaction, she suggests, the penetrator should "put a latex condom on his penis and then put an animal-skin condom over it." To protect *himself,* she adds, the penetrator should "put on an animal-skin condom and wear a latex condom over it."[88] Of course, since *both* partners will probably want to guard against allergic reaction, perhaps the best idea is for the penetrator to slip on three condoms nested one inside the other: an animal-skin one nearest the phallus, a latex one in the middle, and another animal-skin one on top. See also: **latex-induced shock**.

**Condom Olympics.** A safer-sex awareness extravaganza dreamed up by California's Claremont Colleges in 1990, which featured such competitions as the Water-Filled Condom Toss and the Blow-Up-the-Condom-Until-It-Bursts Contest. Julia Karet, di-

*The official symbol of the* **Condom Olympics,** *as proposed by the American Gender Society.*

rector of health education outreach for the six colleges, showed admirable sensitivity when she announced the festival. "We realize that there's people [*sic*] who might be uncomfortable with taking a humorous approach to this very serious topic," said Karet. "We also realize there's a thin line between providing information about health care and doing something that could be interpreted as promoting sex—which is certainly not what we do."[89] See also: **condom relay races; pin-the-condom-on-the-man contests**.

**condom relay races.**   Taking an interactive approach to safer-sex education, Smith College professor Faye Crosby used the occasion of the school's annual Parents' Weekend to conduct a series of "condom relay races," during which parents and students competed against each other to see who could put five condoms on an unpeeled banana the fastest without breaking the banana. Crosby originally thought her tournament had been well conceived, but even though she had been careful to mention **dental dams** during the course of the festivities, several of her students angrily condemned her for "marginalizing lesbians" by not actually using the dams in the races themselves. "It was as if you said, 'oh, well, here are the dental dams—boring, insignificant lesbian sex . . . Now let's get to the really great and fun heterosexual sex,'" Crosby, who has since apologized for her "exclusionary" behavior, quoted her critics as telling her. "I felt terrible!" she confessed.[90] (Note: Professor Crosby is not the only educator to get into trouble for using bananas in connection with condom-use instruction. For details, see: **fructal objectification**.)

**Confrontation Survey.**   In her helpful and practical survival manual *Back Off!*, Martha J. Langelan presents an ingenious "Confrontation Survey," a twenty-question script that women who are no longer willing to "tolerate injustice" can carry with them at all times and use to confront any man they feel is harassing them. It works like this, Langelan writes:

> Turn and face your harasser. Look him in the eye. In a calm, businesslike voice, you say: "That's very interesting. You have

just harassed a woman. Women are conducting a research project on sexual harassment and I want to include you in the survey. I want to take just a minute to ask you a few questions."

The rest is simple. All you do is ask the harasser the twenty questions (which vary slightly depending upon whether the unwelcome behavior you were subjected to was verbal or physical), jot down his answers, and recite the farewell remarks Langelan has scripted for you:

"Thank you. Most women do not think this behavior is a compliment. I expect you not to do it again, to anyone. I appreciate your cooperation with this survey. Good-bye."

Langelan concludes with a mailing address where "completed (or partially completed) surveys" can be sent.[91]

**consensual sex, male-initiated.**    As Catharine A. MacKinnon demonstrates convincingly in *Toward a Feminist Theory of the State*, the concept of "male-initiated consensual sex" is an oxymoron. Writes MacKinnon: "[M]ale initiatives toward women carry the fear of rape as support for persuading compliance, the resulting appearance of which has been considered seduction and termed consent."[92] Men and women attempting to obey the regulations set forth in the Antioch College Sexual Offense Policy would be wise to keep MacKinnon's words of wisdom in mind. See also: **Antioch Rules; intercourse, male-initiated; " 'Yes' means 'no'!"**

**consent, sexual.**    An explicit "yes" in response to a request for the initiation of a sexual act, even when one's partner is demonstrably sober and drug-free, may not be sufficient to prove consent, according to a definition of "unwanted sexual activity" issued by the University of Pennsylvania. "What appears to be consensual, even to the parties involved, may in fact not be so," the university cautions.[93] See also: **Antioch Rules; consensual sex, male-initiated; intercourse, male-initiated; " 'Yes' means 'No'!"**

**consent, sexual, obtained from a person with a multiple personality disorder.** When one wishes to initiate sex with a person who has a multiple personality disorder, obtaining consent only from the specific personality one wants to make love to is insufficient grounds on which to proceed. If Mark A. Peterson, of Oshkosh, Wisconsin, didn't know this on the night in 1990 when he had what he alleged was consensual intercourse with "Jennifer," one of eighteen distinct personalities sharing the body of a former waitress identified in press accounts only as "Sarah," he certainly knows it now. As it turned out, another of Sarah's "selves"—a six-year-old girl named "Emily"—was "peeking" as Peterson and Jennifer made love in Peterson's car, and when Emily told Sarah (the so-called "host" personality) about what she'd seen, Sarah became furious and called the police. At the ensuing rape trial, several of Sarah's personalities—each of whom were sworn in separately—testified against Peterson, including Emily, who demanded a teddy bear before she would agree to take questions from prosecutors. According to the London *Daily Telegraph,* Peterson, who was convicted of second degree assault and sentenced to up to ten years in prison, complained as he left court that he had been prosecuted "for just having a fling with a girl after a date in a coffee shop." "I still don't think she is mentally ill," he added. Sarah, the *Daily Telegraph* reports, was so traumatized by the events that she subsequently developed twenty-eight completely new personalities.[94]

**continuum theories.** In his essay "The War of All Against All," Louis Menand discusses what is fast becoming the prevailing view of gender relations in the 1990s: "the notion that all sexual behavior, from bottom patting to serial killing, falls along a continuum, and that sex is everywhere used to abuse, dominate and oppress." The Antioch Sexual Offense Policy, Menand notes, "articulates precisely this conception of sexual behavior as a continuum . . . the idea being that hand clutching and ear nibbling, if uninvited, are assaultive—like rape, although, of course, much lower on the scale."[95] Similar "continuum theories" have proven invaluable in establishing the link between casual conversation and gynocide (see: **conversation**) and in elucidating the view that there are not just two sexes, but at least five, and possibly an infinite number (see: **intersexual**).

**conversation.** "Cecille," a contributor to Martha J. Langelan's survival manual, *Back Off!*, says men's assumption that "they have the right to engage us in conversation anytime they please" is one of the things that puts women "in fear." Cecille sees unwelcome conversation as part of a spectrum of behavior that includes "invading our space," "commenting on our bodies uninvited," and "pornography." "Verbal attack is the most prevalent form of violence against women," she adds. "It is one of the first steps on the progression that leads to the ultimate violence, murder."[96] See also: **continuum theories; dates, asking for.**

*An example of superficially gender-just, but nonetheless unwelcome,* **conversation.**

**cos.** See: co.

**coself.** See: co.

**cosmetic subjugation.** In a letter reprinted in Joseph Hanson and Evelyn Reed's useful anthology *Cosmetics, Fashions, and the Exploitation of Women,* Helen Baker of Seattle, Washington, points out that cosmetics are "a prize example of the special discrimination that women workers are subjected to." According to Baker, makeup is not a "luxury" that women have a free choice to accept or reject. Rather, she informs us, it is "a grim necessity for the older or not physically blessed woman" who has to compete for employment in a lookist, male-supremacist labor market.[97] In the early 1970s, the Women's Strike for Equality coined a phrase for the oppression Baker describes—"cosmetic subjugation"— and, to combat it, they began providing **Freedom Trash Cans**, where women could deposit lipsticks, compacts, and other accoutrements of their victimization.[98] See also: **beauty myth; fashion profiteers**.

**cosurvivor.** The husband, lover, or sibling of a woman who has survived a rape or rape attempt. As Kathleen Kapila, a social worker at St. Luke's–Roosevelt Hospital in New York City, explained at a "cosurvivorship seminar" she conducted in February 1993, cosurvivors suffer the same feelings of rage and helplessness that survivors do. Therefore, like survivors, they frequently require counseling.[99]

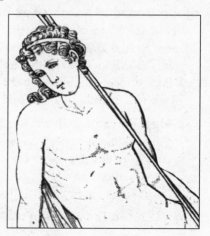

*King Tyndareus of Sparta,* **cosurvivor** *of the rape, by a swan, of his wife, Leda.*

**couple busting.**   A disarmingly simple technique devised by SCUM—the Society for Cutting Up Men—for bringing gender justice to the world. As the organization's founder, Valerie Solanas, wrote in her famous *SCUM Manifesto:* "SCUM will couple-bust—barge into mixed (male-female) couples, wherever they are, and bust them up."[100] See: **couples.**

**couples.**   Before accepting a date, much less agreeing to "go steady" with, live with, or marry a man, a woman owes it to herself—and to her gender—to weigh carefully the following cautionary words about couples from the Leeds Revolutionary Feminist Group:

> The heterosexual couple is the basic unit of the political struc-ture of male supremacy. In it each individual woman comes under the control of an individual man. It is more efficient than keeping women in ghettoes, camps, or even sheds at the bottom of the garden. In the couple, love and sex are used to obscure the realities of oppression, to prevent women from identifying with each other in order to revolt, and from identifying "their" man as part of the enemy. Any woman who takes part in a hetero-sexual couple helps to shore up male supremacy by making its foundations stronger.[101]

See also: **couple busting; tables for two.**

**cow, referring to a woman as a.**   A student's calling another stu-dent a cow is an offense specifically labeled as **Hostile Environ-ment Sexual Harassment** in official guidelines distributed by the state of Minnesota to its public school students and staff.[102] See also: **likening a woman to an animal.**

**Cro-Magnon man within.**   Accord-ing to columnist and men's move-ment leader Asa Baber, it is not (as Douglas Gillette has argued) an "ape within" that men must get in touch

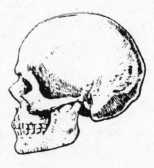

*The skull of a* **Cro-Magnon man,** *an early tool-user and rapist.*

with to find true empowerment, but rather a Cro-Magnon man. Baber writes:

> As men we have special gifts. One of those is the ability to be in touch with the Cro-Magnon man who lives somewhere deep inside our hearts and minds and calls to us. It is vital to remember that this man is not a savage. In no way is he an uncontrolled killer or evil oppressor. . . . Indomitable and invincible and wild, ready to protect and defend and compete, his instinct and perceptions necessary to ensure the survival of the human race, this primitive man at the center of our psyches must be allowed room to live and breathe and express himself.[103]

Before contacting the Cro-Magnon men within them, however, male readers may wish to ponder Susan Brownmiller's account of how a creature similar to the one Baber describes actually invented rape and, by extention, the patriarchal oppression of women. Indeed, she writes, "man's discovery that his genitalia could serve as a weapon to generate fear must rank as one of the most important discoveries of prehistoric times, along with the use of fire and the first crude stone axe."[104] See also: **ape within; parakeet within**.

**dancing too close.** Charles H. Goldstein, senior partner of Goldstein & Kennedy, a Los Angeles law firm whose specialty is representing corporations in labor relations matters, warns that attempting to dance too close to a woman—even if the woman follows the man's lead without apparent resistance—can now be considered sexual harassment. And, says Goldstein, if the excessively close dancing occurs on company time—for example, at an office party—it can lead to legal problems for the offending employee and/or the organization for which he works. To help managers learn more about the legal perils of close dancing and other problem areas such as "hugging" and "kissing under the mistletoe," Mr. Goldstein has narrated a videotape entitled *How to Prevent Sexual Harassment Lawsuits,* which his public-spirited firm generously makes available to clients and nonclients alike for the nominal fee of $79.95 per copy.[105] See also: **standing too close.**

**date rape.** A term coined in 1982 by *Ms.* magazine writer Karen Barrett to describe a sexual offense that Andrea Parrot and Laurie Bechhofer, editors of *Acquaintance Rape: The Hidden Crime,* define as "nonconsensual sex between people who are dating or on a date." A failure to say "no" to the proposition or initiation of sex, Parrot and Bechhofer point out, is not the same as saying "yes" and does not imply consent. Similarly, consent cannot be assumed from interactions on previous dates and "must be obtained on every separate occasion." "To violate or ignore these conditions," they warn their readers, "is to enter the gray zone and take the risk of committing rape."[106]

**dates, asking for.** "Cecille," a contributor to *Back Off!,* an anthology of "resistance strategies" edited by Martha J. Langelan, notes that one of the techniques men use to keep women "in fear" is "assuming they have the right to engage us in conversation anytime they please." As a result, she writes, "characteristics I've come to think of as male—a deep voice, a male body—put me on edge, no matter who the individual man is." Men of conscience might be wise to remember Cecille's message before asking a woman they don't know well for a date.[107]

**dates, paying for.** "On a date," Robin Warshaw advises women readers of *I Never Called It Rape: The* Ms. *Report on Recognizing, Fighting and Surviving Date and Acquaintance Rape,* "pay your own way (or let your date buy the movie tickets and you pay for pizza afterward) so that the date is not interpreted as a transaction in which you 'owe' the man something." Indeed, Warshaw says, "rape counselors and women who have been raped by acquaintances recommend that you run, do not walk, from any man who . . . refuses to let you share any of the expenses on a date and gets angry when you offer to pay."[108] See also: **wormboy**.

**dating.** "In the dating system," Andrea Dworkin warns, "women are defined as the passive pleasers of any and every man," and, as a result, "are coerced into becoming sex-commodities." Dworkin's conclusion: "[W]e must, in order to protect ourselves, refuse to participate in the dating system. . . ."[109]

**Day of Dread.** See: **Super Bowl Sunday**.

**"dear," referring to a woman as.** As Nessa Wolfson and Joan Manes point out in their celebrated essay "Don't 'Dear' Me!," men must never call a woman "dear," because doing so carries "the implication that the addressee is in some way subordinate to the speaker."

**Decade of Genital Appropriation.** A phrase coined by Sally Cline, author of *Women, Celibacy and Passion,* to describe the 1960s, the era when men systematically undermined the legitimacy of all the excuses women have traditionally invoked to avoid being subjected to intercourse.[110] See also: **celibacy; Sexual Revolution**.

**definitional stretching.** A term coined in 1991 by Dr. Neil Gilbert, a professor of social welfare at the University of California at Berkeley, to describe what he suspected might be a deliberate attempt to expand the concept of "rape" to the point where even the most rigorously conducted research would reveal it to be a problem "vastly larger than commonly recognized." As evidence to support his claim, Gilbert offered the discrepancy between a widely quoted *Ms.* magazine study conducted by Dr. Mary P. Koss, which indicated that more than one in four college women had been victimized by at least one rape or rape attempt, and a U.S. national crime survey, which placed the number of American women who might expect to be raped each year at somewhere between one in five hundred and one in one thousand. While acknowledging that government rape statistics tend to be notoriously low, Gilbert cited the facts that (a) any woman answering "yes" to Koss's question "Have you ever had sexual intercourse when you didn't want to because a man gave you alcohol or drugs?" had been counted as a rape survivor, that (b) 73 percent of the women classified by Koss as having been raped had initially failed to characterize their experience as such, and that (c) roughly 41 percent of the "raped" women in Koss's survey had chosen to sleep with their rapists again, as further indications that her numbers might be at least slightly inflated. Gilbert went on to praise activists for "the good job" they had done in "raising consciousness" about rape, and said he had spoken up because of his fear that overzealous "definitional stretching" would ultimately serve only to "trivialize" public perceptions of the true seriousness of the crime, but these disclaimers did not prevent some members of the academic community from questioning his assertions. Sheila Kuehl, for example, a director of the California Women's Law Center, announced that she found herself "wishing that Gilbert himself might be raped and . . . be told, to his face, it had never happened." Placards reading KILL NEIL GILBERT appeared mysteriously on the Berkeley campus. And scores of demonstrators from SOAR (Students Organized Against Rape) gathered in Berkeley's Sproul Square to light candles for rape survivors and to chant over and over again the rhythmic suggestion that Gilbert should "cut it out or cut it off."[111]

**dental dams.** Small sheets of latex, originally developed to help dentists keep their patients' teeth and gums dry during oral surgery, that have become an important tool for protecting women against the spread of sexually transmitted diseases during cunnilingus. Although dental dams are produced in a variety of attractive colors and are now available in at least six flavors (including chocolate), some feel the devices have a tendency to detract from the pleasure of oral sex. Not so, asserts one woman interviewed by the British newspaper *The Guardian*, who talks glowingly of the "fun" to be had "blowing bubbles in the rubber."[112]

**depantsing.** Under the Minnesota Department of Education's guidelines for children of kindergarten age and up, any public school student found guilty of "depantsing"—pulling down a student's pants or pulling up a student's skirt—can be expelled for sexual harassment, and any school that fails to prevent such behavior can be sued for damages by the parents of the offended child. Depantsing, Minnesota sexual-harassment expert Susan Strauss informs us, is also known as **spiking.**[113]

**designated sober monitor.** One of a group of women attending a mixed-gender party who is appointed by her compatriots to watch over and protect them from alcohol-related sex offenses. If, after having had a drink or two, a member of her circle appears to be on the verge of wandering off with a man, it is the duty of the designated sober monitor to walk up to her and say something like "You're drunk, wouldn't you rather go home? You can call him tomorrow." Designated sober monitors have become a fixture at the University of Michigan, and *Newsweek* reports the concept is rapidly gaining popularity at other institutions of higher learning.[114]

**desire.** Sheila Jeffreys, author of *Anticlimax*, assures women that what they're actually experiencing when they think they're overcome by "heterosexual desire" is merely "eroticized power difference."[115] Example: *Vanessa's favorite sexually correct play was* **Eroticized Power Difference** *Under the Elms.*

**Dignity, the Snail.** A puppet character created by the Minnesota Department of Education to teach elementary school children not to let anyone "say anything about our body parts that hurts us."[116] See also: Equality, the Frog; Respect, the Turtle; puppet surrogates.

DIGNITY

Minnesota Department of Education, 1993

**Dignity, the Snail.**

**dildo substitute.** A definition of **penis** offered by the self-styled "Nomadic Sisters" of Saratoga, California.[117]

*A* **dildo substitute.**

**diseasism.** Discrimination against persons living with AIDS, for example, by the temporarily HIV-negative.[118]

**displays of affection in hallways.** See: affection, public displays of.

**dog, pretending to be a.** Many men who wish to practice Dr. Shepherd Bliss's novel therapeutic technique of "joining the world of the four-leggeds" find that pretending to be a dog is a particularly good way to start. Journalist Jon Tevlin learned this firsthand while attending one of Bliss's seminars, an experience that he wrote about in the *Utne Reader:*

> Out of the corner of my eye, I saw Shepherd coming toward me, head down, tufts of white hair ringing a bald spot. . . . Meanwhile I felt a slight presence at my rear, and turned to see a man beginning to sniff my buttocks. "Woof!" he said.[119]

See also: **four-leggeds, joining the world of**.

**dog, referring to a woman as a.** Calling another student a dog is an abuse specifically labeled as **Hostile Environment Sexual Harassment** in the official guidelines the state of Minnesota distributes to its public school students and staff.[120] See also: **likening a woman to an animal**.

**dolphin, pretending to be a.** One of the rites in which British correspondent Mick Brown was asked to participate during the course of a Wild Man retreat he attended in New York's Catskill Mountains in 1992 was to pretend he was a dolphin. (Another was to pretend he was an elephant.) The dolphin exercise was apparently intended to help Brown and his comrades recover the natural animality that the Industrial Revolution drove out of all men back in the nineteenth century, and it's one other men can easily replicate at home.[121] (Note: Any man who pretends to be a dolphin because he's impressed by the acquatic mammal's reputation for virtue is sadly misguided, however. In a hard-hitting editorial in the May–June 1992 edition of *Ms.* magazine, editor Robin Morgan strips away male dolphins' squeaky-clean media image and demonstrates that they're every bit as oppressive as their human counterparts. See: **sex offenders, nonhuman**.)

**dolphin patriarchy.** See: **sex offenders, nonhuman**.

**domestic incarceration survivor.**
A nonpatriarchal term for a woman who is, or once was, a "wife."[122]

*Ivana Trump, a* **domestic incarceration survivor,** *accompanied by her insignificant other, Donald Trump.*

**Don Juan.**  Any man who has taken the trouble to acquire—much less actually read—this dictionary probably already knows that quoting from a blatantly phallocentric poem such as Lord Byron's *Don Juan* represents unconscionable behavior. What he may *not* know, however, is that such quotations may actually be legally punishable. Ian Macneil, former Robert Braucher Visiting Professor of Law at Harvard University, discovered this when he had the poor judgment to assign a textbook that, in the context of describing a typical contract negotiation, reproduced the following lines from *Don Juan:*

> A little still she strove, and much repented,
> And whispering, "I will ne'er consent"—consented.

Bonnie Savage, the ever-alert student head of the Harvard Women's Law Association, immediately issued an "open letter" accusing Macneil of sexism. A quotation "depicting a woman . . . being dominated has no place in a contracts textbook," she declared. The letter—which Savage forwarded to several Harvard Law School officials for their consideration in the event there might be a plan afoot to offer Macneil tenure—also pointed out that the Byron passage implied that "women mean yes when they say no"—a "dangerous misperception" that, she noted, has been widely discredited in "rape law." Although no formal charges were ever pressed, Savage's vigilance did not go unrewarded; less than a year after she wrote her "open letter" the university issued new guidelines covering sexism in the classroom, and Macneil quietly left the Harvard faculty.[123]

**door opening.**  There are at least three reasons, philosopher Marilyn Frye tells us, why a man's opening the door for a woman must be regarded as an impermissible breach of sexually correct etiquette. First, she writes, it

*A man putting the finishing touches on a shameless act of* **door opening.**

sends a clear message that "women are incapable." Second, the detachment of the door-opening act from "the concrete realities of what women need and do not need is a message that women's actual needs and interests are unimportant or irrelevant." Third, and worst of all, this gesture of so-called "male gallantry" imitates "the behavior of servants toward masters," and thus mocks women, who, in this phallocentric society, are "in most respects the servants and caretakers of men."[124]

**double negative linguistic constructions.** Women who accidentally or intentionally behave in a manner they feel others might consider sexually incorrect—such as, for example, being attracted by, or agreeing to marry, a man—may find double-negative linguistic constructions useful when they are required to explain their actions. Consider, for example, feminist legal scholar Catharine A. MacKinnon's response to *New York* magazine correspondent Dinitia Smith when Smith asked her how she could justify having become engaged (to psychoanalyst and repentant womanizer Jeffrey Masson) after having "written that equal relations between men and women are impossible in an unequal society." Explained MacKinnon: "He's not not a man, and I'm not not a woman."[125] Example: *Vanessa's favorite sexually correct French motion picture was* And God Created **Not Not** a Woman.

**drinking and penile driving.** "The law punishes the drunk driver who kills a pedestrian," observes noted date-rape researcher Mary P. Koss. "And likewise, the law needs to be there to protect the drunk woman from the driver of the penis."[126] See also: **alcohol; offering a woman a drink.**

**drum therapy.** A self-help ritual, borrowed from African and precolonial North American cultures, in which men purge themselves of what *American Spectator* correspondent Andrew Ferguson calls "the weak-kneed you-betcha-boss, sorry-honey-I-didn't-mean-it deference" modern culture has thrust upon them by gathering together in "sacred spaces" (two specific examples of such spaces are the loft bordering a freeway in Emeryville, California, where the **Sons of Orpheus** men's group meets each Wednesday evening, and the basement exhibition hall of Stouffer's Arboretum Hotel in Austin, Texas, which hosted the First International Men's Conference in 1991) and banging the bejesus out of drums. (Although any drums will do, those similar in design to those used by indigenous Americans, and "B.D. Drums"—which the *San Francisco Chronicle*'s Alice Kahn describes as instruments that, in the way kosher food is blessed by a rabbi, have been "owned, played and endorsed by Robert Bly"—are among those most highly recommended.)[127] A fast-growing cadre of health professionals extol the psychological and neurophysiological virtues of drumming, or **tactile-vestibular activity**, as many of them prefer to call it. Indeed, *The Dallas Morning News* reports, many companies, including IBM and McDonnell-Douglas, have set up executive drumming circles, which, according to corporate drumming consultant Ray Dillard, help employees learn to develop their "ensemble minds" and "express themselves with confidence."[128] Despite the many apparent benefits of drum therapy, however, it is not without its critics. Native American writer Sherman Alexie, for example, finds a certain irony in "white men's searching for answers" in the same native traditions that they worked so long, and so brutally, to obliterate. Besides, he adds (after apologizing for "supporting a stereotype"), "white men can't drum."[129] And clinical psychologist Laura S. Brown sees men's drumming groups as gravely dangerous, conjuring up visions of the "speculative dystopias" created by novelist Suzy McKee Charnas, in which men "imprison women as slaves and animals who are underfed, raped and then beaten for stealing men's maleness during heterosex." For those tempted to think Brown might be overreacting, she adds the following sober warning:

> Don't tell me "it can't happen here," that no such terrible outcome can arise from something as apparently silly as men in a room with a drum. As a Jew, I know better.[130]

**Dworkin-MacKinnon Law.** An ordinance enacted by the Indianapolis City Council in 1984, which, among other things, permitted any woman offended by material she felt was pornographic not only to sue for its prohibition, but also to collect monetary damages for the harm it caused her. The legislation—drafted by antipornography crusaders Andrea Dworkin and Catharine A. MacKinnon, introduced in the council by an anti-ERA activist, and signed into law by Indianapolis's Republican mayor William Hudnut—was hailed as a major turning point in the struggle against phallocentrism. However, the Eurocentric-white-male-dominated U.S. Supreme Court declared it unconstitutional less than a year after it was passed.[131] See: **Bill of Rights; First Amendment; obscenity.**

# E

**ear nibbling.** A form of assault whose place on the spectrum of sexuality and violence is discussed in the entry on **continuum theories**.

**economic equity.** Andrea Dworkin offers the following reminder to those who feel that pursuit of such goals as equal pay for equal work, equal access to job opportunities, and the elimination of the "glass ceiling" might be more important to the mass of women—and therefore worth more of their time and effort—than an all-out crusade against pornography:

> Women won't be able to get economic equity as long as we're seen as pieces of meat. Pornography determines our economic worthlessness. It is really a form of colonialization of the woman's body. It is the equivalent of land. The people who own it are men.[132]

See also: **equity feminism.**

**efemcipation.** Emancipation, especially as it applies to the liberation and empowerment of women. Bina Goldfield, who coined the term, feels so strongly about eliminating all vestiges of patriarchy from our written and spoken language that she has compiled a volume entitled *The Efemcipated English Handbook* that presents an alphabetical list of hundreds of words in which the syllables "man" and "men" have been dutifully replaced by "fem." Goldfield's list is accompanied by an instruction "femual," which, she explains in her preface, is designed to help you achieve "perfement comfemd ... of an alternative language" and "perhaps inspire you to carry it to as yet undreamed-of possibilities."[133] (Note: Whether or not the efemcipated term "perfement" should itself be efemcipated to become "perfefemt" has been a matter of some debate in feminist linguistic circles.)

**elephant, pretending to be a.** See: dolphin, pretending to be a; four-leggeds, joining the world of.

**emasculation, antidote for.** See: remasculation.

**emotional smothering.** See: smothering, emotional.

**enclosure.** Feminist Barbara Mehrhof suggests that the only reason the word "penetration" is used to describe sexual intercourse in Western culture is that men have been in charge of creating language and have insisted on defining everything from their own perspective. An equally valid term for this particular act, Mehrhof notes, is "enclosure,"[134] and both men and women would show sensitivity and courtesy by using it in their discussions of whether the sex acts they propose or reject are truly consensual. (Note: Although generally admiring of Mehrhof's proposal, some critics have warned that rewriting current rape law to replace the phrase "penetration, no matter how slight" with "enclosure, no matter how limited" could prove counterproductive.) See also: **engulfment; envelopment; nutting; positive language.**

**English.** Patricia A. Harney and Charlene L. Muehlenhard observe that the English language—whose etymology and grammatical rules have been under the control of men for centuries—is one of the "insidious" institutions that make Western culture a "rape-conducive environment."[135] See: **rape-conducive environments.**

**engulfment.** According to linguist Robert Baker, proof—as if proof were needed!—that intercourse is something that men inflict on women is provided by the fact that virtually all the verbs used to describe the man's role are active ("screwed," "fucked," etc.), while those used to describe the woman's role are passive ("was screwed," "was fucked," etc.). Furthermore, Baker argues, "the passive construction of these verbs . . . can *also* be used to indicate that a person is being harmed. . . . [T]he metaphor involved would only make sense if we conceive of the female role in intercourse as that of someone being harmed (or being taken advantage of)." "It is only natural," Baker concludes, "for women to reject such a role, and it would seem to be the duty of any moral person to support their efforts—to redefine our conceptions not only of fucking, but of the fucker (man) and the fucked (woman)." A good way to begin this process, of course, is to change our terminology. For example, says Baker, in a society where a woman's playing the active role in intercourse was not considered abnormal, we might expect to see terms like " 'engulfing'—that is, instead of saying 'he screwed her,' one would say 'she engulfed' him." But better still— as a contribution to "the elimination of gender from our language"—we should use only gender-neutral terms for coitus: e.g., "Dick and Jane did it with each other."[136] See also: **enclosure; envelopment; nutting**.

**envelopment.**  Gloria Steinem's entry in the sweepstakes to find nonphallocentric terms for sexual intercourse. "Try replacing 'penetration' with 'envelopment,' " she suggests, "and see what happens to your head."[137] Example: *"Go get* **enveloped***!" Astrid shouted to a construction worker who was trying to objectify her.* See also: **enclosure; engulfment; nutting; positive language**.

**epicene.**  Belonging to, or having the characteristics of, both the male and the female sexes, and, presumably, any other sexes that lie between them along the human sexual continuum.[138] Example: *Co, cos, coself, tey, ter, tem, ve, vis, and ver are all* **epicene** *pronouns*. See also: **intersexual**.

**Equality, the Frog.**  A puppet character created by the Minnesota Department of Education to teach elementary school children that "everyone deserves the same rights . . . because we are all more alike than different."[139] Before accepting or propagating Equality,

EQUALITY

**Equality, the Frog.**

Minnesota Department of Education, 1993

the Frog's message, women owe it to themselves to read (or reread) what Andrea Dworkin has to say about "equality":

I want to suggest to you that a commitment to sexual equality
with males . . . is a commitment to becoming the rich instead of
the poor, the rapist instead of the raped, the murderer instead of
the murdered.[140]

See also: **Dignity, the Snail; Respect, the Turtle; puppet surrogates**.

**equity feminism.** In her 1994 book *Who Stole Feminism?*, Clark
University philosophy professor Christina Hoff Sommers makes
the controversial assertion that there is a silent majority of women
in academia who make no claims "to unmask a social reality that
most women fail to perceive." According to Sommers, these
women—whom she calls "equity feminists,"

> embrace no specialist feminist doctrines; they merely want for
> women what they want for everyone—a "fair field with no
> favors." . . . Equity feminists are as upset as anyone else about
> the prevalence of violence against women, but . . . because they
> are not committed to the view that men are arrayed against
> women, they are able to see violence against women in the con-
> text of what, in our country, appears to be a crisis of violence
> against persons. . . . To view rape as a crime of gender bias
> (encouraged by a patriarchy that looks with tolerance on the
> victimization of women) is perversely to miss its true nature.
> Rape is perpetrated by criminals, which is to say, it is perpe-
> trated by people who are wont to gratify themselves in criminal
> ways and who care very little about the suffering they inflict on
> others."[141]

The notion of a cadre of equity feminists—whose agenda Sommers insists is well on its way to being realized—has, of course,
been broadly dismissed as "backlash," "simplistic," "self-serving,"
"elitist," and worse.[142] A frequently heard objection is that the
achievement of "equity" by a small minority of pampered upper-
class women does little for the millions who remain oppressed and
victimized, and absolutely nothing to dismantle the "sex/gender
system" itself, which University of Illinois philosophy professor

Sandra Lee Bartky—who calls Sommers "a right-wing ideo-logue"[143]—defines as "that complex process whereby bisexual infants are transformed into male and female gender personalities, the one destined to command, the other to obey."[144] Kim Gandy, executive vice-president of NOW, agrees. "It's as if this group peels off and says, 'We've got ours, the rest of you are on your own, the heck with you,' " she says of Sommers and her cohorts.[145] See also: **power feminism; economic equity; Equality, the Frog**.

**eroticized power difference.** See: desire.

**essentialism.**   Robert S. McElvaine, author of *The Way We Are: Human Nature, Sex and Traditional Values,* defines "essential-ism" as the "heresy" that "there are biological differences between males and females." Nonessentialists, McElvaine writes, believe that "sex identity is entirely a product of culture"—that "all humans at birth are slates that are completely blank except for a few parts that are of no particular significance," and that the old cliché "Susan is of the female persuasion" must now be taken com-pletely seriously.[146] In her book *Gender Trouble,* the celebrated Johns Hopkins University antiessentialist Judith Butler demon-strates how even the most loyal "feminists," by making claims in behalf of a "fictive" category called "women," are actually helping "construct" a gender that members of other "phantas-mic categories" can oppress. A far better strategy, she suggests, is to "deconstruct identity," thereby exposing as "political" the very terms through which "cultural configurations" of sex and gender are expressed.[147] See also: **believing that one is male; gender; gender justice; gender**

*Kim Basinger, a member of a fic-tive category called "women."*

oppression; human beings who happen to have been born penised; humans who were born without a penis; prepatriarchal cultures; sex.

**extended clitoris.** See: penis.

**extraterrestrial rape.** Antonio Villas-Boas, a Brazilian farmer, created a sensation in 1957 when he claimed he had been abducted by aliens and forced to board their spacecraft, where he was allegedly "seduced" by a beautiful blond extraterrestrial with "long, pointy hands." (The alien woman, Villas-Boas told his physician, pointed at her belly after the sex act had been completed to show that the farmer had impregnated her.) Debate has raged ever since about whether the incident actually occurred and, if it did, whether Villas-Boas or the alien was guilty of rape.[148] See: **receptive noninitiation.**

**eye contact, excessive.** When a male professor makes excessive eye contact with female students, he stands a good chance of being

*A blatant example of* **excessive eye contact.**

convicted of "prolonged staring," as a recent sexual harassment case at the University of Toronto demonstrated. For the details, see: **prolonged staring.**

**eye contact, insufficient.** When a male professor fails to make sufficient eye contact with female students, he's contributing to the creation of "a biased climate in the classroom," *The Barnard/Columbia Women's Handbook* tells us. Such a climate, the handbook warns, "may cause a woman to lose confidence in her abilities" or "feel discouraged and/or physically threatened."[149]

*A blatant example of* **insufficient eye contact.**

# F

**failure to remember women's names.** See: women's names, failure to remember.

**false consciousness.** The failure of members of both dominant and subordinated groups to see that their beliefs and values are the products of an oppressive social system and are therefore irrelevant, useless, and totally meaningless. As Catharine A. MacKinnon notes in her book *Toward a Feminist Theory of the State*, "false consciousness" is the most frequently given explanation for why so many women submit willingly—even eagerly—to male domination.[150] See: **internalized oppression; psychological captivity.**

**family, traditional.** If you're a woman who dreams of getting married and having children, warns Vicki Noble, it's time to develop a new plan. Otherwise, you are in danger of being "imprisoned in the cage of the patriarchal family, with rape and murder a constant threat, and no safe place to get away."[151]

*The Brady Bunch, prisoners in the cage of the patriarchal family, with rape and murder a constant threat, and no safe place to get away.*

**fashion profiteers.** According to Evelyn Reed, coauthor of *Cosmetics, Fashions, and the Exploitation of Women*, there are "three main gangs" of "profiteers, exploiters, and scoundrels" who live gluttonously at the expense of "the hypnotized mass of women [they] dragoon or wheedle into their sex commodity market in search of beauty." They are:

1. "The manipulators of female flesh" who put women "by the thousands and tens of thousands" through "various ordeals in their beauty and slenderizing salons," and who are aided and abetted by "the face-lifters, nose-bobbers, and other surgical rescuers of female beauty";
2. "Those who paint and emulsify this manipulated flesh with cosmetics, dyes, lotions, emulsions, perfumes, etc."; and
3. "Those who decorate the manipulated and painted flesh" by ordaining "a round-the-clock fashion circus," which compels women not only to acquire outfits for "mornings, afternoons, cocktails, evening, night, and bedtime," but also to collect "a vast collateral assemblage of 'accessories' to 'go with' whatever they are supposed to go with."[152] See also: **beauty; cosmetic subjugation**.

**favors.** If a man attempts to bestow a favor on a woman, she owes it to herself not to accept it. The reason, Hunter College professor Sue Rosenberg Zalk reminds us, is that although doing a favor "seems to indicate a fondness for the person, it may well be a vehicle for rendering the woman submissive, dependent and obliged."[153] See also: **flowers**.

**feeling loved.** Any woman in a "white-dominated society" who "feels loved" by her male partner is probably just deluding herself, National Book Award–winning poet Adrienne Rich indicates in an essay reprinted in Laura Lederer's useful anthology *Take Back the Night*. Indeed, as author Carolyn See notes in *The New York Times Book Review*, Rich seems "more than just a little bit hot under the collar" on the subject, as evidenced by the following passage:

> Whatever her caste and privilege, [she] is carnally hated, meant not to be merely dominated or humiliated in daily life, but beaten in bondage, forced to eat feces, her nipples rubbed raw with pincers, her body fed into a meat grinder.[154]

**female flesh, manipulators of.** See: fashion profiteers.

**female genitalia.** See: genitalia, female.

**female orgasm.** See: orgasms, female.

**fembot.** A term coined by Mary Daly to describe the "archetypical role model" into which patriarchy seeks to force all women.[155] Fembots who are displayed publicly (e.g., on television programs or in beauty pageants) for the purpose of turning "numberless" other women into "mummified/numb-ified" clones of themselves are referred to by Daly as **numbots.**[156]

**femininity.** See: internalized oppression.

**feminist vegetarianism.** See: meat eating; stomach that has no ears, the.

**femstruation.** A gender-just improvement upon "menstruation" suggested by celebrated linguistic reformer Bina Goldfield.[157] See: efemcipation.

**fence sitter.** A biphobic term used by gay men and lesbians, and some heterosexuals, to disparage members of the bisexual community.[158]

**ferms.** A term coined by Anne Fausto-Sterling, a Brown University geneticist and intersexual rights advocate, to describe individuals who possess ovaries and some aspects of male genitalia but who do not have testes. Fausto-Sterling, a leader in the struggle to overthrow the two-party sexual system, feels there are at least five sexes, and possibly more.[159] See also: **herms; merms; intersexual; two-party sexual system.**

**fifties-nostalgia parties.** A fifties-nostalgia party is not an acceptable place for a man to take a woman on a date because, as Dean Hilda Hernandez-Graeville of Harvard has pointed out, racism was particularly rampant in America during that specific time period. Indeed, Hernandez-Graeville has called upon her university to place an outright ban on such parties.[160] (Note: Sixties-nostalgia parties are not an appropriate substitute for fifties-nostalgia parties. See: **Decade of Genital Appropriation.**)

**filial rape.** The rape by a father of his son. In "Dirt and Democracy," an article in *The New Republic,* Alan Wolfe discusses Andrea Dworkin's view that since "sex is power, nothing else" and "every man is a beast," virtually all fathers have the potential—if not a longing—to violate their own children. "She tells me, for example," Wolfe writes, "that I have refrained from raping my son not because I love him, but because of the fear that when he grows up, he might rape me back."[161]

**finger cots.** Small latex sheaths that fit over one's fingers. An increasing number of advocates of "less dangerous sex" now recommend that both partners wear finger cots or, better still, latex gloves, during heavy petting.[162] See also: **latex gloves; latex-induced shock.**

**fin slapping.** See: **sex offenders, nonhuman.**

**First Amendment.** As John Stoltenberg points out in his essay "Confronting Pornography as a Civil-Rights Issue," the First Amendment protects only *"those who have already spoken* from state interference" [The italics are Stoltenberg's]. Women are among those specifically not protected, Stoltenberg argues, because they "have been systematically excluded from public discourse by civil inferiority, economic powerlessness, and violence." Pornography in particular, he notes, "silences women," while "the rich pornography industry spends millions of dollars on lawyers to protect its right to keep saying to women, in effect: 'You are nothing but a whore and men should be able to do anything they want to you.'" In the face of these facts, Stoltenberg concludes, reexamination of the blind adherence the so-called "progressive legal community" pays to the First Amendment is long overdue.[163] See also: **Bill of Rights; Dworkin-MacKinnon Law; virtual rape.**

**first kiss.** See: **kissing.**

**flattery.** Before accepting a compliment from a date or sex partner, women would be wise to recall Cheris Kramarae and Paula Treichler's definition of "flattery": "praise commonly given to women in substitution for money and occupational status." According to Kramarae and Treichler, admiring remarks, such as kind words about a woman's appearance, are often nothing more that an attempt by men "to keep women happily in their traditional place."[164] (Indeed, because they may violate the "unwelcome verbal conduct" provision of the Civil Rights Act of 1964, unsolicited compliments can subject the complimentor to prosecution if the complimentee objects.) Example: *"Giving me praise in substitution for money and occupational status will get you nowhere," snapped Hélène to the honey-tongued lothario.* See: **flattery, withholding; clothing, verbal comments about; love notes.**

**flattery, withholding.**  Before failing to offer a compliment to a date or sex partner, men would be wise to recall Claudette McShane's description, in her helpful guidebook *Warning! Dating May Be Hazardous to Your Health!,* of men's systematic need to "humiliate and embarrass the women they're with in order to maintain their supposed superior status." "A man," she adds, "can't allow a woman to feel as though she may be adequate because he fears he could lose control and she may dethrone him in his superior position."[165] See: **flattery.**

**flipping.**  Boys in the fourth grade or higher who are found guilty of "flipping"—the traditional elementary school ritual of flipping up a little girl's skirt—are now punishable as **sexual harassers** under a new California state law that went into effect in January 1993. "Flipping . . . is terribly embarrassing and humiliating," explains California state senator Gary K. Hart, who sponsored the legislation. Nan Stein, of the Wellesley College Center for Research on Women, agrees; indeed, she considers flipping to be nothing less than **gendered terrorism.**[166]

**flowers.**  The presentation of flowers by a man before escorting a woman on a date

*Instruments of ritual violation being delivered to a victim before the kill.*

is a definite no-no, according to feminist scholar Andrea Dworkin. "The traditional flowers of courtship," she advises us in *Letters from a War Zone*, "are the traditional flowers of the grave, delivered to the victim before the kill. The cadaver is dressed up and made up and laid down and ritually violated and consecrated to an eternity of being used."[167] See also: **favors.**

**food play.** The Terrence Higgins Trust, an AIDS support group, recommends erotic "food play" as a low-risk, high-fun alternative for those who find the physical, ethical, or political risks of "penetrative" sex unacceptably high.[168] Before you or your partner initiate or consent to a food-play session, however, you should be aware that the University of Maryland at College Park has placed "holding or eating food provocatively" on its official list of "unacceptable gestures and non-verbal behaviors that may be in violation of campus policy on sexual harassment."[169] See: **provocative eating.**

**food-service rape.** In a *Newsweek* guest editorial, reprinted in *Nation's Restaurant News,* Connecticut waitress Stacey Wilkins recounts in harrowing detail how a group of male "country-club tennis buddies" refused to cut their match short, arrived at the restaurant where she worked a full 15 minutes after closing time, dawdled endlessly over the pizza they somehow conned the restaurant's owner into supplying, and then "violated" her by ordering dessert. "Tears streamed down my face," Wilkins writes. "This was a watershed: the culmination of a decade of abuse. I am now at the breaking point." Indeed, Wilkins concludes, her experience was nothing less than an "emotional rape."[170]

*A dessert, similar to the one used in the brutal **food-service rape** of Stacey Wilkins.*

**foreplay.** *Scarlet Women* magazine defines "foreplay" as "what men have to do to get women to open their legs voluntarily."[171] And, writes Anne Koedt, since foreplay was "a concept created for male purposes," it "works to the disadvantage of many women." "As soon as the woman is aroused," Koedt explains, "the man changes to vaginal stimulation, leaving her both aroused and dissatisfied."[172] See also: **foreplay, chatter during; foreplay harassment.**

**foreplay, chatter during.** College women who don't feel their institution's sexual-offense rules offer adequate protection against men who might try to talk them into engaging in unwelcome sex acts would be wise to keep chatter during foreplay to a minimum. Indeed, as *The New Yorker* magazine has pointed out, a major shortcoming of the Antioch Sexual Offense Policy is that, by demanding a running dialogue between sex partners, it actually

*Survival Strategy #1: Minimizing* **chatter during foreplay.**

aids and abets men who are adept at using persuasive language to seduce women.[173]

**foreplay harassment.** An offense that Kenneth C. Cooper, author of "The Six Levels of Sexual Harassment," classifies as a Level 4 violation: more flagrant than "aesthetic appreciation," "mental groping," and "social touching," but less serious than "sexual abuse" and "ultimate threat." Among the behaviors that Cooper classifies as "foreplay harassment" is a male manager's brushing up against a female employee "as if by accident."[174] See also: **aesthetic appreciation; mental groping; social touching**.

**foreskin restoration movement.** The growing trend among determined male circumcision survivors to "re-create" their foreskins, either by surgery or by using an ingenious stretching technique, involving weights and adhesive tape, invented by movement leader Jim Bigelow. The two reasons men most frequently cite for "uncircumcising," as Bigelow calls his stretching process: (1) They believe that restoring their penis's natural covering will allow it to regain the sensitivity it has lost from years of unprotected rubbing up against their underwear; and (2) they want to erase the pain—both physical and emotional—they suffered when their parents permitted infant circumcision to be performed on them without their consent. "Having a foreskin has restored to me a completeness, a psychological sense of wholeness which was missing," enthused Bigelow after spending four years perfecting his own process on himself.[175] See also: **BUFF; NOHARMM; keratinization; RECAP; UNCIRC; uncircumcising**.

**four-leggeds, joining the world of.** One of the best ways to "recover the wild man" that lives deep within the male psyche, says men's movement leader Dr. Shepherd (né Walter) Bliss, is "to temporarily leave the world of the two-leggeds" and join him "in the world of the four-leggeds." "You may find yourself behaving like these four-leggeds," Bliss tells the men who attend his seminars. "You may be scratching the earth, getting in contact with the dirt and the world around you." At this point, says Jon Tevlin, who wrote about Bliss in the *Utne Reader*, people usually start pawing at the ground.[176] See also: **ram, behaving like a; gorilla, dressing up as a; proud serpent's tail, rooting one's body to the ground with one's.**

**Freedom Trash Cans.** Special wastebaskets, commissioned in the early 1970s by the Women's Strike for Equality, in which women were encouraged to deposit their perfume bottles, compacts, lipsticks, etc., as a protest against their "cosmetic subjugation."[177] See: **cosmetic subjugation.**

**free speech.** University of Hawaii law professor Mari Matsuda has recommended a strict campus speech code under which anyone making a remark that proved offensive to women and minorities would be subject to punishment. Offensive remarks made by women and minorities about white men, however, would still receive First Amendment protection. "Hateful verbal attacks upon dominant group members by victims are permissible," she explains.[178]

**French kissing.** It's rape, antisexism crusader Rus Ervin Funk points out, whenever a man puts any body part or object into a woman's mouth without her express consent.[179] Knowing this, male readers will certainly want to make sure they don't move from "regular" kissing to tongue kissing until they're absolutely convinced that their partners want them to proceed. Indeed, even in consensual situations, people may want to eschew French kissing, suggests nurse practitioner Josephine Bolus of the Kings County Hospital Center in Brooklyn, New York, because it can "bring you into contact with . . . blood or saliva." "It's nearly impossible to get [sexually transmitted] diseases by kissing with your mouth closed," she reminds us.[180]

**friendly pats.** A "friendly pat," the Working Women's United Institute informs us, is one of the many specific behaviors that constitutes workplace sexual harassment.[181]

**frigidity.** See **heterosexual celibacy.**

**fructal objectification.**   It's a very poor idea to use a banana to demonstrate how to use a condom, especially if you attempt to "enrich" your presentation with so-called "humorous" remarks. Toni Blake, an instructor at the University of Nebraska, found this out the hard way (no pun intended) when she introduced a banana as a prop during her class on human sexuality and observed, while discussing the proper "timing" for condom application, that men, not unlike basketball players, sometimes "dribble before they shoot." One of Blake's male students immediately pressed sexual harassment charges against her, accusing her of "objectifying his penis" and, as a result, creating a "hostile academic environment for him as a man." In a triumph for the new appropriateness, Blake's department chairman decided that, at least while the case was pending, she should be relieved of her human sexuality teaching duties.[182] (Note: The booklet used by Antioch College to present its Sexual Offense Policy to incoming students features a "flip-book movie" of a condom being applied to a banana, an unpardonable example of **fructal objectification** that the American Gender Society trusts will be expunged from future editions.)

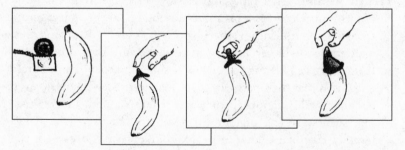

*Images from an Antioch College flip-book depicting
a condom being applied to a banana—an unpardonable
example of* **fructal objectification.**

**fucking.**   "Nothing is less an act of love and more an act of ownership [and] violation," opines Andrea Dworkin, "than fucking."[183]

See also: **coitus; enclosure; engulfment; envelopment; intercourse; nutting; outercourse; vagina-specific fucking.**

**fucking, vagina-specific.** See: vagina-specific fucking.

**furniture moving.** When a man moves heavy furniture for a woman, he may *seem* to be helping her. But, Nancy Henley instructs us in her book *Body Politics*, the gesture is actually one of a whole range of strategies called "protection rackets" that men employ to keep women from realizing they're perfectly capable of coping with their environment without male intervention. The moral for our women readers is clear: The next time you want to rearrange those sofas, tables, and chairs, do it yourself![184] See: **protection rackets.**

*Survival Strategy #2: Nipping* **furniture moving** *in the bud.*

**gender.** Although many use the terms "sex" and "gender" interchangeably, such usage is incorrect and misleading, Virginia Prince reminds us in her essay "Sex, Gender and Semantics." "Sex" should be used, she says, only to describe unequivocal *biological* functions—such as making eggs or sperm—while "gender" should be seen as a purely *cultural* phenomenon, "the accumulation of information and behavior patterns that are passed on from generation to generation." Thus, she points out, such terms as "male" and "female" refer to *sex,* while "girl," "boy," "man," and "woman" refer to *gender.*[185] See also: **essentialism; sex; vagina-specific fucking.**

**gender advisor.** Brown University medical science professor Anne Fausto-Sterling's term for a counselor qualified to help intersexuals decide whether to maintain their natural position on the female-male continuum or to enlist the aid of "a surgical shoehorn" in an effort to become what Western society deems a "normal" man or woman.[186] See: **intersexual; two-party sexual system.**

**gender community.** A sexually correct term for transvestites, transsexuals, and transgendered persons. As Alan Hamilton points out in his *Sexual Identity and Gender Identity Glossary,* some members of the gender community also "identify as members of the sexual minority community" (i.e., they are also gays, lesbians, or bisexuals). But, it's important to note, many others are heterosexuals.[187] See: **sexual minority community.**

**gender dysphoria.** Alan Hamilton, in his *Sexual Identity and Gender Identity Glossary,* defines this as "unhappiness or discomfort experienced by one whose sexual organs do not match one's gender identity."[188] Example: *Renée Richards's sexual reassignment surgery not only addressed her* **gender dysphoria,** *but also greatly improved her tennis ranking.* See: **gender identity; preoperative transsexual.**

**gendered terrorism.** A term Nan Stein, a project director at the Wellesley College Center for Research on Women, uses to describe elementary school boys' chronic predilection for flipping up girls' skirts.[189] See: **flipping.**

**gender harassment.** P. Franklin, J. Moglin, P. Zatling-Boring, and R. Angress, authors of "Sexual and Gender Harassment in the Academy," define "gender harassment" as verbal behaviors such as "remarks, jokes, and innuendoes," that are "directed at women because they are women." "These behaviors," they add, "may or may not be aimed at eliciting sexual cooperation from women."[190]

**gender identity.** According to Alan Hamilton's *Sexual Identity and Gender Identity Glossary,* the term "gender identity" is used to denote one's "psychological gender role: *masculine* or *feminine.*"[191] See: **gender role; gender dysphoria.**

**gender justice.** A system of morality based on the principle that, since (to quote antipatriarchal activist Harry Brod) "the process by which we all become engendered is a process of manufactured difference being imposed on us,"[192] every action, attitude, behavior, convention, custom, institution, law, and relationship based on this "manufactured difference" must be abolished, modified, or replaced.

**gender oppression.** Poet Cheryl Clarke defines this as "the male exploitation and control of women's productive and reproductive energies on the specious basis of a biological difference."[193]

**gender reconciliation facilitators.** Men and women confused about the appropriate way to relate to members of the opposite sex have nothing to lose—and everything to gain—by seeking the services of a "gender reconciliation facilitator." Such facilitators are also recommended for resolving the increasing number of arguments about whether it is men or women who are more oppressed in Western society.[194] For more information about engaging gender reconciliation facilitators, contact:

The Menswork Center
1950 Sawtelle Boulevard, Suite 34
Los Angeles, CA 90025
(213) 479-2749

See also: **Saint Monica, pilgrimages to the statue of.**

**gender role.** Alan Hamilton's *Sexual Identity and Gender Identity Glossary* defines "gender role" as a set of "arbitrary rules, assigned by society, that define what clothing, behaviors, thoughts, feelings, relationships, etc., are considered appropriate and inappropriate for members of each sex."[195] See also: **gender identity; gender dysphoria.**

**genital myth.** Author Sally Cline's term, patterned after Naomi Wolf's famous coinage the **beauty myth,** for the political "construct" that forces women to go on having sex when, as Joan Smith of the British newspaper *The Independent* puts it, "they would rather listen to opera or Joan Armatrading." The myth is "policed" by a group of people Cline refers to as the "genital mythmasters."[196] See also: **beauty myth; Genital Power Elite.**

**Genital Power Elite.** A term for men popularized by Sally Cline, author of *Women, Celibacy and Passion,* a book in which she argues that women's best chance for success in the struggle against male oppression is to avoid "sexual intercourse and general genital thrashing about."[197]

*The Three Stooges, members of the*
**Genital Power Elite.**

**genitalia, female.** Here's what "Kit," a woman whose interview with Sally Cline is quoted in Cline's book, *Women, Celibacy and Passion,* has to say about female genitalia: "Men go on about that bit of the body all the time. Male sexuality centers on women's genitals as if that's what it's about. Well it isn't."[198]

**ghettoes, keeping women in.** See: couples.

**giving up a seat for a woman.** Be warned: When a man offers to give up his seat for a woman, he's not *really* trying to be respectful. On the contrary, Nancy Henley cautions in *Body Politics,* the gesture—so generous on the surface—is actually a clear, if ironic, attempt by the man to assert his superior ability to cope. And to make matters worse, Henley advises, "men who temporarily role-play at subservience, by, e.g., opening a door [or] giving up a seat, do not, like real servants, fade into the woodwork but instead gain attention as a primary focus of the ritual."[199]

**glove.** A street-slang term for "condom." It reached broad public consciousness as part of the phrase "No glove, no love," a slogan designed to popularize the concept that to protect herself from HIV infection, a woman should withhold sexual intercourse from any man who is not wearing a condom. See: **"No glove, no love."**

**gloves, latex.** See: latex gloves.

**glow-in-the-dark condoms.** In connection with their safer-sex awareness program, the six Claremont Colleges, located in California's San Gabriel Valley, recently made "glow-in-the-dark condoms" available to all their students. Each of the novelty condoms, which cost $1 apiece, comes with a specific warning that it should not be used as a contraceptive or to prevent the transmission of diseases.[200]

**God, our queen and lover.** As part of her mission to remove "sexist and dominant" references from Jewish prayers, Philadelphia rabbi Rebecca Alpert refers to God as "she" and "queen." She also finds "images of inequality between the exalted divine and the lowly human" objectionable, and urges that God should instead be spoken of as "lover, friend, companion, partner." John Leo, reporting on Alpert's crusade in *The San Diego Union-Tribune*, offers a new first line for Psalm XXIII: "God is my girlfriend, I shall not want . . ."[201]

**Goddess in the Office Workshops.** Professional women who want to learn how to use witchcraft to stop sexual harassment or prevent corporate takeovers may be interested in attending a "Goddess in the Office Workshop" run by feminist witch Zsuzsanna Emese Budapest, the woman who (according to editor Kay Leigh Hagan) deserves credit for "sparking/creating" the Goddess Movement.[202] You can arrange for one to be held in your area by writing to:

> Goddess in the Office Workshops
> P.O. Box 11353
> Oakland, CA 94611

See also: **Goddess Movement; bergamot oil; Hot Foot powder; pig's tongue.**

**Goddess Movement.** A loosely organized, broad-based movement whose goal is to resurrect the spirituality of the ancient, female-centered, goddess-worshiping religions that many archaeologists believe thrived until (as Douglas Todd of the *Vancouver Sun* phrases it) "patriarchal religions came in to mess things up." Among the many popular manifestations of the Goddess Movement are:

- a renewed interest in Wicca (Old English for "witch"), a form of nature worship that reigned in ancient Europe;
- the celebration of female divinity, as embodied in "Mother Earth," whose seasonal rhythms, closely echoing female reproductive cycles, have inspired thousands of women to gather for ritual observances of such occasions as equinoxes, solstices, new moons, and the annual Perseid meteor shower;
- new reverence for such specific deities as ancient Greece's Gaea, the Navajos' Changing Woman, and Asia's Kuan Yin;

- the production, by a small bakery in upstate New York, of chocolate cookies molded in the shape of the Venus of Willendorf, the world's oldest known example of goddess statuary (you can buy them at $9 per pound);
- the founding, by feminist witch Zsuzsanna Emese Budapest, of the Susan B. Anthony Coven #1, and the institution, also by Budapest, of "Goddess in the Office" Workshops; and
- the admission to the faculty of the Institute of Culture and Creative Spirituality, located on the campus of Holy Names College in Oakland, of the noted witch and Goddess Movement leader, Starhawk.

The reaction of the patriarchy to Starhawk's appointment was swift and hardly surprising: Rev. Matthew Fox, the director of the Institute of Culture and Creative Spirituality, was sentenced by his Roman Catholic superiors to a year of public silence. This incident has led to ominous talk of renewed "witch hunts" and reminders that the traditional association of witchcraft with satanism is, to quote the *Los Angeles Times*'s Irene Lacher, a "bad rap imposed on Goddess paganism by its Christian opponents." "No true witches today practice human sacrifice, torture, or any form of ritual murder," Starhawk assures us in her book *The Spiral Dance.* "Anyone who does is not a witch, but a psychopath."[203] See also: **Goddess in the Office Workshops; prepatriarchal cultures; Venus of Willendorf; wombmoon.**

**going to a man's apartment.** Carol Pritchard, author of *Avoiding Rape On and Off Campus,* has some good advice for all college-age women: "Think carefully before you go to a male friend's apartment," she writes. "Do not expose yourself to any unnecessary risk."[204] See also: **one-on-one time.**

**gooching.** Accusing a man of rape without justification. The term gained currency in England after finance clerk Susan Gooch was convicted of "attempting to pervert the cause of justice" by falsely charging two men with assaulting her. One was a stranger whom she picked up in a Covent Garden restaurant and proceeded to have consensual sex with in a shop doorway and on a tube train (in full view of the driver); the other was a colleague, who was home watching television at the time.[205] (Note: According to Catherine Comins, assistant dean of student life at Vassar College, men who are gooched may actually benefit from the experience. For details, see: **rape, false accusations of.**)

**gorilla, dressing up as a.** Among the innovative therapeutic techniques the world-famous Sterling Institute of Relationships uses to enrich men's ability to interact with others is getting them to dress up as gorillas, beat their chests, and stage fistfights.[206] See also: **ape within; four-leggeds, joining the world of; ram, behaving like a.**

**"Gotcha" stickers.** On the night of March 21, 1991, women undergraduates at Duke University dramatized the constant danger *all* women face from rapists by ambushing solitary male students and plastering them with fluorescent orange "Gotcha" stickers. Just how much reeducation may be required, however, was demonstrated by the reaction of junior biology major Michael Fritz, who told a *New York Times* correspondent he hadn't been "worried or frightened" when a woman stuck her head through the door of the room where he was studying and asked him if he was alone. He was, the *Times* reports, "merely surprised when she stuck a sticker on him. 'I know there's no danger of my ever being raped,' Mr. Fritz said. 'I'm on the wrestling team and stuff, and I really don't have a whole lot of fear.' "[207]

**Goya's "The Naked Maja."** See: **art "masterpieces" featuring nude women.**

**groin, kicking a man in the.** See: **kicking a man in the groin.**

**groping, mental.** See: **mental groping.**

**guilt, men's.** It's perfectly natural for men to feel guilty about what they've *done*—after thousands of years of rape, subjugation, and brutality, how could they not? But Starhawk, author of *The Spiral Dance: A Rebirth of the Ancient Religion of the Great Goddess,* has heard that more than a few men are also feeling guilty about who they *are,* and she doesn't like it. "Some woman gave birth to you, shaped your male body inside her," she reminds her male readers. "Honor her by taking pride in yourself."[208] Unfortunately, Starhawk's well-meaning exhortation has only served to increase the already considerable burden of men's inappropriate guilt. See also: **guilty men.**

**guilt, women's.** See: **making a woman feel guilty (as a means of obtaining sex).**

**guilty men.**  One of the two large classifications—the other is "macho pigs"—into which social commentator Cynthia Heimel says all today's men can be divided. Guilty men, writes Heimel, "who know and hate that women have been oppressed for centuries," are "no fun at all, because guilt causes low self-esteem and general wimpiness. Guilt makes men clutch their heads and mutter, then fall asleep with their clothes on."[209] See also: **macho pigs.**

**gun control (as a form of sex discrimination).**  Self-defense advocate Karen McNutt notes that gun control "perpetuates the victim status of women" by making it more difficult for them to pursue their careers in urban areas, which, while offering the greatest opportunity for professional advancement, are also the most crime-ridden. Encouraging women to carry weapons would free them from fear, McNutt writes, thus empowering them to "compete successfully in the business world." "For too long women have accepted the roll [*sic*] of natural victim," she concludes. "This must stop."[210]

**gurgling.** See: **ram, behaving like a.**

**gynandrous love.**  A more appropriate term for the type of ideal love that Ann Ferguson originally described as "androgynous."[211] See: **androgynous love.**

**gynandry.**  University of Massachusetts philosophy professor Ann Ferguson defines "gynandry" as an optimal type of personal development that transcends the outmoded, stereotypical labels "masculine" or "feminine"—and all the "negative and distorted personality characteristics" associated with them. Unfortunately, Ferguson writes, our present-day "sexist society" considers anyone who dares to express the "traits, skills and interests" associated with gynandry "a social outcast or deviant." In the ideal future world that Ferguson envisions, however, it will "no longer matter" whether one is a man or a woman, and this problem will disappear.[212] (Note: To learn why it's inappropriate to refer to gynandry as "androgyny," and how gynandry can improve your sex life, see: **androgynous love**.)

**gynocide.**   Andrea Dworkin defines this as "the systematic crippling, raping and/or killing of women by men . . . the relentless violence perpetrated by the gender class men on the gender class women." "Under patriarchy," Dworkin concludes sadly, "gynocide is the ongoing reality of life lived by women."[213] See also: **androcide**.

**Halloween.** Andrea Dworkin suggests that Halloween should be renamed "Witches' Eve" in memory of "the nine million women" who, over the past three hundred years, have been branded as witches and slaughtered by European and American men. "Let us together make it a time of mourning," she writes, "for all women who are victims of gynocide, dead, in jail, in mental institutions, raped, sterilized against their wills, brutalized."[214]

**Halloween parties.** No women—not even those who choose to ignore Andrea Dworkin's suggestion that Halloween should be recast as a night of mourning for the victims of gynocide—should allow themselves to be talked into attending a Halloween party without first recalling that the majority faction of the Student Senate at the University of Wisconsin at Madison has voted to prohibit campus-wide masquerade balls. Their reasoning: The anonymity afforded by wearing masks permits men to "poke," "pinch," and inflict "rude comments" upon women without fear of punishment.[215]

**hamburgers.** According to Jeremy Rifkin, author of *Beyond Beef,* hamburgers can cause wife beating. "The statistics linking domestic violence and quarrels over beef are both revealing and compelling," he writes. To illustrate his point, Rifkin offers the following quote from a battered woman: "It would start off with him being angry over a trivial thing like cheese instead of meat on a sandwich."[216] See also: **meat eating; stomach that has no ears, the.**

**hand clutching.** For a discussion of why hand clutching is "assaultive," see: **continuum theories.**

**hand-drum-assisted communication.** Jamal Mohmed, a therapeutic drumming specialist from Dallas, Texas, observes that hand drums can be just the thing to "open up" psychiatric patients who normally have difficulty communicating. "It's like the drum gives them another voice to speak through, and since it's not their voice, they feel freer to use it," he says.[217] Men who find it hard to share their emotions with women, or who feel shy about making the explicit verbal requests required under the Antioch Sexual Offense Policy, might want to try bringing a small hand drum along with them on their next date to use as an ice-breaker, as a confidence booster, or as a trusted "other voice" to help communicate a desire for intimacy. See also: **drum therapy; puppet surrogates; tactile-vestibular activity**.

*A* **hand-drum-assisted** *policy activation request being rejected by a woman using a puppet surrogate.*

**handshakes.** Attempting to shake the hand of one's date—even a date one has never met before—is an act to be assiduously avoided by men and women alike. As Nancy Henley tells us in *Body Politics,* the handshake is "a masculine ritual of recognition and affirmation [that] serves to perpetuate male clubiness and exclude women from the club."[218] Thus, a man who shakes the hand of a woman is, at the very least, showing insensitivity that borders on sexism; a woman shaking the hand of a man is conspiring in the erasure of her own gender.

*Former British prime minister Margaret Thatcher conspiring in the erasure of her own gender.*

**harassers, prepubescent.** Evidence—as if evidence were needed!—that men are never too young to become sexual abusers comes from an elementary school in Virginia, where a second-grade boy was recently found guilty of sexual harassment for pinching a female schoolmate in "a private area." Needless to say, the young harasser was summarily expelled.[219] See also: **depantsing; Dignity, the Snail; Equality, the Frog; flipping; gendered terrorism; Respect, the Turtle; snuggies; tickling.**

*A potential* **prepubescent harasser.**

**harassment, in vitro.**  See: in vitro sexual harassment.

**harassment, metaphorical.**  See: metaphorical harassment.

**headgear, sexually objectionable.**  According to Susan Strauss and Pamela Espeland, authors of *Sexual Harassment and Teens: A Program for Positive Change*, "wearing an obscene hat" is one of the ominous examples of "sexually harassing behavior" that have been reported in U.S. high schools.[220]

**heavy petting.**  See: petting; blue balls.

**helping a woman move furniture.**  See: furniture moving.

**Hepwa.**  The ancient West African god of Deep Masculinity. An increasing number of Western men—especially those involved in the mythopoetic men's movement—have found that raising their voices in supplication to Hepwa can help improve their ability to relate to women. It's apparently particularly helpful to be drumming at the time one invokes Hepwa's spirit, so men who plan to seek the deity's help during an upcoming date may want to consider bringing their drums along.[221] See also: **drum therapy; hand-drum-assisted communication; Sons of Orpheus.**

**herms.**  Brown University intersexual rights advocate Anne Fausto-Sterling's term for those whom dominant-culture medical professionals call "true hermaphrodites"—individuals possessing one ovary and one testis. As Fausto-Sterling and an increasing number of others have pointed out, the division of the human race into only two sexes is an artificial construction of Western society; herms are one of at least five "gradations" that lie along the spectrum from female to male.[222] See also: **ferms; intersexual; merms; two-party sexual system.**

**het.**  A colloquial term for "heterosexual," often—though not always—implying bemusement or condescension on the part of the speaker.[223]

**Hets.**

**heterosexism.** A handout distributed by the Smith College Office of Student Affairs defines "heterosexism" as the "oppression of those of sexual orientations other than heterosexual, such as gays, lesbians and bisexuals." "This can take place," the handout adds, "by not acknowledging their existence."[224] See also: *Romeo and Juliet*.

**heterosexual celibacy.** The appropriate term for what, in less enlightened times, might have been called **frigidity**. The new phrase is more accurate, Dale Spender suggests, because it demonstrates that, unlike male impotence, frigidity is not a failing, but rather a *conscious choice*—"a form of power against the oppressor, a form of passive resistance."[225] See also: **sexual deprivation (as a motive for relationship termination)**.

**heterosexuality.** In an illuminating essay in *This Bridge Called Our Back: Writings by Radical Women of Color,* Cheryl Clarke defines "heterosexuality" as "a diehard custom through which male-supremacist institutions insure their own perpetuity and control over us. Women are kept, maintained, and contained through terror, violence, and spray of semen."[226] For a woman to engage in it, therefore, is nothing less than treason; indeed, Andrea Dworkin warns, "unambiguous conventional heterosexual behavior is the worst betrayal of our common humanity."[227] See also: **compulsory heterosexuality; heterosexual sexual identity**.

*A woman betraying her common humanity by engaging in* **heterosexuality.**

**heterosexuality, compulsory.** See: compulsory heterosexuality.

**heterosexuality, optional.**  See: compulsory heterosexuality.

**heterosexual sexual identity.**  Heterosexual sexual identity is neither innate nor "natural," Shulamith Firestone informs us in *The
Dialectic of Sex*. Indeed, she intimates, human babies are born
bisexual, and the majority turn into heterosexuals only as a by-
product of the power dynamics of the "patriarchal nuclear family."
According to Firestone, the process works likes this: Boys and girls
discover early in life that their father has more power than their
mother. Both, "in order to get power for themselves," soon recog-
nize they have to reject the mother as a love object: the boy because
he sees his father as an all-too-potent competitor and "potential
castrator," and the girl because "the only way as a girl she can attain
power is through manipulating the father. So she becomes a rival to
her mother for her father's love. The girl comes to identify with her
mother and to choose her father and later, other men for love
objects; while the boy identifies with his father, sublimates his
attraction to his mother into superego (will power), and chooses
mother substitutes, other women, for his love objects."[228]

**himbo.**  A term used by *Boston Globe* correspondent Judith Gaines,
among others, to describe a sexy but mindless man. The "himbo"
stereotype is becoming increasingly evident in the mainstream
media, Gaines notes, most notably in a spate of advertisements
featuring nude or seminude men. Such images, she points out, can
be beneficial in that they allow men to see how it feels to be sexually exploited; indeed, she tells us, Boston advertising executive
John Carroll calls the trend "equality by subtraction" because "it
drags men down to the level where women already suffer." But
Adam Thorburn, who conducts research on sexism and the media
at Sarah Lawrence College, sees the objectification of men not as a
step toward parity between the genders but as just another device
for subjugating women. Ads featuring undressed females typically
reveal their weakness, openness, and vulnerability, Thorburn
notes, while undressed males "show their muscularity, like a coat
of armor made by their own flesh."[229]

**ho!** A Native American expression meaning "I understand." Joseph Jastrab, a "facilitator of the inevitable" from New Paltz, New York, suggests that grunting it while a man is baring his soul to you is an excellent way to encourage intimacy.[230] Jastrab's specific experience with "ho!-grunting" is apparently confined to mytho-poetic men's retreats, but there's no reason to think the practice wouldn't also be helpful to couples in dating or love relationships who want to affirm efforts by their partners—male *or* female—to share their deepest feelings. Before grunting "ho!" to your significant other, however, two pieces of cautionary advice are in order: (1) Make sure the object of your affections is not among those outraged by what Native American writer Sherman Alexie calls the " 'Indians 'R' Us' commodification" of indigenous customs and artifacts[231]; and (2) If you're a man grunting at a woman, be certain that she doesn't mistake your cry of "ho!" ("I understand") for "ho" (African-American slang for **sex-care provider**).

**holding hands.** See: **affection, public displays of.**

**homophobia.** A term that originally meant an irrational fear of same-sex attraction but, as Alan Hamilton points out in his *Sexual Identity and Gender Identity Glossary,* is now used to describe "all aspects of the oppression of lesbians, gay men, and bisexuals." "This oppression," Hamilton writes, "ranges from not including LesBiGays in one's circle of friends, and media reports on and representations of LesBiGays in society, through the cold shoulder, snide comments, verbal harassment, assault, rape, and murder based on the target person's (perceived) sexual identity."[232] (Note: Before using the term "homophobia," readers should be advised that the philosopher Richard D. Mohr rejects it in favor of "fear of gays" or "fear of lesbians." His reasoning: The word "homophobia" is "morally misleading" because it transforms bigotry into "an abstract clinical illness" that "relieves the individual of social and moral responsibility."[233]) See also: **LesBiGay; biphobia; homophobic laughter.**

**homophobic laughter.** Students convicted of this offense at Sarah Lawrence College can be placed on "social probation," be required to write a "reflection paper" on **homophobia,** and be sentenced to perform ten hours of community service. That's the punishment undergraduate Marlin Lask received after he allegedly laughed when his friend John Boesky called fellow Sarah Lawrence student Peter Nichols a "faggot." The defamatory epithet was apparently uttered after Nichols had used "effeminate" gestures to mock Boesky's performance in a college play, and had also uttered disparaging remarks about the financial conduct of Boesky's famous father, Ivan. Boesky has since apologized for his conduct and has promised never again to "use words that perpetuate problems in our society." But Lask, who seems to have learned nothing from his experience, has enlisted the aid of the New York Civil Liberties Union in an attempt to "clear" his record, and has decided to pursue his studies elsewhere.[234]

**honey.** "Honey," as profeminist Alan Alda has noted, is an inappropriate address label "unless you are a bear talking to your lunch."[235] How then should a woman respond to this so-called "term of endearment"? Mona Howard suggests a devastating pair of ripostes to hurl back at any man who subjects her to it: "Young Lad" if he's younger than thirty, and "Old Man" if he is older.[236]

**hostile environment sexual harassment.** A category of sex discrimination that was first identified by legal scholar Catharine A. MacKinnon and that, thanks largely to her efforts, was officially classified in 1980 by the U.S. Equal Employment Opportunity Commission as a civil rights violation. The EEOC categorizes hostile environment sexual harassment as any "unwelcome verbal or physical conduct" that creates an "intimidating, hostile, or offensive working environment," a landmark definition under which previously unpunishable offenses, such as writing an unsolicited love letter to a fellow employee, publicly displaying a photo of one's wife wearing a bathing suit, telling off-color jokes around the water cooler, and leaving one's newspaper open to a page on which a bra advertisement appears, have been successfully out-lawed and/or prosecuted.[237] See also: **quid pro quo sexual harass-ment; right not to be offended.**

**Hot Foot powder.** Feminist witch Zsuzsanna Emese Budapest sug-gests to career women that "Hot Foot powder," which one can obtain from one's neighborhood occult supply store or from a specialty catalog, can work wonders in getting men to stop harass-ing them. "It is a white powder that will sink undetectably into the carpet," Budapest writes in *The Goddess in the Office,* "and the idea is to sprinkle it somewhere where your harasser will walk. Before you sprinkle the powder, hold your hands over it, project your will into the substance, and say three times:

> You will now rise, you will now walk,
> You will now fly, you will now disappear.
> Out of my life, out of this office,
> Out of this project, out of my world.
> Blessed be!"[238]

See also: **bergamot oil; pig's tongue.**

**house niggers.** A term used by Catharine MacKinnon to describe the Feminists Against Censorship Taskforce (FACT), a group founded by Betty Friedan, Adrienne Rich, Rita Mae Brown, and other women who have somehow become convinced that the right of free speech might eventually prove more useful to those oppos-ing patriarchy than constitutionally sus-pect curbs on the dissemination of explicitly sexual materials. "The labor movement had its scabs," says MacKin-non, "the slavery movement had its Uncle Toms, and we have FACT."[239]

**housewifery.** "Since housewifery and pros-titution have the same structure," argues

*A woman perpetrating an act of* **housewifery.**

Ann Ferguson, "it is hypocritical to outlaw one and not the other." While she would ideally like to see the elimination of both, Ferguson acknowledges that "capitalist patriarchy" is not likely to support the prohibition of housewifery. Therefore, as an interim step, she advocates "the elimination of legal sanctions against prostitution."[240]

**hugging.**  See: dancing too close.

**human beings who happen to have been born penised.**  One of the terms John Stoltenberg, author of *Refusing to Be a Man*, uses to describe the individuals who used to be called "men" until Stoltenberg and others discovered that gender was merely a "political and ethical construction."[241] See: essentialism; human creatures with a Y chromosome; human infant who is accidentally born with an elongated genital; humans who were born without a penis.

*Sylvester Stallone, a* **human being who happens to have been born penised.**

**human creatures with a Y chromosome.**  A nonessentialist term for "men" coined by clinical psychologist Laura S. Brown.[242] See also: essentialism; human beings who happen to have been born penised; Y chromosome.

**human infant who is accidentally born with an elongated genital.**  An admirably sexually correct phrase used by John Stoltenberg, author of *Refusing to Be a Man*, to describe what is traditionally known as a "male baby."[243]

**human sexual spectrum.** See: intersexual; continuum theories.

**humans who were born without a penis.** A phrase created by John Stoltenberg to emphasize the fact that men's age-old tendency to consider women "different" (and presumably inferior) on the basis of the accidental and totally unimportant fact that they don't possess a phallus is arbitrary, unreasonable, and discriminatory. Some feminists have argued that Stoltenberg's term is phallocentric, since it defines women in terms of a male organ that women *don't* possess, rather than a female one that they do. However, the growing number of individuals who agree with Stoltenberg that gender differences are merely a political construct reject alternate usages like "humans who were born vagi- naed" on the grounds that such phrases inflate the importance of the sex organ in determining a person's identity.[244] See: **human beings who happen to have been born penised.**

*Hillary Rodham Clinton, a* **human who was born without a penis.**

**humor and jokes about sex or women in general.** Bernice Sandler, director of the Project on the Status and Education of Women of the Association of American Colleges, cites the shocking statistic that between 20 and 30 percent of all women attending college experience "sexually harassing behaviors" at some point during their undergraduate careers. One of the specific behaviors they are forced to endure, she notes, is "humor and jokes about sex or women in general."[245] See also: **intellectual harassment; mopping jokes; stupid-women jokes.**

**hurting women.** Before a woman consents to allow a man—even a man she knows well and trusts—to have sex with her, she would be well advised to reflect on the following warning from Andrea Dworkin: "The hurting of women is . . . basic to the sexual pleasure of men."[246]

**hypnotic regression.** A psychotherapeutic technique that practitioners employ to help subjects remember, often in startling detail, traumatic incidents of sexual abuse, or even of extraterrestrial abduction and rape, which they otherwise might never have recalled, and which may, in fact, not have occurred.[247] Also known as **repressed memory therapy**.

# I

**ideal love.** See: androgynous love.

**ideological jock straps.** *Ms.* magazine says John Stoltenberg's book of essays, *Refusing to Be a Man,* "rips the ideological jock straps off" the "myths about male sexual identity." "Anybody out there who *can't* think of a guy who needs it?" the magazine goes on to ask.[248]

**inappropriate innuendo.** According to a training manual distributed at Swarthmore College, inappropriate innuendo is an offense that lies within the "spectrum of incidents and behaviors" encompassed by the term **acquaintance rape.**[249]

**insignificant other.** A former husband, wife, boyfriend, girlfriend, or lover.[250]

**institutional power.** Access to political, economic, and interpersonal power (such as networking and social acceptance) within the dominant culture. As a handout distributed by the Smith College Office of Student Affairs points out, a group needs such power in order to be able to oppress other groups, and thus only men can be guilty of sexism. Even if women should wish to "return the favor," they lack the resources to do so.[251]

**intellectual harassment.** A term coined by the Modern Language Association Committee on the Status of Women to describe such behaviors as "easy dismissal of feminist writers"; "automatic deprecation of feminist work as 'narrow,' 'partisan,' and 'lacking in rigor'"; and "malicious humor directed against feminists."[252]

**intercourse.** Before agreeing to, or commencing intercourse, especially with a new partner, it's useful for a woman to pause for a moment and remember—and perhaps share with her companion—Andrea Dworkin's oft-quoted observation that "intercourse is the pure, sterile, formal expression of men's contempt for women."[253] See also: **coitus; outercourse.**

**intercourse, gender-neutral terms for.** In his essay " 'Pricks' and 'Chicks': A Plea for 'Persons,' " linguist Robert Baker demonstrates that virtually all the verbs in the English language used to describe coitus are "active" when applied to males and "passive" when applied to females. For example, he notes, we say "Dick screwed Jane," or "Dick fucked Jane," but "Jane was screwed by Dick," or "Jane was fucked by Dick." Clearly, a more appropriate way for lovers to discuss intercourse would be to use gender-neutral language. Examples of such constructions cited by Baker are: "Dick and Jane made love to each other," "Dick and Jane slept with each other," and "Dick and Jane did it with each other."[254] See also: **enclosure; engulfment; envelopment; nutting.**

**intercourse, male-initiated.** Men who think a woman's express consent gives them a license to commence intercourse are playing with fire, according to *Ms.* magazine's recently retired editor-in-chief, Robin Morgan. "Rape," she has written, "exists any time sexual intercourse occurs when it has not been initiated by the woman out of her own genuine affection and desire."[255] See also: **Antioch Rules; consensual sex, male-initiated; "Yes means no!"**

**internalized oppression.** As French philosopher Michel Foucault has pointed out, members of subjugated groups often so thoroughly internalize the "disciplines" imposed upon them by the ruling class that they actually end up policing themselves, without any need for outside control. In her book *Femininity and Domination,* University of Illinois feminist theorist Sandra Lee Bartky argues convincingly that women in the Western democracies, who seemingly choose the "feminine lifestyle" of their own free will, are actually victims of internalized oppression:

> No one is marched off for electrolysis at the end of a rifle. . . . Nevertheless . . . the disciplinary practices of femininity . . . must be understood as aspects of a far larger discipline, an oppressive and inegalitarian system of sexual subordination. . . . The woman who checks her makeup half a dozen times a day to see if her foundation has caked or her mascara run, who worries that the wind or rain may spoil her hairdo, who looks

frequently to see if her stockings have bagged at the ankle, or who, feeling fat, monitors everything she eats, has become, just as surely as the [prison] inmate, a self-policing subject, a self committed to a relentless self-surveillance. This self-surveillance is a form of obedience to patriarchy.[256]

See also: **beauty myth; cosmetic subjugation; false consciousness; psychological captivity.**

**intersexual.** A member of one of the many sexes (Brown University medical science professor Anne Fausto-Sterling specifically defines at least three[257]) that lie between "male" and "female" on the human sexual spectrum. Any readers who think intersexuality is of no overriding concern to them are not only guilty of blatant heterosexism—they also have another think coming. As Rus Ervin Frank reminds us in *Stopping Rape: A Challenge for Men:*

> The truth is that males and females, on the physiological and biochemical level, actually exist on a continuum. On one extreme is male and on the other is female. Most of us fall somewhere in between, merging the two. For example, the penis is structurally little more than an extended clitoris, testicles little different from vaginal walls. Additionally, we all have extremely variant levels of estrogen and testosterone—the chemicals thought to be responsible for some of the differences between being female and being male.[258]

In other words, practically speaking, we are *all* intersexuals. See: **gender; sex.**

**in vitro rape.** The in vitro fertilization of an egg cell with sperm from a donor who has not been expressly approved in advance by the biological mother.[259] See also: **in vitro sexual harassment.**

*A potential **in vitro rape** survivor.*

**in vitro sexual harassment.** Making "unwelcome or irrelevant comments"—e.g., exclaiming "What a dish!"—about in vitro egg cells is increasingly being defined as harassment.[260] See also: **in vitro rape.**

**Iron John.** See: **mythopoetic men's movement; New Warrior Weekend Adventures; Wild Man within.**

**Jell-O.**  See: metaphorical harassment.

**Jews, new.**  See: new Jews.

**jock straps, ideological.**  See: ideological jock straps.

**justifiable rape.**  In *The Morning After,* Katie Roiphe wrote:

> The image that emerges from feminist preoccupation with rape
> and sexual harassment is that of women as victims, offended by
> a professor's dirty joke, verbally pressured into sex by peers.
> This image of a delicate woman bears a striking resemblance to
> that '50s ideal my mother and the other women of her genera-
> tion fought so hard to get away from. They didn't like her pas-
> sivity . . . her excessive need for protection. . . . But here she is
> again. . . . Only this time it is the feminists themselves who are
> breathing new life into her.

Well, Wheelock College sociology professor and anti-rape-van
crusader Gail Dines has read *The Morning After,* and she sees
Roiphe for what she is—"a traitor . . . the Clarence Thomas of
women." But Dines is confident that, in time, Roiphe will pay the
inevitable price for her inappropriate opinions. "[When] she walks
down the street," Dines told *Newsweek,* "she's one more
woman."[261] See also: **lesson-rapes; rape vans**.

**keratinization.** Surgeon Thomas Ritter points out in his trendsetting self-help book *Say No to Circumcision* that years of abrasive rubbing against diapers and underpants without the protection of a foreskin can cause the glans of the phallus to build up a thick layer of the fibrous protein keratin, a process that causes it to become "dry, dull, leathery, brownish," and, therefore, less sensitive to sexual stimulation. California psychologist Jim Bigelow agrees: "I get letters from older men who say sex with their circumcised penis is like having intercourse with the elbow," he says. Fortunately, Bigelow has perfected a technique for reversing the keratinization process: a procedure for "re-creating" the foreskin, which he calls uncircumcising.[262] See also: **BUFF; circumcision survivors; foreskin restoration movement; NOHARMM; RECAP; UNCIRC; uncircumcising.**

**kicking a man in the groin.** As part of her Women's Empowerment in the '90s course, feminist self-defense specialist Paxton Quigley teaches students the proper method of kicking a man in the groin. "You have to get in close," she says wryly, "because it's such a small area."[263] See: **Women's Empowerment in the '90s.**

**kissing.** Men, before you plant a kiss on the mouth of your date, girlfriend, domestic partner, or wife, you'd better be sure she's ready and willing to accept it! If she isn't, it's rape, according to Rus Ervin Funk, author of *Stopping Rape: A Challenge for Men,* whose definition of the term specifically includes "forced contact or penetration of the mouth by any object or body part."[264] Example: *Vanessa's favorite sexually correct detective novel was Mickey Spillane's* **Forcibly Contact or Penetrate My Mouth** *Deadly.* See also: **affection, public displays of; blowing kisses; osculatory rape.**

# L

**latex gloves.** Safer sex advocates are increasingly recommending that anyone who plans to engage in heavy petting should don a pair of latex gloves—or a set of finger cots—before beginning. It's also a good idea to wear latex gloves or finger cots when removing a used condom from one's penis because, as nurse practitioner Josephine Bolus reminds us, such condoms are "covered on the outside with the female's secretions and on the inside with the male's—both of which may harbor disease." All the latex items must then be wrapped in tissue paper and disposed of immediately, Bolus warns. And when you're done, she concludes, "remember to wash your hands."[265] See also: **finger cots.**

**latex-induced shock.** The conscientious use of latex condoms, dental dams, finger cots, and gloves may indeed, as many "safer sex" advocates insist, be the most reliable "barrier" method of preventing the transmission of sexual diseases. But anyone relying on such devices should be aware that they may be even more dangerous than the infections they're designed to prevent. A recent study conducted at the Henry Ford Clinic in Detroit concluded that over 6 percent of the population is allergic to latex, with contact capable of triggering acute reactions ranging from sniffles to hives to swelling of the genitals to nausea and even to "anaphylactic shock," which is potentially life-threatening. And the number of those at risk is increasing dramatically, warns Dr. Ronald R. Brancaccio of the New York University Medical Center, because even if one is not *currently* allergic to latex, continued use of latex safer-sex devices can actually lead to the *development* of such an allergy. "Epidemics are not usually discussed in terms of contact allergy, but we are in the midst of one to natural rubber latex," the doctor concludes gravely.[266] (Note: Abstinence, of course, is the one foolproof way to counter the threat of latex-induced shock. But there are other solutions—for details, see: **condom layering.**)

**legalized prostitution.** See: marriage.

**legalized rape.** See: marriage.

**LesBiGay.** A contraction of "lesbian, bisexual, and gay" used as a colloquial term for the sexual minority community and its members. As a means of preventing the word from being interpreted as pertaining only to lesbians and gays, bisexual activists insist that the "L," the "B," and the "G" always be capitalized.[267] See also: **sexual minority community.**

**less dangerous sex.** Sex educator Kent Mast, cofounder of Respect, Inc., rejects, as do most of his colleagues, the term "safe sex" as hopelessly overoptimistic. But Mast considers the phrase that is most commonly used in its place, "safer sex," to be a misnomer as well. "There is no safe sex or safer sex," he says. "There is only less dangerous sex."[268]

**lesson-rapes.** Robin Morgan notes that feminist college students have become prey to "lesson-rapes"—"acts based on the theory that all these frustrated feminists need is a good rape to show 'em the light."[269] (Note: Readers should be careful not to confuse the "lesson-rapes" condemned by Morgan with those encouraged for the purpose of demonstrating to cynical members of the patriarchy the seriousness of the sexual violence epidemic currently sweeping the United States. For example, after Berkeley professor Neil Gilbert published a series of articles questioning the accuracy of alarmingly high rape statistics reported by researcher Dr. Mary Koss, Sheila Kuehl, the director of the California Women's Law Center, remarked: "I find myself wishing that Gilbert himself might be raped and . . . be told, to his face, it had never happened."[270])

**letting the turtle do the talking.** See: **Respect, the Turtle.**

**likening a woman to an animal.** Men must stop likening women to animals, warns Andrea Parrot, author of *Coping with Date Rape and Acquaintance Rape,* who cites such behavior as a quintessential example of "sexual **objectification.**" Two forms of likening women to animals that Parrot specifically condemns: referring to a woman as a "chick" and making barking noises at a woman "because she is such a 'dog.'" Furthermore, Parrot points out, likening a woman to an animal is not merely *offensive;* it is actually *actionable* as sexual harassment "if the woman hears the comments."[271] (Note: Men who just can't resist likening women to animals, even when there are no women within earshot, should be aware that their comments are not only sexist but also *speciesist,* and may be considered objectionable, not just to any animal rights activists who happen to be listening, but also to the animals themselves.) See also: **cow, referring to a woman as a; dog, referring to a woman as a; pig, calling a woman a; sex object**.

**lingerie.** "If men really are turned on by all that awful underwear," suggests Jane Rule, author of *The Hot-Eyed Moderate,* "then maybe they should have been wearing it all along."[272]

**lip licking.** The University of Maryland at College Park includes "licking lips or teeth" in the official list of "unacceptable gestures and nonverbal behaviors" it says "may be in violation of campus policy on sexual harassment."[273]

**list exchanging.** A safer-sex technique recommended by "Elsa," a woman described by psychotherapist Sharyn Wolf in her book *Guerilla Dating Tactics.* "Elsa keeps a computer printout of her sexual partners in her wallet," Wolf tells us. "There are a few names scratched in by hand at the bottom. When she's with a guy she likes, she hands him the list and asks for his. She offers her fax number just in case he wants to send it to her."[274]

**literary sperm salesmen.** Author Sally Cline's term for male writers—she specifically mentions Norman Mailer, Henry Miller, and Kingsley and Martin Amis—who are "obsessed with exploitative and penetrative sex."[275]

*Norman Mailer, a* **literary sperm salesman.**

**looking at nature through masculine eyes.** In order to become "more potent, generative, and embodied"—not to mention gaining in "power" and "maturity"—men need to learn to "look at nature with masculine eyes," advises Aaron R. Kipnis, the well-known gender reconciliation facilitator. "With fresh eyes, wiped clean of a feminist perspective which claims nature as Goddess alone," Kipnis instructs his readers, "seek the images of masculinity in nature. Those erect, thick, tall trees, do they remind us of mother or something else? What about those mountain peaks that thunder at their summits and sometimes explode, covering the earth with rich, fertilizing ash? Are these the Earth Mother's breasts? How do they appear to you?"[276] See also: **tree, tying one-self to the top of a.**

**lookism.** The Smith College Office of Student Affairs defines "lookism" as "the belief that appearance is an indicator of a person's value; the construction of a standard for beauty/attractiveness; and oppression through stereotypes and generalizations of both those who do not meet that standard and those who do."[277] See also: **aesthetic appreciation.**

**lookist dating.** Choosing to go out or have sex with people because one finds them "attractive," or electing *not* to date or sleep with individuals whose appearance one finds repugnant, are, of course, blatant examples of inappropriately lookist dating behavior. A growing number of "beautiful" women and "handsome" men are coming to realize that using their looks to attract dates is also an insidious form of lookist discrimination.[278] See: **lookism.**

**love.** Andrea Dworkin defines romantic love as "the mythic celebration of female negation." "For the female," she adds, "the capacity to love is exactly synonymous with the capacity to sustain abuse and the appetite for it."[279] Example: *Vanessa's favorite sexually correct movie was* **The Mythic Celebration of Female Negation** Is a Many-Splendored Thing.

**love, androgynous.** See: **androgynous love.**

**love, gynandrous.**  See: androgynous love.

**love, ideal.**  See: androgynous love.

**loved, feeling.**  See: feeling loved.

**love notes.**  Men who are afraid that their verbal requests for dates will be rebuffed might assume that written letters—especially flattering, nonpressuring ones—are a viable alternative. Before sending such a missive, however, they might consider the case of the federal income tax agent in San Mateo, California, who wrote a love note to one of his IRS colleagues, praising her "style and élan" but pledging not to bother her again if she rejected him. The woman sued him under the "unwelcome verbal conduct" provision of the Civil Rights Act of 1964, and, because she was able to convince the court that any "reasonable woman" would indeed have found the agent's letter "unwelcome," won. Thus was established the important legal precedent that even "well-intentioned compliments" can qualify as illegal sexual harassment.[280] See also: **flattery**.

# M

**mace substitute, environmentally friendly.** For women who want to be able to incapacitate potential attackers but don't want to foul the atmosphere in the process, feminist self-defense advocate Paxton Quigley is marketing an "all-natural" mace substitute.[281] (Note: For information on Quigley's line of designer handguns and other products she has created for the "armed sisterhood," see: **Women's Empowerment in the '90s.**)

**macho pigs.** One of the two categories into which social commentator Cynthia Heimel says all today's men can be divided. "Macho pigs," Heimel writes, "don't care" that women have been oppressed for centuries, "and never will. Your average woman knows to just ignore the macho guys unless they get in her face and she has to kill them."[282] (For Heimel's opinion of the other of the two categories into which today's men can be divided, see: **guilty men.**)

**Mahler, Gustave.** Editorialist Michael Costello urges men not to take women to concerts featuring works composed by Gustave Mahler, because Mahler's music, according to "feminist musicologist" Susan McClary of the University of Minnesota, is "filled with themes of male masturbation."[283] (Note: McClary has a similar problem with the works of Richard Strauss, so it's probably a good idea to avoid them, too.)

**Gustave Mahler,** *a sexually suspect composer.*

**making a woman feel guilty (as a means of obtaining sex).** In their essay "Nonviolent Sexual Coercion," Charlene N. Muelenhard and Jennifer L. Schrag name "making a woman feel guilty" as one of the principal types of "verbal coercion" men employ to obtain sex from women. (Perhaps on the assumption that most women wouldn't be interested in initiating sex with a man or wouldn't stoop to using guilt as a means of persuasion, "making a *man* feel guilty as a means of obtaining sex" is not listed in Muelenhard and Schrag's catalog of offenses.)[284] Men should take note that a growing number of corporations and academic institutions (including Antioch College) specifically cite "verbal coercion" as a punishable sex offense;[285] indeed, Cornell University's Andrea Parrot categorizes it as "soft rape."[286] See: **soft rape.**

**male.** *Women & Guns* magazine proposes the following definition for "male": "A quaint anachronism, once useful for protection of females, but rendered obsolete by contemporary firepower."[287] See: **Women's Empowerment in the '90s.**

**male bashing.** As Steve Greaves pointed out in an influential letter to *Yoga Journal,* "male bashing" is a "self-justifying, reactive, male sexist term." Therefore, any time a man uses it in response to criticism of his gender's "competitive power-striving, wars of conquest and domination against women and nature," he is merely confirming women's worst suspicions.[288]

**male bonding.** The "ultimate male bond," Catharine MacKinnon observes in *Only Words,* is "that between pimp and john."[289]

**male feminism.** See: **profeminism; womb envier.**

**male parasitism.** Philosopher Marilyn Frye uses the term "male parasitism" to describe men's tapping of, and dependence upon, "the strength, energy, inspiration and nurturance of women" to keep themselves going. As Frye explains it:

> Men are drained and depleted by their living by themselves and with and among other men, and are revived and refreshed, re-created, by going home and being served dinner, changing to clean clothes, having sex with the wife; or by dropping by the

apartment of a woman friend to be served coffee or a drink and stroked in one way or another; or by picking up a prostitute for a quicky or for a dip in favorite sexual escape fantasies; or by raping refugees from their wars (foreign and domestic).

"The ministrations of women," Frye concludes, "be they willing or unwilling, free or paid for, are what restore in men the strength, will and confidence to go on with what they call living."[290] See also: **Patriarchal Imperative.**

**male self-control.** See: self-control, male.

**male sexual identity.** In his book *Refusing to Be a Man*, John Stoltenberg explains that "male sexual identity—the belief that one is male, the belief that there is a male sex, the belief that one belongs to it"—is a complete fiction, a "political and ethical construction" created by men for the sole purpose of oppressing women. To keep his readers focused on this crucial point, he frequently substitutes such phrases as "human beings who happen to have been born penised" and "humans who were born without a penis" for the more traditional terms "men" and "women."[291] See: **essentialism.**

**malicious humor.** The Modern Language Association Committee on the Status of Women includes "malicious humor against feminists" on the official list of oppressive behaviors it classifies as "intellectual harassment."[292] See: **intellectual harassment.**

**manipulated emotional labor.** A term used by British celibacy advocate Sally Cline to describe female orgasm."[293] Example: "*Oh, Brad,*" *moaned Desirée* (*not her real name*), "*that was the best* **manipulated emotional labor** *I ever had!*" See also: **orgasms, female.**

**manipulators of female flesh.** See: fashion profiteers.

**man's apartment, visiting.** See: going to a man's apartment.

*manusturbatus interruptus.* See: masturbation, female.

**marital slave.** The late poet Audre Lorde's term for what was formerly called a "wife."[294] See also: **premarital slave.**

*A **marital slave** being colonized by a sexual terrorist.*

**marriage.** Andrea Dworkin calls marriage "legalized rape."[295] Dale Spender prefers the term "legalized prostitution."[296]

*A decorative pastry used in **rape-legalization** ceremonies.*

**marriage ceremonies.** See: **weddings.**

**masculinity, regreening of.** Noted gender reconciliation facilitator Aaron R. Kipnis suggests that one reason many men feel alienated and disconnected—and, by definition, unable to approach relationships in a "fecund, life-affirming" manner—is that they try to relate to nature by communing only with Mother Earth, without realizing that there's a Father Earth, too, with whom they desperately need to connect. "Our work ahead," Kipnis writes, is to reclaim the "archetypal energy" of the Green Man—one of the "ancient masculine gods of the earth" (*Wingspan* magazine editor Christopher Harding reminds us that the Green Man "persists in our popular culture" as "the Green Giant of frozen pea fame"[297]). But just how can modern men begin the process of connecting with the Green Man—a process that Kipnis calls the "regreening of masculinity"? Well, one way, Kipnis says, is to tie yourself to the top of a tree. "Feel the strength and ancient, deeply rooted power of the Green Man who dances, sways, and shudders with the wind," he writes. "Of course," he adds, "this is dangerous. So don't go up without proper training, safety equipment, and a buddy to secure you."[298]

**masquerade balls.** See: Halloween parties.

**masturbation, female.** Sally Cline, author of *Women, Celibacy and Passion,* tempers her plea for a universal renunciation of coital penetration by somewhat grudgingly offering the rare women among her readership who actually enjoy genital stimulation permission to masturbate. She then goes on to recommend the *manusturbatus interruptus* approach perfected by an acquaintance of hers named "Sue," who always stops manipulating herself just before the moment of orgasm. While the less enlightened among us might find this technique unnecessarily frustrating, Sue lauds it as a form of "tantra yoga" that helps her achieve "my goal of a circled space."[299] (Note: If Sally Cline had consulted our dictionary before writing *Women, Celibacy and Passion,* she would undoubtedly have used the more gender-equitable term **msturbation,** rather than "masturbation," to describe Sue's activities.)

**masturbation, male.** Wheelock sociology professor Gail Dines feels strongly that men must not be permitted to use fantasy images of women as an autoerotic aid—so strongly, in fact, that she bases much of her crusade against the sale and distribution of pornography on her opposition to this practice. "Women weren't put on this world to facilitate masturbation," she told an audience at Harvard who had come to see her famous slide show featuring images of women being brutalized, adding that the availability of *Playboy* magazine for on-premises use in college libraries didn't particularly worry her since men were unlikely to masturbate there.[300]

**matrilineal cultures.** See: prepatriarchal cultures.

**" 'Maybe' means 'no'!"** If a woman says she "isn't sure," Donna Jackson advises men in her helpful "Rape Awareness List for Nice Guys," "assume the answer is no and let it go."[301]

**meat eating.** According to Carol J. Adams, author of *The Sexual Politics of Meat,* meat eating and male dominance are "overtly associated." Therefore, she argues, the only appropriate option for enlightened women is vegetarianism. Adams warns her readers that they might find other feminist issues more worthy of their concentration. Indeed, she confesses, she herself was once preoccupied with things like "women victimized by male violence," which left precious little time for spreading the message that "the presence of meat proclaims the disempowering of women." But then—perhaps as a result of her scholarly work in the field of critical theory—she saw the light: "The sexual politics of meat . . . are not separate from other pressing issues of our time. . . . By my own silencing, I endorsed the dominant discourse that I was seeking to deconstruct."[302] See also: **hamburgers; stomach that has no ears, the.**

*A woman being disempowered by* **meat eating.**

**mental groping.** A form of sexual harassment, more serious than "aesthetic appreciation," defined by Kenneth C. Cooper, author of "The Six Levels of Sexual Harassment," as a male manager's staring at a female employee in a manner that makes her feel he is "undressing her with his eyes."[303] (It is worth noting that it would be considered **lookist**, and therefore equally objectionable, if the manager in question were to stare at a woman in a way that made her feel that he was "*dressing* her with his eyes"—i.e., obscuring physical features he deemed unattractive by covering them in his mind with additional clothing.) See also: **aesthetic appreciation; lookism; social touching**.

**mental rape.** A term used by Lamesa Whitson, a speaker at a meeting of the Alabama Board of Education, to characterize the teaching of condom use to the state's high school students as a means of combating the spread of AIDS. "These examples of safe techniques are nothing more [*sic*] than mental rape of an innocent child," the United Press International quoted Whitson as saying.[304] The phrase "mental rape" has also been employed by Mary Sue Hubbard, wife of Church of Scientology founder L. Ron Hubbard, to describe disillusioned church archivist Gerald Armstrong's removal of some ten thousand pages of her husband's papers from church headquarters in an effort to demonstrate that Mr. Hubbard was "virtually a pathological liar when it comes to his history, background and achievements";[305] and by Dr. Gregory G. Patrick, a Pennsylvania lung specialist, to portray the "violation" and "brutalization" he felt when a malpractice suit was filed against him.[306]

**merms.** Intersexuals who possess testes, and some aspects of female genitalia, but who do not have ovaries. According to Brown University geneticist Anne Fausto-Sterling, who coined the term, merms are just one of at least three discrete sexes that lie between the male and female poles on the human sexual spectrum.[307] See also: **ferms; herms; intersexual; two-party sexual system**.

**metaphorical harassment.** It's a pity that tenured professor J. Donald Silva didn't have a chance to read our dictionary before using the example "Belly dancing is like Jell-O on a plate—with a vibrator under the plate" to explain the meaning of the word "simile" to his creative writing class at the University of New Hampshire. If he had, he might have been spared the indignity of being brought up on sexual harassment charges, formally reprimanded, and suspended from his teaching duties.[308]

*Jell-O on a plate, the key element in a notorious case of* **metaphorical harassment.**

**mister-ectomy.** Boston College professor Mary Daly notes that this is "the most foolproof solution" to "The Contraceptive Problem." Mister-ectomy is "tried and true, and therefore taboo," she adds.[309] See also: **misterics**.

**misterics.** Mary Daly defines "misterics" as "uncontrollable and mysterious fits (thought by some to be caused by testicular disturbances)." They are, she observes, a "common psychoneurotic manifestation of mister-ectomy anxiety."[310] See: **mister-ectomy**.

**mistletoe.** Moorhead State University in Minnesota has officially banned the use of mistletoe as a holiday decoration. "Mistletoe tends to sanctify uninvited endearment," Moorhead State president Rolland Dille explains.[311]

**Mistletoe,** *an infamous uninvited-endearment sanctifier.*

**monosexual.** Alan Hamilton, in his *Sexual Identity and Gender Identity Glossary,* defines a monosexual as "one who has significant sexual and romantic attractions primarily to members of one sex."[312] Straights, gays, and lesbians are all monosexuals, and Andrea Dworkin, for one, does not approve. "An exclusive commitment to one sexual formation," she writes, "whether homosexual or heterosexual, generally means that one is, regardless of the uniform one wears, a good soldier of the culture programmed effectively to do its dirty work."[313]

*President Bill Clinton,*
*a* **monosexual.**

**mopping jokes.**  Under the University of Michigan's speech code (which a white-male-dominated federal court has since deemed unconstitutional), a male student was brought up on sexual harassment charges for slipping the following joke under a female student's door:

> Q. How many men does it take to mop a floor?
> A. None, it's a woman's job.[314]

See also: **stupid-women jokes.**

**more-oppressed-than-you competitions.**  Columnist Cynthia Heimel's term for debates between women who point out that their gender has had to endure centuries of subjugation under male patriarchy, and the growing chorus of men, led by Warren Farrell and John Lee, who feel *they* are the **new Jews**—even more abused and victimized by society than women. Women should resist the temption to engage in such competitions, Heimel warns, because "we would always win, and that would bring on more [male] guilt." "They have enough already," she concludes.[315] See also: **gender reconciliation facilitators; guilty men; oppression of white males; success objects.**

**mouse within.** See: parakeet within.

**Mozambique.** Feminist pro-gun activist Paxton Quigley's name for one of the self-defense techniques she teaches in her **Women's Empowerment in the '90s** course. Quigley describes the practice drills she has devised for the "Mozambique"—which consists of pumping two bullets into a man's body and one into his head—as "awfully fun to do."[316] See also: **murder.**

**msturbation.** A nonpatriarchal term for female autoeroticism.[317]

**murder.** University of Colorado graduate student Kristen Asmus, in an oft-quoted article in the *Colorado Daily,* suggests helpfully that murder might be the answer to the sexual harassment problem. "Women will begin to fight back," she predicts. "Women will begin to kill men if they have to."[318] See also: **androcide; castration; Mozambique.**

**mythic celebration of female negation.** See: love.

**mythopoetic men's movement.** Christopher Harding, editor of *Wingspan* magazine, defines this as "a freewheeling exploration of male sprituality and male psychology (especially from a Jungian perspective), which encourages men to delve into their psyches by reintroducing them to literature, mythology and art."[319] The movement, which owes its remarkable popularity to such best-selling books as Robert Bly's *Iron John* and Sam Keen's *Fire in the Belly,* is characterized by an impressive array of personal growth activities (all of which are covered in detail elsewhere in this book): ritual drumming, chanting, and screaming; participating in neo-primitive "Wild Man weekend gatherings"; pretending to be dolphins, rams, or elephants; making pilgrimages to the statue of Saint Monica in Southern California; donning gorilla suits and staging fistfights; tying oneself to the top of trees; and reenacting (some would say expropriating) Native American rites such as the sweat

lodge, the talking stick council, and the warrior initiation ceremony. These activities have "far-reaching benefits for individual
couples, families, and society in general," Harding enthuses,
because they encourage intimacy and provide "opportunities and
safe container-spaces for the catharsis of pent-up anger and rage
that might otherwise be expressed dysfunctionally at home."[320]
Forensic psychologist Laura S. Brown, however, views Bly, Keen,
and their followers somewhat less optimistically: "Hitler, too,"
she writes, "looked to myth and legend . . . to feed his murderous
visions of reality; he, too, relied upon ritual, upon the special
bonds between men, to build his movement."[321]

**"Naked Maja."** See: art "masterpieces" featuring nude women.

**narcissistic gratification.** See: praising a woman's accomplishments.

**necrophilic energy.** According to Boston College **thealogian** Mary Daly, men combine a "frantic fixation" upon the life-loving female energy they lack—an energy she terms **biophilic**—with a "frantic indifference" to the destruction they wreak upon the women who possess it. Daly characterizes this combination of "need/attraction" and indifference as "necrophilic"—"not in the sense of love for actual corpses, but of love for those victimized into a state of living death."[322] See also: **biophilic energy; male parasitism; Patriarchal Imperative.**

**networking (as a method of branding potential sexual abusers).** As Claudette McShane points out in *Warning! Dating May Be Dangerous to Your Health!,* women can help each other prevent dating abuse by "networking"—that is, by spreading the word about men who are known or suspected to have engaged in nonconsensual verbal or physical behavior of a sexual nature at some time in the past. (An effective means of accomplishing this, popular at Brown University and other educational institutions, is to scrawl the names of alleged offenders on the walls of bathroom stalls.) But McShane uses a harrowing example to demonstrate that "breaking the conspiracy of silence" will only work if women overcome their natural tendency to discount clear warnings from rivals that a man is a potential abuser:

> For Brenda, even when a former girlfriend of Daryl called to tell her that Daryl was violent, she didn't believe it. Instead she considered the former girlfriend jealous and petty. Only later when Brenda was nearly killed, did she realize the kindness of her warning.[323]

(An additional word of caution: Before engaging in such networking, women would be wise to ascertain if talking—even in private—about the sexual behavior of others is a violation of any particular speech code that may be in effect at their school or place of business. For example, the sexual harassment code at Amherst-Pelham High School in Amherst, Massachusetts, specifically lists "spreading sex gossip" as an offense that can lead to a parent conference, detention, suspension, expulsion from school, or even referral to the police.[324])

**new Jews.**    Men's rights advocate Warren Farrell, author of *The Myth of Male Power,* is convinced that men are the "new Jews" because they have become the scapegoats of an increasingly Nazi-like feminist movement.[325] Andrea Dworkin, on the other hand, argues that women are even *more* victimized than the Jews were in Nazi concentration camps, because male pornographers portray their victims as if they actually *enjoy* being brutalized. "No one," she reminds us, "not even Goebbels, said that the Jews liked it."[326] See also: **more-oppressed-than-you competitions.**

**Newton's Rape Manual.**    University of Delaware philosopher Sandra Harding observes that since scientific inquiry is essentially an act of patriarchal aggression, *Newton's Principles of Mechanics* might more appropriately be named *Newton's Rape Manual.*[327] See also: **science.**

*Newton's Rape Manual.*

**New Warrior Weekend Adventures.**    Perhaps the best-known of the many **Wild Man weekend gatherings** organized by the burgeoning mythopoetic men's movement, "New Warrior Weekend Adventures" are a continuing series of retreats designed to attract men who feel that macho roles are no longer appropriate, but that feminist activism has made them more responsive to women's emotions than to their own. As Doug Stanton, who participated in one of the weekends, wrote in *Esquire,* these men—mostly well-educated middle-class whites who pay hundreds of dollars apiece to attend—congregate in training compounds in the woods where, after being assigned animal nicknames such as Brother Marmot or Brother Water Buffalo, they "growl and yodel, weep and moan, drum their brains out and chant their lips off" in a quest to "reclaim an inner, primal, ruddy Wild Man—the New Warrior's hairy mentor—who lumbers through Robert Bly's best-selling book *Iron John* like an absentminded bigfoot with a degree in social work." Each New Warrior Weekend Adventure ends in a climactic initiation rite during which, Stanton reports, "naked, yodeling men beating their chests and prancing with weenies akimbo around a bonfire of patio candles" are officially pronounced "warriors." According to one woman interviewed by Stanton, her husband's weekend in the woods vastly improved the intimacy of their relationship. "I'm more in touch with his emotions because he is," she proclaimed. Another woman, the wife of a Wisconsin warrior-dentist, noticed a different kind of result: From now on, her mate informed her, "we're going to leave the toilet seat *up!*"[328]

**"No glove, no love."** A slogan designed to help women give men the message that, because the overwhelming majority of those carrying the HIV virus are male, a man cannot expect a woman to have penetrative sex with him unless he agrees to wear a condom.[329] See: **glove.**

**NOHARMM.** An acronym for the National Organization to Halt the Abuse and Routine Mutilation of Males, a San Francisco–based group that aids recovering circumcision survivors by providing them with confidential survey forms on which, as the director, Tim Hammond, phrases it, they can record "their own feelings of betrayal."[330] If you'd like to receive a copy of this survey form, you can get one by contacting:

NOHARMM
P.O. Box 460795
San Francisco, CA 94146

See also: **BUFF**; circumcision survivors; foreskin restoration movement; keratinization; **RECAP**; **UNCIRC**; uncircumcising.

**" 'No' means 'no'!"**   A slogan that has become the rallying cry of the anti-date-rape movement. Just how accurately this catchphrase reflects women's true behavior is revealed in a study conducted by professor Charlene N. Muehlenhard and her graduate student, Lisa Hollabaugh, which showed that a mere four out of ten college women had ever said "no" to sex when they really meant "yes."[331] "When a woman says 'no,' chances are that she means it," concluded Muehlenhard.[332]

**nonhuman sex offenders.**   See: sex offenders, nonhuman.

**nonrape (as a weapon of male domination).**   As antisexism activist Rus Erving Funk points out, men who *don't* rape use the men who do to paint themselves as "good" men who wouldn't rape "and then argue that we deserve the praise and support of women—basically because we don't do something horrible to them." Such arguments are an all-too-familiar strategy, Funk argues, for maintaining men's position of dominance over women.[333]

**nude slides in class presentations.**   A report issued by a committee charged with planning "diversity education" for incoming freshmen at the University of Pennsylvania listed "nude slides in class presentations" as an example

*A **nude slide** of the Venus of Willendorf, the earliest known example of sexually harassing art.*

of sexual harassment.[334] See also: **art "masterpieces" featuring nude women**.

**numbot.** See: fembot.

**nutting.** A word coined by feminist linguists Midge Lennert and Norma Willson to provide an active term for what women do while men are "screwing" them; the time has long since come, they imply, for women to be seen as equal partners in the act of intercourse.[335] Andrea Dworkin informs us, however, that such equity is a masochistic fantasy. Intercourse, she writes, is "the most systematic expression of male power over women's bodies," and any woman who enjoys it has merely "internalized and eroticized" her own subordination.[336] See also: **enclosure; engulfment; envelopment; positive language**.

**objectification.** The dehumanization—either literal or figurative—of individuals and groups in order to exploit them for one's own sexual, economic, or political purposes. In Andrea Dworkin's view, "objectification may well be the most singly destructive aspect of gender hierarchy." "Living in the realm of male objectification," she adds, "is abject submission, an abdication of the freedom and integrity of the body, its privacy, its uniqueness, its worth in and of itself because it is the human body of a human being."[337]

**objectification, fructal.** See: fructal objectification.

**obscenity.** Largely as the result of a brief cowritten by feminist law scholar Catharine A. MacKinnon, the Canadian Supreme Court reworded its legal definition of "obscene" so that it would cover material that "degrades and dehumanizes women," as opposed to that which "offends morals."[338] One of the first of the thousands of books to be banned under the new statute was *Woman Hating,* by Andrea Dworkin, MacKinnon's longtime compatriot in the antipornography movement. (As writer Susie Bright describes it, "a Canadian customs official took one look at Dworkin's title . . . and . . . using MacKinnon's criterion of banning anything that 'degrades women,' refused the book entry."[339])

**offering a woman a drink.** Any man who hopes he might be able to persuade his date to engage in sexual activity would be extremely well advised not to offer her an alcoholic beverage. The reason: Noted rape researcher Mary P. Koss now officially classifies as a "rape survivor" any woman who answers "yes" to the question, "Have you ever had sexual intercourse when you didn't want to because a man gave you alcohol or drugs?"[340]

**one-on-one time.** One of the best ways women can avoid being sexually assaulted, Josh McDowell advises in *It Can Happen to You: What You Need to Know About Preventing and Recovering* *from Date Rape,* is to place strict limits on the quantity of "one-on-one time" they permit their dating partners to share with them. "When you spend excessive amounts of unprogrammed time alone with a man . . . especially at night, you are asking for trouble," warns McDowell. "Eliminate that possibility by encouraging double dates and group activities."[341] See also: **going to a man's apartment.**

**on-line cross dressing.** *The Village Voice*'s term for the ever more common practice of logging on to a computer bulletin board or electronic "chat" service using a gender identity different from the one an individual usually assumes in the "real" world. Those considering whether or not to engage in such virtual gender-bending are faced with a moral dilemma, *The Voice* points out: "Is changing or obscuring biology truly dishonest, or rather an expression of one's inner self(s). And might the human body be just a quaint relic in the realm of the textual body?"[342] See also: **virtual rape.**

**opening the door for a woman.** See: **door opening.**

**oppression of white males.** Here's comforting news for white male readers distressed by the responsibility they bear for the ongoing oppression of women: According to John Lee, publisher of *MAN!* magazine and one of the leaders of the men's movement, American white males have been every bit as abused and victimized as women and "just didn't realize it"! But doesn't the fact that white males run the country and are widely considered to be the most privileged group in the world weaken Lee's argument, *Newsweek*'s Jerry Adler wanted to know. Absolutely not, Lee countered. In fact, the very power that society has given white males has turned them into " 'success objects,' valued only for their salaries—a complementary form of oppression to that which values women only as 'sex objects.' " "No wonder men are rebelling," Adler concluded.[343] See also: **sex objects; success objects.**

**optional heterosexuality.** See: **compulsory heterosexuality.**

**oral sex condoms.** Condoms specially designed to prevent the spread of disease during fellatio. Oral sex condoms come in either traditional or flavored varieties; "Janice," a woman interviewed by hattie gossett for an article in *Essence* magazine, notes that the mint ones offered by Schmid Laboratories under the brand name "Sheik" are particularly tasty.[344]

**orgasms, female.** Any woman who enjoys—or *thinks* she enjoys—orgasms will be illuminated by Sally Cline's description of them, in her 1993 book *Women, Celibacy and Passion,* as "a form of manipulated emotional labour which women worked at in order to reflect men and maintain men's values."[345]

**osculatory rape.** A nonconsensual kiss. The term gained currency after antisexism crusader Rus Ervin Funk offered, in his book *Stopping Rape: A Challenge for Men,* a blanket definition of rape that included "forced contact or penetration of the mouth by any object or body part."[346]

**outercourse.** An increasingly popular term whose most frequent meaning is "nonpenetrative sex," or, as columnist Suzanne Fields prefers to put it, "everything but."[347] For example, Marion Brown, coordinator of counseling at the Whitman-Walker Clinic in Washington, D.C., includes "hugging," "kissing," "massaging," and "toe-sucking" in her definition of "outercourse." However, the British newspaper *The Guardian* takes exception to the breadth of this usage, preferring to see the word limited to descriptions of "sexual arousal without bodily contact."[348] Joanne Goff, a member of the New York City Board of Education's AIDS Advisory Council, endorses *The Guardian*'s view and then some: Because she believes that "sexual arousal is a continuum," and, therefore, that even the most "innocent" indulgence in erotic activity can "set you on the road towards intercourse," she is convinced that the practice of "outercourse," as taught to the city's school children, should entail total abstinence from sex.[349] See also: **continuum theories.**

**ovarimony.** An appropriate term for a woman's act of giving witness. "I protest the use of the word 'testimony' when referring to a woman's statement," wrote Rachel W. Evans in a famous letter to *Ms.* magazine, "because its root is 'testes' which has nothing to do with being female. Why not use 'ovarimony'? Think it sounds funny? Think it sounds funnier than 'testimony'?"[350]

**Pandora's Box.**  A pathetically androcentric mythical metaphor, which not only blames women for humanity's failings, but also, by its very name, seems to imply that female genital sexuality is the repository of all evil. As a nonpatriarchal substitute, the American Gender Society suggests "Prometheus's Sac."[351]

**parakeet within.**  When mythopoetic men's movement adherents attempt to contact the apes living deep within their psyches, accept warrior nicknames like Brother Grizzly Bear or Brother Water Buffalo, "root their bodies to the ground with their proud serpents' tails," gurgle like rams, or pretend to be elephants, they are honoring the precolonial warrior tradition of communing with their "spirit animals." However, says Native American writer Sherman Alexie, the white men who participate in such rituals tend to overlook an extremely important point: "A warrior does not necessarily have an animal inside him at all," he writes. "And if there happens to be an animal, it can be a parakeet or a mouse just as easily as it can be a bear or a wolf."[352] See: **ape within; Wild Man within; New Warrior Weekend Adventures; proud serpent's tail, rooting one's body to the ground with one's.**

**patriarchal family.**  See: **family, traditional.**

**Patriarchal Imperative.**  According to philosopher Marilyn Frye, men live parasitically off the strength, energy, and nurturing of women, and therefore have a relentless urge to "have access" to them. Frye calls this drive the "Patriarchal Imperative," and she suggests that systematically denying men the access they crave may be the key to women's empowerment. "It is always the privilege of the master to enter the slave's hut," she writes. "The slave who decides to exclude the master from her hut is declaring herself not a slave."[353] See also: **male parasitism.**

*Survival Strategy #3: Preempting the* **Patriarchal Imperative.**

**patriarchy.** *The Encyclopedia of Feminism* defines "patriarchy" as "the universal political structure which privileges men at the expense of women."[354] Andrea Dworkin prefers to call it "relentless gynocide." "Under patriarchy," she explains, "no woman is safe to live her life, or to love, or to mother children. Under patriarchy, every woman is a victim, past, present and future. Under patriarchy, every woman's daughter is a victim, past, present and future. Under patriarchy, every woman's son is her potential betrayer and also the inevitable rapist and exploiter of another woman."[355]

**pats, friendly.** See: friendly pats.

**paying for a date.** See: dates, paying for.

**pedagogy.** Those considering attending a mainstream university may rethink their plans once they've heard what Jane Gallop, a professor of English at the University of Wisconsin at Milwaukee, has to say about the "pedagogy" they're likely to find there. "Pederasty" would be a more apt word for it, opines Gallop, since the so-called "instruction" proceeds on the theory that a "greater man penetrates a lesser man with his knowledge," while the empty student is a "receptacle for the phallus."[356]

**penile dekeratinization.** See: keratinization.

**penile driving.** See: drinking and penile driving.

**penile personification.** Cornell University professor Andrea Parrot, author of *Coping with Date Rape and Acquaintance Rape,* defines this as "the practice of referring to a penis by a proper name other than that of the man it is attached to, for example, George, or Henry, or Horatio, or more recently in the movie *Peggy Sue Got Married* as 'Lucky Chuckie.'" Personification of the penis, Parrot warns, is "very dangerous," because the man no longer has to take responsibility for the activities of his own penis. As examples of this process, she cites the familiar expression, "The little head thinks for the big head," which implies that the penis has a brain, and the following line of dialogue: "Lucky Chuckie has a mind of his own and made me do it."[357]

**penis.** The self-styled "Nomadic Sisters" of Saratoga, California, authors of *Loving Women,* define "penis" as "a dildo substitute."[358] Antirape activist Rus Ervin Funk prefers to think of it as an "extended clitoris."[359]

**penis envy.** See **vagina gratitude; womb envier.**

**penis guard.** A controversial device, conceived by Amaechi Larry Esekody of The Woodlands, Texas, designed to help rapists—potential or otherwise—protect themselves against **sociosexual vigilantism.**[360]

**penis length, bragging about.** Bragging about the length of one's penis has been officially categorized as **hostile environment sexual harassment** by the Minnesota Department of Education. All public school males—from kindergartners through high school children—are potentially punishable under state law if they are found guilty of this offense.[361]

**penis-length positioning.** *Ad Week* columnist Bob Garfield's term for the strategy of making an otherwise "nonsexy" product appealing by implying that men who use it are so confident about the size of their genital organs that they have no need to overcompensate by surrounding themselves with phallic symbols. As an example of penis-length positioning, Garfield cites an advertisement in which a woman, after belittling the owner of a powerful sports car, sees a handsome man drive up in a four-cylinder Hyundai Elantra and remarks: "I wonder what *he*'s got under the hood!"[362] Some critics have suggested that campaigns such as Hyundai's are antipatriarchal since they depict women as sexually assertive and men as passive sex objects, but the prevailing view is

*The Hyundai, a* **penis-length positioned** *product.*

that, since they glorify the importance of the penis, they are highly demeaning to women.

**penis-shaped erasers.** The inherent justice of employees' being able to hold the companies they work for responsible for maintaining a totally nonhostile working environment was demonstrated early in 1994 when one of Continental Airlines' bulk-seat sales representatives, Vol Stephen Davis III, sued the corporation for failing to prevent female coworkers from "sexually harassing" him by "openly complaining about their lack of a sex life with their husbands" and by placing "pencils with erasers shaped like penises" in his office. According to Davis, he had to obtain psychiatric counseling because of the harassment.[363]

**peop.** A singular form of "people," pronounced "peep." The word, first popularized in Worcester, Massachusetts, was apparently coined to provide speakers desirous of avoiding the "son" in "person" with a gender-fair alternative.[364] Example: *As a womon and a* **peop** *of color, the late poet Audre Lorde was doubly oppressed.*

**perfume.** Perfume is "headachy," Jane Rule tells us in *The Hot-Eyed Moderate,* and if men are so crazy about it, well, "then maybe they should have been wearing it all along."[365]

**person living with AIDS.** A phrase that stresses the positive concept that AIDS is a condition that can be *lived* with, and which therefore is increasingly felt to be the only appropriate term for describing an individual with acquired immune deficiency syndrome. Since the very mention of the word "AIDS" has been known to trigger diseasist and homophobic impulses in an unfortunately large percentage of the populace, many prefer to use the two recognized abbreviations for "person living with AIDS"—**PLA** and **PLWA**—rather than the phrase itself.[366]

**persons presenting themselves as commodity allotments within a business doctrine.** See: prostitutes.

**petting.** According to *Commentary* magazine, more and more sex educators are warning their students that, to guard against the possibility of contracting or transmitting STDs during heavy petting, it's advisable to wear a finger cot or a latex glove. Saying you can't find finger cots or latex gloves in your local store is not a valid excuse for failing to wear them: You can order them easily over the phone from Condomania by calling (800) 772-3354.[367]

**"Pet Your Dog . . . Not Your Date."** Placards emblazoned with this clever proabstinence slogan and a truly irresistible illustration of a puppy are available from the Christian fundamentalist organization Respect, Inc. Displaying a "Pet Your Dog . . . Not Your Date" poster not only helps prevent innocent women from being colonized; it's also a way of paying tribute to Catharine A. Mac-Kinnon, Andrea Dworkin, Gail Dines, and others for having the courage to forge new bonds of unity between left and right for the larger purpose of reforming America's antiquated freedom-of-speech and right-to-privacy laws.[368] (Note: Before ordering a "Pet Your Dog . . . Not Your Date" poster, readers should be aware that the animal-rights organization People for the Ethical Treatment of Animals condemns not only the use of the word "pet," but also the practice of confining nonhuman creatures in one's house or apartment.[369])

Pet Your Dog . . .

. . . Not Your Date.

SAVE SEX
FOR MARRIAGE.

*A* **"Pet Your Dog . . . Not Your Date"** *poster.*

**phallogeneric term.** Boston College **thealogian** Mary Daly defines this as "a pseudogeneric term which, while pretending to include women, in reality conveys the message that only men exist."[370] Examples include such words as "mankind," "chairman," and the pronoun "he," when used generically. See also: **positive language**.

**phallogocentrism.** The use, by the white male heterosexual establishment, of such discredited devices as "reason" and "logic" to
maintain a position of sexual and political control.[371]

**phalloquialisms.** Phrases such as "penetrating insight," "contest
entry," and "magazine insert," which, because they evoke images
of patriarchal or rapist behavior, are now considered "inappropriate" by an ever-widening circle of gender-sensitive language
experts.[372]

**photographs of one's wife wearing a bathing suit.** An historic
1991 ruling by federal judge Howell Melton officially designated
as "workplace misconduct" the display on one's desk or office wall
of a picture of one's wife wearing a bathing suit or any other outfit "not suited to or ordinarily accepted for the accomplishment of
routine work."[373]

**picking up women.** See: dates, asking for.

**pig, calling a woman a.** Characterizing a woman as a pig constitutes "unlawful sexual harassment," according to attorney Joe
Yastrow, an expert on hostile environment offenses who was interviewed by the *Chicago Tribune.* Indeed, says Yastrow, a company
that condones one of its male employee's calling a female
employee a pig is legally punishable, even if the individual uttering
the illicit epithet does not occupy a management position.[374] See
also: **likening a woman to an animal.**

**pig, comparing a man to a.** Comparing a man to a pig is grossly
unfair to the pig, according to thirty indignant animal-lovers who
wrote letters to the editors of *Time* protesting the magazine's deci-
sion to illustrate a Valentine's Day, 1994, cover story by Lance
Morrow entitled "Are Men Really That Bad?" with a doctored
photograph of a pig's head stuck on the body of a man. The com-
plaint made by Mary Peterson of Bloomfield, Connecticut, that
"Pigs aren't lazy, stupid or mean; they're resourceful, intelligent
and forgiving," was representative of most of the correspondence

*Time* received. However, Martha L. Fast of Ojai, California, chose to see things in a more positive light: "By adding a pig's head to your composite man," she observed, "you increased his I.Q. at least 20 points."[375]

**pig's tongue.** A key ingredient in a powerful anti-verbal-harassment spell that feminist witch Zsuszanna Emese Budapest claims she learned from a Yoruba priestess. If you're a woman who's being harassed, Budapest writes in *The Goddess in the Office*, all you need do is visit your local butcher and buy the pig's tongue; cut it open and rub it with black pepper; write the name of your harasser backward nine times in black ink on a piece of white paper; smear some of your own urine on the paper; fold the paper away from yourself until it can be crammed into the pig's tongue (it's crucial to keep a mental picture of the harasser's tongue in your mind while you're doing the cramming); press a rusty nail through the whole package; take the tongue "as far as you can get from your house within a reasonable time"; dig a hole and bury the tongue; and, finally, fill in the hole and pee on it. "Then leave and don't look back," Budapest concludes. "Within a moon the harasser should change his behavior or leave the office."[376] See also: **bergamot oil; Hot Foot powder.**

**pin-the-condom-on-the-man contests.** The University of California at Davis demonstrated just how enlightened campus attitudes toward sex and dating have become when, to celebrate Valentine's Day, 1994, they decided to forego traditional dances and "mixers" in favor of a weeklong, campus-wide "pin-the-condom-on-the-man" contest. "There is an outline of a man with a bull's-eye where the condom would go," explained Jennifer Glasse, the student coordinator of the event. "You spin the person around and if they hit the bull's-eye, they win." The prize? A keychain designed to hold condoms.[377] See also: **Condom Olympics; condom relay races.**

**PLA.** See: **person living with AIDS; PLWA.**

**plastisurgiholicism.** A condition defined by *Guardian* correspondent Andrew Wilson as "an addiction to plastic or cosmetic surgery." Although pressure from the male-controlled beauty and fashion industries and men's stubborn predilection for selecting young and attractive women to be their sexual partners are frequently cited as the underlying causes of plastisurgiholicism, research conducted by Eileen Bradbury of the Withington Hospital in Manchester, England, demonstrates that another institution of patriarchy, father-daughter sexual abuse, may be an even more important culprit. "Some women think that by changing a certain feature, they'll be able to erase traumatic memories," she explains. Bradbury's theory is supported by Roseanne Arnold, whose tummy tuck, liposuction, and nose job would seem to qualify her as a plastisurgiholic. "Every time I looked in the mirror, I would see my dad," Arnold writes in her autobiography, *My Lives.* "It's hard to look at your abuser in the mirror every day. . . . To me, it [plastic surgery] felt like a way of reversing the shit that had happened to me. It was part of my physical recovery."[378]

**PLWA.** The most frequently used acronym for **person living with AIDS**, a phrase which, because it stresses the fact that AIDS is a condition that can actually be *lived* with, is increasingly considered to be the most appropriate term for referring to anyone with acquired immune deficiency syndrome. A second acronym, **PLA**, is also quite common.[379]

**policy activation.** A synonym for "initiating sex" that has gained currency at Antioch College since the institution's famous Sexual Offense Policy was adopted. Indeed, Antioch's Dean of Students, Marian Jensen, notes that the phrase has evolved into a come-on: "Would you like to activate the policy?"[380] See: **Antioch Rules**.

**pornographer-kidnappers.** See: **rape vans**.

**positive language.** One of the best and most practical day-to-day weapons women and men can employ against patriarchy is "positive language," which the *Encyclopedia of Feminism* defines as "the use of the feminine for every indefinite or generic reference in speaking or writing. (For example: 'God in *her* infinite wisdom...'; 'Each student should finish her work...'[381]) A major victory in the crusade for positive language was won when the *University of California at Davis Law Review* announced that, effective immediately, it would permit only feminine generic pronouns to appear within its pages. There was to be just one exception to this policy, readers were informed: When referring to criminal defendants, the magazine would use only *masculine* generic pronouns.[382] Example: *"All right, ladies, I want each of you back in his cell right now," barked the women's prison warden in a commendable display of* **positive language.**

**postcoital nonconsent.** The formal retraction or repudiation, by a party to a completed act of sexual intercourse, of consent expressly given by that party before the act was initiated. Among the many accepted legal grounds for postcoital nonconsent are (1) the consenting party was under the influence of alcohol at the time the consent was given; (2) the consenting party was under the influence of a recreational or prescription drug at the time the consent was given; (3) the consenting party felt obliged or psychologically intimidated at the time the consent was given; and (4) the sex didn't turn out the way the consenting party hoped it would.[383]

**poststructural feminism.** A branch of feminism based on the proposition that every thought is a political thought and every statement is a political statement. In this context, poststructural feminists argue, such concepts as "biological difference," "heterosexual attraction," "ideal beauty," "common sense," "logic," "facts," "truth," and "reality" can be seen for what they are: "fictive constructs" created by men to oppress women. (Note: One small problem with this otherwise unassailable philosophy, writer Nicholas Davidson has pointed out, is that it fails to explain why poststructural feminism is not itself a "fictive construct.")[384]

**potential rapists.** All living males who have reached the age of puberty. The term exploded into the public consciousness after the

Women's Coalition for Change, a group of undergraduate women at the University of Maryland, posted the names of thousands of the university's male students at various key locations around the campus and labeled each and every one a "Potential Rapist."[385] See also: **potential survivors; stickering**.

*U.N. secretary-general Boutros Boutros-Ghali, a* **potential rapist.**

**potential survivors.**  All living females who have not, as yet, "survived" a rape; the implication is that, sooner or later, sexual violence will come to them, too. As legal scholar Catharine MacKinnon puts it: "To be about to be raped is to be gender female in the process of going about life as usual."[386]

**power feminism.**  Naomi Wolf's version of what Clark University professor Christina Hoff Sommers calls "equity feminism." "It is time," Wolf proposes in *Fire with Fire,*

> to abandon orthodoxy, sloganeering, ideological posturing, and life lived on the margins for marginality's sake.... And we must be wary of new definitions of harassment that leave no mental space to imagine girls and women as sexual explorers and renegades.... Power feminism sees women as human beings—sexual, individual, no better or worse than their male counterparts— and lays claim to equality simply because women are entitled to it.... Here at the crossroads of power, we see our majority status, and understand that much of our fate is ours to choose.... We have reached a moment at which sexual inequality, which we think of as being the texture and taste of femininity itself, can begin to become a quaint memory of the old country—if we are not too attached to it to let it go.[387]

There are, of course, many more possible objections to Wolf's concept than can possibly be summed up in the space available to us here, but a surprising number of them are neatly encapsulated in an Internet message posted by Georgetown sociology professor Suzanna Walters shortly after *Fire with Fire* was published: "Wolf's book," opined Walters, "is trash, and backlash, and everything nasty (including homophobic and racist)."[388] See also: **equity feminism.**

**praising a woman's accomplishments.** Women, don't be fooled! When your male lover praises your accomplishments, he may *seem* to be acting benevolently, but, cautions Hunter College professor Sue Rosenberg Zalk, this is "frequently" not the case at all. In fact, Zalk explains in "Men in the Academy: A Psychologi-

*A man obtaining narcissistic gratification by* **praising** *his lover's* **accomplishments.**

cal Profile of Harassment," what is manifested as a man's "care and concern" is often rooted in "the narcissistic gratification obtained from his lover's achievements. She 'belongs' to him and her achievements are his and reflect on him. She, or rather the relationship, has become part of his identity."[389]

**premarital slave.**   A betrothed woman.[390] See also: **marital slave.**

*Noted psychoanalyst Jeffrey Masson and his* **premarital slave,** *Catharine A. MacKinnon.*

**preop TS.**   See: preoperative transsexual.

**preoperative transsexual.**   Alan Hamilton's *Sexual Identity and Gender Identity Glossary* defines a "preoperative transsexual" as "one who is actively planning to switch physical sexes, mostly to relieve gender dysphoria." The term is most frequently encountered in its abbreviated form, **preop TS.**[391] See: **gender dysphoria.**

**prepatriarchal cultures.**   Following the lead of the late UCLA archaeologist Marija Gimbutas, a growing number of feminist scholars have come to believe that in Stone Age Europe, a female-centered, goddess-worshiping, matrilineal culture held sway—a culture in which nature was revered, harmony reigned between the sexes, and war was virtually unknown. According to this theory, marauding, patrilineal Indo-European hordes swept out of the steppes of Central Asia in the fifth century B.C. and decimated this egalitarian society, imposing a domineering, materialistic, patriarchal culture whose unhappy legacy we're still suffering from today.[392] As appealing as Gimbutas's utopian idea may be—indeed, it has helped feed the explosion of today's Goddess Movement—a contingent of feminist academicians at least as large as the matrilinealists consider it extremely counterproductive and dangerous, because it is "authoritarian"—that is, it merely seeks to impose one gender-hierarchical "construct" in place of another—and because it is "essentialist"—i.e., it serves to perpetuate the oppression-conducive fiction that there are important differences between women and men. (At least that's what Johns Hopkins humanities professor Judith Butler *seems* to be saying when she writes: "The postulation of the 'before' within feminist theory becomes politically problematic when it constrains the future to materialize an idealized notion of the past or when it supports, even inadvertently, a reification of the precultural sphere of the authentic feminine."[393] It is statements such as this, apparently, that led Donna Haraway of the University of California at Santa Cruz to characterize Butler's arguments as "lucid" and "witty."[394]) See also: **essentialism; Goddess Movement; Venus of Willendorf.**

**procreation without sex.** See: **turkey-baster insemination.**

**profeminism.** Since it would be highly presumptuous for any man—even one who endorses the aims of feminism—to call himself a feminist, male antisexists have adopted the term "profeminism" to describe their philosophy. However, women should be alert to the fact that many males who profess a belief in women's issues—especially those sophisticated enough to term themselves profeminists—may be doing so for the sole purpose of seducing women. Indeed, as "Peter," a member of the New York Anti-Sexist Men's Action Network, confessed to Katie Roiphe: "We have to ask to what extent is a commitment to feminism on the part of a man an attempt to get a woman into bed. To deny that's true at all would be preposterous."[395] See also: **womb envier.**

**prolonged staring.**  In an historic ruling that proved just how powerful government regulation can be in deterring the objectification of women, University of Toronto chemistry professor Richard Hummel was convicted in 1989 of "prolonged and intense staring" while swimming in a campus pool; according to Hummel, the total cost of the case and its defense was over $200,000. Although a few observers have deemed the penalty excessive (columnist Barbara Amiel, for example, described the Hummel affair as "the utter debasement of the genuinely serious nature of sexual harassment"), there is little doubt that Hummel—and every other man who hears about his case—will think twice before ogling in the future.[396] (*Failing* to ogle, it should be noted, also carries certain risks; see: **eye contact, insufficient.**)

**Prometheus's Sac.**  See: **Pandora's Box.**

**Prospective Queer Parents.**  See: **sperm-egg mixers.**

**prostitutes.**   Since the word "prostitutes" unfairly stigmatizes women forced by patriarchal capitalism to sell their bodies in order to eke out a living, and because, as Dale Spender points out in *Women of Ideas and What Men Have Done to Them,* it is virtually impossible to define it without including "wives," who "also exchange services in return for support,"[397] several less judgmental terms have been coined to replace it. Among the most useful: **sex workers,**[398] **sex-care providers,**[399] **sexual surrogates,**[400] and (to cite an official report recently issued by the city of Allentown, Pennsylvania) **persons presenting themselves as commodity allotments within a business doctrine.**[401]

**prostitution.**  See: **candlelight dinners; housewifery;** and **marriage.**

**protection rackets.**  Nancy Henley's term for things men do that appear to be helpful to, or protective of, women, but which are in fact designed for the purpose of "keeping women passive" and instilling in them a "feeling of inability to cope." Perhaps the most ironic instance of this ploy is a man's offer to walk a woman home. "Since the threat is mainly one of attack by men, and since the main defense is a male escort," Henley notes, the arrangement is actually a form of extortion identical to that "employed by criminal gangs."[402] See: **furniture moving**.

**proud serpent's tail, rooting one's body to the ground with one's.** Men, if you want to free yourselves from the twin burdens of isolation and repressed pain, psychologist Dr. Shepherd Bliss has a suggestion for you: "Root your body to the ground with your proud serpent's tail." Writer Andrew Ferguson had the opportunity to watch Bliss lead men through a veritable plethora of such exercises during an inspirational "bodywork" session held in the basement exhibition hall of the Stouffer Arboretum Hotel in Austin, Texas. The meeting culminated, Ferguson wrote in *The American Spectator*, when Bliss whispered "Now let go!" over the PA system, and the congregation exploded in a chorus of "whimpers, sobs, shuddering grunts from the solar plexus, [and] high-pitched beseeching whines." "Listen!" Bliss responded. "Hear the sounds of men!"[403] (Note: Informal research conducted by the American Gender Society confirms that rooting your body to the ground with your proud serpent's tail is not only a first-rate means of getting in touch with your feelings; it also serves as a dandy excuse for turning down unwanted dinner invitations.) See also: **four-leggeds, joining the world of**.

**provocative eating.** The University of Maryland at College Park includes "holding or eating food provocatively" on its official list of "unacceptable gestures and non-verbal behaviors that may be in violation of campus policy on sexual harassment."[404]

**prudes.** As Mary Daly points out in *Pure Lust*, the word "prude" is "derived from the French *prudefemme*, meaning wise or good woman, and is rooted in the Old French *prode*, meaning good, capable, brave. Prude has the same origins as *proud*." Only in an unremittingly patriarchal society, Daly notes, could the word "prude" be used disparagingly, and the reason why is obvious: The "phallic lusters" and "thrusters" are threatened by "women who are wise, good, capable, brave, and—especially—[by] Proud Women."[405]

**pseudomedical advice.** The University of Maryland at College Park includes the offering of "pseudomedical advice" such as "A little Tender Loving Care (TLC) will cure your ailments" on its official list of "unacceptable verbal behaviors that may be in violation of campus policy on sexual harassment." Lest there be any misunderstanding, the university points out that such advice does "not necessarily have to be specifically directed at an individual to constitute sexual harassment."[406]

**psychological captivity.** An official glossary of terms circulated at the University of Pennsylvania defined this as a state in which "prejudiced images and attitudes ['perpetuated by dominant society'] influence the behavior of subordinates." The term was provided to university facilitators to help them explain, among other things, why a female graduate student would be deluding herself if she thought she had fallen in love with a male graduate-student teaching assistant or a professor, and why the latter would be guilty of sexual harassment if he agreed to date her.[407] See also: **false consciousness; internalized oppression.**

**public displays of affection.** See: **affection, public displays of.**

**puppet surrogates.** Because women in Western society have been taught by the patriarchy to "be nice" and "not make waves," it is often hard for them to be assertive, or to deliver unwelcome messages. As a solution to this problem, an increasing number of women are turning to "puppet surrogates"—hand puppets who can deliver the message for them. For example, "Paula," a member of the Mohawk Nation who serves as an "anti-bias training facilitator," used a dog and a teddy bear puppet to direct traffic at the 1992 National Women's Studies Association Conference in

Austin, Texas ("Teddy and his friend say it's time to go back inside," one attendee quoted her as saying).[408] Similarly, women can use such puppets as the Minnesota Department of Education's Respect, the Turtle, to deny sexual consent to men whom they're afraid of confronting directly. See also: **Dignity, the Snail; Equality, the Frog; Respect, the Turtle.**

*Survival Strategy #4: Using a* **puppet surrogate.**

**quid pro quo sexual harassment.** An offense defined by legal policy expert Ellen Frankel Paul as the "extortion of sexual favors by a supervisor from a subordinate by threatening to penalize, fire or fail to reward." Such extortion has historically been treated as criminal by the American justice system and, since the 1970s, it has specifically been recognized as a form of discrimination punishable under Title VII of the Civil Rights Act of 1964.[409] See also: **hostile environment sexual harassment.**

**ram, behaving like a.** A great technique men can use to "recover" the primitive vitality that modern industrial society has driven out of them, suggests noted psychologist Dr. Shepherd Bliss, is to try "behaving like the most masculine of all animals—the ram." Correspondent Jon Tevlin was fortunate enough to be present when Bliss led a mythopoetic men's gathering in a "behaving-like-a-ram" session. "You may find unfamiliar noises emerging from your throats!" Bliss encouraged his disciples, at which point, Tevlin reports, the air became filled with a joyous chorus of "gurgles and bleats."[410] See also: **four-leggeds, joining the world of; dog, pretending to be a; gorilla, dressing up as a.**

**rapability (as the defining characteristic of femaleness).** Writes Catharine A. MacKinnon: "To be rapable, a position that is social not biological, defines what a woman is."[411] See also: **rape (as the defining characteristic of maleness).**

**rape.** Author Susan Brownmiller, who is widely praised as being the first to perceive rape as an expression of political power rather than a crime of sexual passion, defines it as "nothing more or nothing less than a conscious process of intimidation by which *all* men keep *all* women in a state of fear."[412] University of Michigan legal scholar Catharine MacKinnon notes that, in her view, the term is applicable "whenever a woman has sex and feels violated."[413]

**"rape," careless use of the term.** Catherine Comins, assistant dean of student life at Vassar, sees careless use of the term "rape" as a valuable weapon in the battle against patriarchal oppression. "To use the word carefully would be to be careful for the sake of the violator, and the survivors don't care a hoot about him," she explains.[414] See also: **rape, false accusations of.**

**rape, definitional stretching of.** See: definitional stretching.

**rape, extraterrestrial.** See: extraterrestrial rape.

**rape, false accusations of.** According to Catherine Comins, assistant dean of student life at Vassar, an unjust accusation of rape can be just the ticket when one is trying to educate men about their inherent capacity for violence. "They have a lot of pain," she explained to *Time* magazine in 1991, "but it is not a pain that I would necessarily have spared them. I think it ideally initiates a process of self-exploration. 'How do I see women?' 'If I didn't violate her, could I have?' 'Do I have the potential to do to her what they say I did?' Those are good questions."[415] (Note: The American Gender Society suggests one additional good question: "How would I like to spend the next ten to fifteen years of my life in prison for a crime I didn't commit?")

**rape, filial.** See: filial rape.

**rape, food-service.** See: food-service rape.

**rape, invention of.** See: Cro-Magnon man within.

**rape, in vitro.** See: in vitro rape.

**rape, justifiable.** See: justifiable rape.

**rape, legalized.** See: marriage.

**rape, men's ability to prevent themselves from committing.** "Let's just face it," Kristen Asmus advises in "Blaming the Dress," an essay she wrote for the *Colorado Daily*. "The men in our society cannot control themselves." As discouraging as this fact might seem, however, Asmus does see a solution. "Women will start fighting back," she predicts hopefully. "Women will begin to react with as much violence as men have mustered against them."[416] See also: **castration; murder; sociosexual vigilantism.**

**rape, mental.** See: mental rape.

**rape, osculatory.** See: osculatory rape.

**rape, soft.** See: soft rape.

**rape, telephone.** See: telephone rape.

**rape, verbal.** See: verbal rape.

**rape, virtual.** See: virtual rape.

**rape (as a weapon of male domination).** "Regardless of the intent of individual men who rape," Rus Ervin Funk tells us in *Stopping Rape: A Challenge for Men,* "as a result all women have fewer opportunities. Men use the fear, the threat, and the silence surrounding rape to keep ourselves in a dominant position over women."[417] See also: **nonrape (as a weapon of male domination).**

**rape (as a weapon used by men to gain political office).** According to antisexism crusader Rus Ervin Funk, control of the world's political institutions is one of the many benefits *all* men derive from the rapes *some* men commit. "How are you supposed to run for office when it's unsafe to go out at night?" he asks.[418]

**rape (as the defining characteristic of maleness).** "The act of prevailing upon another to admit of penetration without full and knowledgeable assent," John Stoltenberg writes in *Refusing to Be a Man,* "so sets the standard in the repertoire of male-defining behaviors that it is not at all inaccurate to suggest that the ethics of male sexual identity are essentially rapist."[419] See also: **rapability (as the defining characteristic of femaleness).**

*Albert Schweitzer, an individual with an essentially **rapist** sexual identity.*

**rape-conducive environments.** In their essay "Factors that Increase the Likelihood of Victimization," Patricia A. Harney and Charlene L. Muehlenhard point out that there is "abundant evidence" linking traditional (i.e., patriarchal) gender-role attitudes and sexually aggressive behavior. Therefore, they argue, it's logical to assume that any institution that promotes "traditional gender roles and male dominance" is also helping to create a "rape-conducive environment." The catalog of such institutions provided by Harney and Muehlenhard is, unfortunately, too long to reproduce here in its entirety. However, in the interest of helping our female readers protect themselves, we offer this abridged list:

1. "the socialization of college and graduate students by professors";
2. "dating rituals";
3. "marriage";
4. "women's position in the workplace";

*Survival Strategy #5: Functioning within a* **rape-conducive environment.**

5. "nonverbal interpersonal behavior"; and
6. "the English language."

"Compared with the effects of violent pornography," Harney and Muehlenhard conclude ominously, "the effects of these institutions are probably more subtle—and thus more insidious."[420]

**rape culture.** American and European culture, for example. As Rus Ervin Funk points out in *Stopping Rape: A Challenge for Men,* Western society qualifies as a "rape culture" because it "supports and actively encourages men to rape women, people of color, children, and gay men and lesbians."[421]

**rape of nature.** A phrase used to define "scientific inquiry" by a task force charged by the state of New Jersey with coming up with a set of "feminist scholarship guidelines" for the teaching of science at the university level.[422] See: **science.**

*Marie Curie, a* **rapist of nature.**

**rape vans.** Vans owned by pornographer-kidnappers who, according to Wheelock College professor Gail Dines, use them to roam the streets of New York, adding to America's ever-rising daily toll of sexual violence. The pornographer-kidnappers, Dines explains, drag unsuspecting women into the vans, where they are raped on camera. The pornographer-kidnappers then sell the rape videos through commercial outlets for enormous profits, Dines reports. But, she claims, because society still insists on protecting such videos under the First Amendment, the pornographer-kidnappers remain above prosecution. (The depth of this problem is reflected by the fact that, as Wendy Kaminer reports in the *Atlantic*

*Monthly,* the official in charge of monitoring New York's sex industry claims he has never even *heard* of rape vans.)[423]

**rapist recidivism.** A term coined to characterize the revelation by 42 percent of the women categorized as rape victims in a famous *Ms.* magazine survey that they had gone on to have sex again with their alleged assailants. When Neil Gilbert, a professor at the University of California at Berkeley, suggested that this unexpectedly high incidence of rapist recidivism indicated that the definition of "rape" used in the survey might have been overly broad, a crowd gathered on the Berkeley campus and demanded that Gilbert "cut it out or cut it off."[424] See: **definitional stretching.**

**rapists, potential.** See: potential rapists.

**RECAP.** An acronym for **RECover A Penis,** a support group for circumcision survivors interested in restoring their foreskins. RECAP was founded in 1990 by R. Wayne Griffiths, a contract administrator with the Central Contra Costa Sanitary District, and Tim Sally, a San Francisco masseur.[425] See also: **BUFF; circumcision survivors; foreskin restoration movement; keratinization; NOHARMM; UNCIRC; uncircumcising.**

**receptive noninitiation.** A name offered by Sue Rosenberg Zalk, director of the Center for the Study of Women and Society at the State University of New York, for the offense a man is guilty of when he reciprocates the sexual advances of a woman whom he outranks in a hierarchy. The unequal power relationship makes the man's "concession" to the woman's overtures a clear case of sexual harassment, Zalk tells us. Any attempt by the man to excuse his behavior on the grounds that the woman seduced *him* is, she says, "a transparent rationalization." The fact that the woman "asked," she points out, "is not an explanation for why he complied." "A woman would never get away with offering such an excuse," she concludes.[426] (Note: Since, as Susan Estrich has written, "women in today's society are powerless relative to men," *any* male response to a woman's sexual initiative can—and should—be regarded as an example of receptive noninitiation.)

*A man committing a blatant act of* **receptive noninitiation.**

**"Refuse to be a victim."** The theme of a special advertising campaign launched in late 1993 by the newly antipatriarchal National Rifle Association to convince women to purchase handguns.[427] See: **Women's Empowerment in the '90s.**

**regreening of masculinity.** See: **masculinity, regreening of.**

**remasculation.** Men who feel they have been emasculated—by their mothers, by their love partners, by the feminist assault on patriarchy, by life in general—may find solace in a remasculation ritual observed by *Esquire* correspondent Doug Stanton during a **New Warrior Weekend Adventure** retreat that he had the good fortune to attend. As Stanton tells it, a member of the New Warrior Weekend Adventure staff (a man whose Warrior name was

"Scowling Beaver") began the festivities by juggling two oranges in front of one of Stanton's fellow attendees (who'd been assigned the nickname "Jackrabbit" for the occasion). "I want my balls back, Mother!" Jackrabbit began bellowing; in response, Scowling Beaver ordered all the other weekenders to form a barricade around Jackrabbit. Stanton picks up the action from there:

> "Give 'em to me you bitch!" Jackrabbit screams. He crashes into us with a sweaty *whump,* reaching for the oranges, blood draining from his face. We stop him. He backs up, rockets ahead again.
>
> "I can't go on," he groans.
>
> "You can *do* it!" we yell.
>
> "MOTHER OF GOD!" He's never felt this strong before! He's always been an accountant, and now the Wildman's energy beats in his heart, his guts, his balls! No, wait, not his balls, his mother has his balls. She turned him into a wimp, always told him to be a good boy, never let him piss in the sink. He raises his left hand—his *sword!*—and charges, panting like a plow horse, busting through the knot of men, emerging on the other side.
>
> He halts, stunned, spins on his feet, and stares murderously at the oranges, like a psychopath in a fruit market. Scowling Beaver hands over the fruit, what he's paid $550 for at the door.
>
> "I got 'em back! I got 'em back!" Jackrabbit shouts gleefully.
>
> He hops to the stone ledge, sticks a plastic baseball bat between his legs, and waves his new weenie at us, his exhausted face streaming with joy.

"This is the most amazing thing I've ever seen," Stanton concludes humbly.[428] See: **New Warrior Weekend Adventures; Wild Man within.**

**repressed memory therapy.** See: hypnotic regression.

**Respect, the Turtle.** A puppet character created by the Minnesota Department of Education to teach elementary school students to be aware of their "private places."[429] Women who are anxious to keep men from pawing them, but shy about confronting them directly, might consider bringing a Respect puppet along on their

next date and letting
the turtle do the talk-
ing when it's time to
say "no." See also:
**Dignity, the Snail;
Equality, the Frog;
puppet surrogates.**

**RESPECT**

Minnesota Department of Education, 1993

**Respect, the Turtle.**

**right not to be offended.** Author Jonathan Rauch's term for a new
legal principle that, he asserts, is rapidly taking root in Western
society.[430] As columnist John Leo summarizes it, the basic premise
behind the right not to be offended is that "negative feelings must
not be felt," and that, "if they are felt, then someone must be penal-
ized for it."[431] Despite the fact that this new doctrine is more than
occasionally in conflict with the First Amendment of the U.S. Constitution and that a few other messy details remain to be worked
out (such as how and when to suspend the due process rights of
those doing the offending), the use of feelings as a trump card is (to
quote Leo again) "becoming pervasive."[432] Catharine A. MacKinnon's declaration that "I call it rape whenever the woman feels
violated"[433]; Rus Ervin Funk's definition of sexual assault as
"unwanted sexual contact as *defined by the victim/survivor* [Funk's
italics]"[434]; and the contention, offered in the Princeton University
pamphlet *What You Should Know About Sexual Harassment,* that
harassment is any sexual attention "that makes a person feel
uncomfortable"[435] are all textbook assertions of the right not to be
offended. See also: **hostile environment sexual harassment.**

**romance.** A couple about to embark on a moonlight cruise would
do well to bear in mind Andrea Dworkin's pithy and thought-pro-
voking definition of "romance": "rape embellished with meaningful looks."[436]

***Romeo and Juliet.*** Dismissing Shakespeare's *Romeo and Juliet* as a "blatantly heterosexual love story," Jane Hardman-Brown, head teacher of the Kingsmead School in the London borough of Hackney, refused a grant of free tickets that would have allowed her students to see a ballet based on the play. "It does not explore the full extent of human sexuality," Hardman-Brown explained, leaving to further debate the question of whether Shakespeare's work might be rewritten to include characters whose love affairs reflect alternative lifestyles or should instead simply be banned outright.[437] See also: **Shakespeare; heterosexism**.

**rule of thumb.** When men use the phrase "rule of thumb" in the presence of a woman, they leave themselves open to the charge of being "sexist, patriarchal and insensitive." The reason, Stephanie Schorow reported in a widely quoted article disseminated by the Associated Press, is that the term originated with a sixteenth-century British law that "limited to the thickness of a thumb the stick that could be used by men to beat their wives."[438] (Note: Even the most cursory investigation of the etymology of the phrase "rule of thumb" would reveal that the term has absolutely no relation to wife-battering. It evolved, instead, from the practice among carpenters of using the length of their thumbs as a guide in measuring wood.[439] Nonetheless, since most of the women who encountered Schorow's dispatch are probably unaware of its inaccuracy, men would be well advised to avoid saying "rule of thumb" in mixed company.)

**safe sex.** An inaccurate and outmoded name for the set of behaviors now called **safer sex**.[440]

**safer sex.** The sexually correct term for precautions taken during lovemaking to reduce the chances that one might contract or transmit AIDS or another STD. **Safe sex** is no longer considered an appropriate designation for such precautions, because it fails to acknowledge, as "safer sex" does, that no sex practice, including using a condom, offers foolproof protection. The life-or-death importance of this distinction was highlighted by Valerie Cephas in an attack, published in *Newsday,* on the New York City Board of Education's sex-education program. "If the failure rate for parachutes were the same as for condoms," wrote Cephas, "there would be no skydivers!"[441] See also: **less dangerous sex.**

**SAFFIR (Seattle Area Fat Feminist Inspiration and Rage).** See: **sizeism.**

**Saint Monica, pilgrimages to the statue of.** At the intersection of Wilshire Boulevard and Ocean Avenue in Santa Monica, California, on a precipice overlooking the Pacific Ocean, stands a statue of Saint Monica that *LA Weekly* columnist Michael Ventura feels everyone interested in gender reconciliation must visit. Writes Ventura:

> The piece has an air of wanting to be ignored and it gets its wish. It is as though the sculptor had been frightened of his own idea. Plainly, whether he knew it or not, his idea had been to sculpt the image of a woman onto a phallus. Walk around the statue. From behind, it is an erection plain and simple and only slightly abstract. From the front, a woman of minimal lines has taken her place within, or on the surface of, the penis.

According to Ventura, the sculptor's psyche must have traveled back to the Neolithic era when "it was not unusual to sculpt images of the Great Goddess onto carvings of the erect penis." Did

**Statue of Saint Monica,** *Santa Monica, California.*

such carvings symbolize "the masculine and the feminine *cohabiting the cock itself*?" Ventura wonders.

> If the cock is also feminine, then where does "feminism" hide and where does "macho" run? . . . Simplicities like "feminine or masculine" or "straight and gay" are shallow beside these ancient stones. . . . The erection, which the feminist and the macho alike have seen as such a one-note, one-purpose organ, is less a sword than a wand.

"Statue transcends self and becomes a piece of psychic archaeology," Ventura concludes.[442]

**Saint Uncumber.** See: Uncumber's Day.

**Sarah, the Spider.** An arachnid who introduced herself to Boston College **thealogian** Mary Daly and played a pivotal role in inspiring *Websters' First New Intergalactic Wickedary of the English*

*Language,* the groundbreaking feminist lexicography Daly compiled "in cahoots with" Jane Caputi.[443]

**science.** According to the "Feminist Scholarship Guidelines" issued by the New Jersey Project, a task force charged with reforming public schools, centuries of so-called "scientific inquiry" have left us with little more than a "white, male, Eurocentric, heterosexist, and elite view of 'reality.' "[444] Feminist theorist Elizabeth Fee, who is quoted in the New Jersey Project report, explains the patriarchal "construct" that led to this unfortunate set of circumstances: "Mind was male" she writes, "nature was female, and knowledge was created as an act of aggression—a passive nature had to be interrogated, unclothed, penetrated, and compelled by man to reveal her secrets."[445] Philosopher Sandra Harding, of the University of Delaware, makes the same argument a bit more succinctly: Science, she says, is "marital rape, the husband as scientist forcing nature to his wishes."[446] ("What about *women* scientists?" columnist Michael Costello wonders. "Are they lesbians?"[447]) See also: *Newton's Rape Manual.*

**scissors sign.** Supporters of sociosexual vigilante Lorena Bobbitt, reports *Vanity Fair* magazine, "have transformed the V-for-Victory sign into a symbol of solidarity by making scissorlike motions with their fingers."[448] See also: **sociosexual vigilantism.**

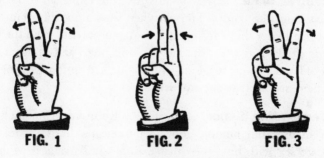

**FIG. 1**            **FIG. 2**            **FIG. 3**

*Instructions for making the* **scissors sign.**

**screwing.** See: coitus; enclosure; engulfment; envelopment; intercourse; nutting; vagina-specific fucking.

**SCUM.** An acronym for the Society for Cutting Up Men, an organization founded by Valerie Solanas in the 1970s whose goal, eloquently stated by Solanas herself in her famous *SCUM Manifesto,* was to save the world from male domination by getting rid of the men themselves.[449] See: **androcide.**

**second virginity.** Concerned that young women who have already experienced intercourse may have less incentive than their uninitiated sisters to enjoy the medical and spiritual benefits of what British feminist Sally Cline calls "celebrating celibacy," U.S. public-school abstinence educators have come up with the concept of "second virginity" to establish new moral ground on which teenagers can get off to a fresh nonstart.[450]

**seduced, allowing oneself to be.** See: receptive noninitiation.

**seduction.** According to Andrea Dworkin, the only real difference between seduction and rape is that "in seduction, the rapist bothers to buy a bottle of wine."[451] Knowing this, a man interested in protecting himself against prosecution may want to consider bringing along some Pinot Grigio or a nice Chardonnay on his next date.

**self-control, male.** Any woman who thinks she can count on a man's ability to control himself when she's alone with him on a date had better think again, Kristen Asmus advises us in the *Colorado Daily.* But when the inevitable happens and things do get out of hand, Asmus suggests, women *do* have options.[452] (For two of them, see: **castration; murder.**)

**self-deprecating humor.** According to Robin Morgan, if a man's "self-deprecating humor" about being rejected leads a woman to initiate sex with him, then that man is—in "a radical feminist" sense of the term—guilty of rape.[453]

*Survival Strategy #6: Coping with* **self-deprecating humor.**

**serial killing.** See: tickling; continuum theories.

**sex.** A term that Virginia Prince, author of "Sex, Gender, and Semantics," insists must be used only to describe specifically *biological* differences, such as the male production of sperm and the female production of eggs. As adherents of the burgeoning antiessentialist movement have demonstrated, all other distinctions—such as the arbitrary division of the human race into "men" and "women"—are purely cultural, and can be dismissed as differences of **gender.**[454] See also: **essentialism; gender.**

**sex-care providers.** See: prostitutes.

**sex-commodities.** Andrea Dworkin's term for what "the dating system" coerces women into becoming. How can women prevent this from happening? By refusing to participate in the dating system, says Dworkin.[455] Example: *Vanessa's favorite sexually correct TV show was "The* **Sex-Commodity** *Game*. See also: **women-as-property model**.

**sexism.** The Smith College Office of Student Affairs defines "sexism" as "the stereotyping of males and females on the basis of their gender; the oppression of women by society in the belief that gender is an indication of ability."[456] Because it's possible to infer from such definitions that men as well as women can be victims of sexist oppression, Andrea Dworkin uses the term "women-hating" instead.[457]

**sexists.** "[I]n a racist, classist and sexist society we have all swallowed oppressive ways of being, whether intentionally or not," Brandeis University women's studies professor Becky Thompson has written. "Specifically, this means that it is not open to debate whether a white student is racist or a male student is sexist. He/she simply is."[458] See: **false consciousness**.

**sex objects.** Individuals, typically women, valued primarily in terms of sexual appeal or as a source of sexual gratification. By turning women into sex objects, Meri Nana-Ama Danquah writes in *The Washington Post*, the male-dominated culture creates the notion "that we are powerless and useless unless meeting the needs—whatever they may be—of men."[459] See also: **beauty myth; success objects**.

**sex offenders, nonhuman.** Humans aren't the only species whose males are guilty of sexual abuse, and Robin Morgan, the crusading editor of *Ms.* magazine, has finally put an end to the cover-up, at least insofar as it applies to dolphins. "Dolphins, loved by everyone except certain

*Flipper, a notorious* **nonhuman sex offender.**

recalcitrant tuna fishermen, are not as gentle as we have sentimentalized them to be—if they're male," warns Morgan. "Dolphin males conspire to kidnap fertile females, and then will keep a kidnapped female 'in line' by physical threat or action: fin slapping, biting, or charging into her with the full force of their bodies."[460]

**Sexual Abuse Bowl.** See: **Super Bowl Sunday.**

**sexual assault.** Rus Ervin Funk, coordinator of the Men's Anti-Rape Resource Center, classifies as "sexual assault" any "unwanted sexual contact as *defined by the victim/survivor*" (his italics). Individuals on dates should keep this in mind before touching their companions or allowing their companions to touch them.[461]

**sexual assault, frequency of.** According to Margie Metch of New York City's Task Force Against Sexual Assault, one in five dates ends in assault. Based on these numbers, if you're a college woman who dates just once a week you can reasonably expect to survive 41.6 sexual assaults before you graduate (not to mention the dozens of other attacks to which you were *already* subjected during your high school years).[462] Is it any wonder that Vicki Noble, author of *Shakti Woman: Feeling Our Fire, Healing Our World*, writes: "Women are more in danger from men they know than our soldiers are from 'enemies' on the battlefield!"?[463]

**sexual bribery.** A form of sexual harassment specifically recommended for proscription by the Supreme Court of the State of New Jersey (and also by many other public and private institutions). "Sexual bribery" is defined as: (a) the solicitation of "sexual activity or other sex-linked behavior" by promise of reward; or (b) the presentation of gifts or other favors in an attempt to foster such activity or behavior.[464] See: **candy; dates, paying for; flowers.**

**sexual coercion.** See: **soft rape.**

**sexual consent forms.** Deborah Gallo, an avid student of the legal issues involved in consensual dating, has published "a little black book of sexual consent forms," guaranteed to prevent "embarrassing courtroom imbroglios" between dating partners (assuming, of course, that both parties agree to sign before making first contact). But don't plan on saving money by creating your own version of such a document unless you're willing to risk being the defendant in an infringement suit; Gallo, who doubles as a real estate agent in Toronto, has already filed for a patent on her form. "Naturally," she explained to a *Life* magazine reporter, "the knockoff threat is constant."[465] See also: **signatures, women's, on sexual consent forms**.

**sexual deprivation (as a motive for relationship termination).** "Telling a woman that her refusal to have sex was changing the way they felt about her" is specifically listed by Charlene Muelenhard and her colleague Jennifer Schrag in their catalog of men's offenses that can be categorized as "sexual coercion."[466] Since a sexual coercion conviction can lead to suspension from an increasing number of universities (Antioch College, for example), college men would be well advised not to use an absence of sexual activity as a justification for breaking up with their significant other.[467]

**sexual gratification.** Women must work hard to prevent sex with men from being too enjoyable. That's the gist of remarks made by Simone de Beauvoir during an interview conducted by Alice Schwartzer in 1976. "The worst thing," the famous novelist and essayist informed Schwartzer, "is for women to find so much happiness in sexuality that they become . . . slaves to men," thus strengthening "the chain that binds them to their oppressor."[468]

**sexual harassment.** Lists of specific offenses officially proscribed as "sexual harassment" vary widely from institution to institution, from city to city, and from state to state (this dictionary alone details literally scores of forbidden behaviors). But perhaps the most useful *general* definition of the term may be found in *What You Should Know About Sexual Harassment,* a pamphlet distributed at Princeton University, which describes it as "unwanted sexual attention that makes a person feel uncomfortable or causes problems in school or at work, or in social settings."[469] The key word to keep in mind here is "uncomfortable": As Rus Ervin Funk warns in his helpful book, *Stopping Rape: A Challenge for*

*Men*, "it is the survivor"—not some impartial deliberative body relying on abstract legalistic definitions—"who defines what is and what isn't appropriate behavior."[470] See also: **right not to be offended.**

**sexual identity community.**  See: **sexual minority community.**

**sexual imposition.**  An offense officially defined by Antioch College as "nonconsensual sexual contact." ("Sexual contact," the college explains, "includes the touching of thighs, genitals, buttocks, the pubic region, or the breast/chest area."). Under the Antioch Rules, sexual imposition may lead to criminal prosecution, and/or institutional sanctions "up to and including expulsion or termination of employment."[471]

**sexually oriented conversation.**  Josh McDowell, author of *It Can Happen to You: What You Need to Know About Preventing*

*Survival Strategy #7: Avoiding* **sexually oriented conversation.**

*and Recovering from Date Rape,* advises women that to prevent rape, they should do their best to keep the mood between themselves and their dates from becoming sexy and to keep the conversations they hold with men from turning to the subject of sex. "If you feel the atmosphere or conversation becoming sexually oriented, try to change the mood or subject of conversation," he advises.[472]

**sexually suggestive reading material.** U.S. federal judge Howell Melton struck a valiant blow for the right of women everywhere not to be offended when he issued a ruling officially prohibiting, as "hostile environment sexual harassment," the bringing of "sexually suggestive or demeaning" reading material into any workplace located within his jurisdiction.[473] See: **hostile environment sexual harassment; right not to be offended.**

**sexual minority community.** Lesbians, gay men, and bisexuals. Be wary of using the phrase "sexual minority community" in connection with transsexuals, however: While some qualify as members of this group, Alan Hamilton warns us in his *Sexual Identity and Gender Identity Glossary,* many others do not. (Note: The term "sexual minority community" is also offensive to lesbians, gays, and bisexuals who feel that the word "minority" stigmatizes them by branding them as "different" or "abnormal." Some individuals in this category may prefer to be called members of the **sexual identity community.**)[474]

**sexual negligence.** A term coined by the Harvard-Radcliffe Undergraduate Council to describe a category of offenses in which a perpetrator proceeds with sexual activity in a situation "where there is neither mutual consent or expressed unwillingness." While noting that such offenses are, of course, "criminal," the Council recommended, in a 1992 report, that punishments for them should be less severe than those meted out in cases where unwillingness is actively expressed.[475]

**sexual objectification.** See: **objectification.**

**sexual offense advocate.** The title Antioch College confers on the officials it charges with counseling—or hearing complaints from—those covered by its sexual offense policy. Jason Vest, of *The Washington Post,* notes that the choice of this particular term was a "curious" one.[476]

**sexual offense policy.** See: Antioch Rules.

**sexual offers in the workplace (as a factor in the oppression of white males).** Those who argue—as an increasing number of men do—that upper and middle-class white males are more oppressed than women in Western society cite as an example the fact that women, individually and as a group, have more opportunities than their male colleagues to gain promotions by responding to sexual offers from their employers.[477] See also: **oppression of white males; success objects**.

**sexual reassignment surgery.** Alan Hamilton's *Sexual Identity and Gender Identity Glossary* defines this as "a surgical procedure which changes one's primary sexual organs from one sex to another (penis to vagina or vagina to penis)." The term is often used in its abbreviated form, **SRS**.[478]

**Sexual Revolution.** According to British feminist Sheila Jeffreys, the only freedom women gained from the so-called "Sexual Revolution" of the 1960s was "the freedom ... to take pleasure from their own erotic subordination."[479] See also: **Decade of Genital Appropriation**.

**sexual surrogates.** See: prostitutes.

**sexual terrorism.** John Stoltenberg, author of *Refusing to Be a Man,* informs us that this is one of the two principal means by which the male flourishes as a sexual entity. (The other is "acts of force.")[480]

**sex workers.** See: prostitutes.

**Shakespeare.** John Banville, in an *Irish Times* article defending London school teacher Jane Hardman-Brown's declaration that

Shakespeare's *Romeo and Juliet* is a "blatantly heterosexual love story" (see: ***Romeo and Juliet***), points out that Hardman-Brown's detractors have lost sight of "the central issue, which is the question of Shakespeare's politics, sexual and otherwise, and the effect his plays may have in maintaining establishment values." The truth, Banville notes, is that "Shakespeare was at the least a very meek artist in a savagely repressive time, and at worst a self-serving reactionary." And besides, Banville concludes, the play "is not very good, heretical as it may be to say so."[481]

**Shakespeare,** *a self-serving reactionary.*

**shaking hands.** See: handshakes.

**sheds at the bottom of the garden, keeping women in.** See: couples.

**signatures, women's, on sexual consent forms.** When it comes time for a man to evaluate the legal weight of a woman's signature on a sexual consent form, Andrea Dworkin recommends a healthy dose of skepticism. "If you can force someone to fuck a dog," she offers helpfully, "you can force them to sign a contract."[482] See: sexual consent forms.

**significant other.** A gender-inclusive, nonheterosexist improvement upon such outmoded terms as "husband," "wife," "spouse," "boyfriend," "girlfriend," and "lover."[483]

**size-acceptance movement.** A coalition whose members have banded together to fight discrimination against individuals with larger-than-average body images and to discredit the notion, perpetuated by the **beauty myth,** that "thin is beautiful."[484]

**size-affirmative dating.** Making a special point of dating individuals with alternative body images, as a protest against the **fashion profiteers** who set artificial standards for attractiveness in order to exploit both women's and men's fears of sexual rejection. Size-affirmative dating is also sometimes referred to as **body-image-inclusive dating**.

**sizeism.** Discrimination by the temporarily fit against those whose body image does not conform to the norms set by the dominant culture.[485] The women of Seattle Area Fat Feminist Inspiration and Rage (SAFFIR) raised America's consciousness about the evils of sizeism when they showed up at a scholastic fashion show and staged an impromptu but ingenious pageant involving naked Barbie dolls, fake blood, and a toilet bowl. Wrote *Seattle Times* correspondent Wylie Wong, who was fortunate enough to witness the event:

> Barbie dolls were everywhere. Nude Barbie dolls with nooses around their necks. Clothed Barbie dolls in coffins. A toilet bowl filled with empty food cartons and diet books—and a nude Barbie doll—sat on the sidewalk.

The high point of the demonstration, in Wong's view, was the apparition of SAFFIR member Diana Mackin, who paraded along the street

> with a pink set of scales chained around her ankle. Fake blood oozed out of her stomach and thighs to show where women sometimes undergo surgery to get rid of fat.

Despite the success of the protest, however, not all the women competing in the fashion show were willing to admit they were collaborating in a squalid celebration of body image exclusionism. "It's a great way to get money," enthused contestant Cyndee Hubner, a twenty-one-year-old tap dancer who said she planned to use any cash she won to help pay her own way through dental school.[486]

**smacking sounds.** See: blowing kisses.

**smothering, emotional.** The notion that a man could be "enveloped and smothered" by a mother, lover, or wife is "a paranoid fantasy," Will Roscoe, author of *The Zuni Man-Woman*, informs us. "Women don't have the power in this culture to do that to men," he says.[487]

**snuggies.** "Snuggies"—defined as "pulling [another student's] underwear up at the waist so it goes in between the buttocks"—occupies sixteenth place on the list of "examples of sexually harassing behaviors reported in U.S. high schools" that Susan Strauss and Pamela Espeland provide in their book *Sexual Harassment and Teens: A Program for Positive Change.* Just how serious an offense Strauss and Espeland consider snuggies to be is indicated by the fact that the two items immediately following it on their list—in seventeenth and eighteenth places, respectively—are "sexual assault and attempted sexual assault" and "rape."[488]

**SOAR (Students Organized Against Rape).** See: definitional stretching.

**social touching.** Since it's difficult—if not impossible—to distinguish between a "friendly touch" and a "sensual touch" (the difference may depend entirely on the state of mind of the person doing the touching), Kenneth C. Cooper, author of "The Six Levels of Sexual Harassment," warns male managers against any "social touching" of employees. Indeed, he classifies it as "Level 3" sexual harassment, more serious than **aesthetic appreciation** and **mental groping**, but less grievous than **foreplay harassment.**[489]

**sociosexual vigilantism.** A term coined by noted Australian feminist activist Stephanie Morris to describe Lorena Bobbitt's emasculation of her abusive husband, John Wayne Bobbitt. Although Morris characterizes Ms. Bobbitt's removal of Mr. Bobbitt's penis as "a bold and courageous act of feminist self-defense" and praises Ms. Bobbitt as "a potent symbol of female empowerment," she finds herself forced to concede that "some women question the political prudence of 'sociosexual vigilantism.'" And indeed, the

*Lorena Bobbitt, a celebrated* **sociosexual vigilante.**

remarks of Paul Biagi, interviewed in a New York City bar by a reporter for Reuters News Service, would seem to support the view that more time is needed before society as a whole, dominated as it has been by thousands of years of oppressive patriarchy, is prepared to accept Ms. Bobbit as (to quote Morris again) "a symbol of innovative resistance against gender oppression everywhere." "Let's face it," said Biaggi, "she'll never get another date."[490] See also: **bobbitt; bobbittectomy; castration; penis guard.**

**soft rape.** Andrea Parrot, author of *Coping with Date Rape and Acquaintance Rape,* defines this as nonconsensual sexual intercourse ("or other sexual act") in which "coercion (pressure or intimidation) or threat of coercion," rather than actual physical force, is used to gain the victim's compliance.[491]

**sons, why fathers tend not to rape their own.**  See: filial rape.

**Sons of Orpheus.**  The act of communal drumming, writes **tactile-vestibular** therapist Bruce Silverman, can lead men "through a portal to a lower world, the animal world, the instinctual realm where spirits and ancestors roam, where Orpheus sought Eurydice, his lost love." And what better way for men to rediscover their connection with nature and their capacity to relate meaningfully to women and other men than to join a drumming circle like Silverman's "Sons of Orpheus," where every Wednesday night inside the group's "ritual space"—a whitewashed loft bordering a freeway in Emeryville, California—dozens of ordinary men from all walks of life "become the sons of the Greek hero who sang his grief to both gods and men with such power that the 'trees crowded round him' and the rocks were 'softened by his notes' "?[492] (Note: *Newsweek* correspondent Jerry Adler attributes this magical transformation to the almost indescribable racket generated by Silverman and his adherents. "How else are you going to get the attention of the gods," he asks, "especially when your ritual space is right next to an expressway?"[493])

**Sophia.**  A female incarnation of the divine, mentioned in the Book of Proverbs and elsewhere in the Bible. Those who wish to honor Sophia may wish to use the following prayer, which was introduced at a 1994 conference of Protestant **thealogians** as part of a communionlike "women's sexuality and sensuality affirmation ritual" that also involved the sharing of milk and honey:

> Our maker Sophia, we are women in your image; with the hot blood of our wombs we give form to new life. With nectar between our thighs we invite a lover. . . . With our warm bodily fluids we remind the world of its pleasure and sensations.

Presbyterian officials estimate that adverse reaction to the prayer, the affirmation ritual, and the conference as a whole will cost the national church $2.5 million in contributions by the end of 1995. But Patricia Rumer, general director of Church Women United, dismisses such complaints as backlash. "Men need to silence this kind of thing in order to be in control," she told *The New York Times*.[494] See also: **Christa, Daughter of God; God, our queen and lover; Goddess Movement; thealogian.**

**sperm-egg mixers.** Gatherings, such as those sponsored by Prospective Queer Parents of Berkeley, California, at which gays and lesbians compare medical histories and family trees in hopes of starting a "non-traditional family." When a satisfactory match is found, according to a report in the January 1994 issue of *Heterodoxy*, a contract is signed, the man chosen to father the child ejaculates into a cup, and the prospective mother, "armed with a turkey baster or syringe, sucks up the semen and injects it into the uterus."[495] See also: **baster babies; turkey-baster insemination.**

**spiking.** See: depantsing.

***Sports Illustrated Swimsuit Issue.*** Frank Rich of *The New York Times* has made an important discovery about the *Sports Illustrated Swimsuit Issue:* Men aren't attracted to the women in it. "Indeed, the pictures are not even sexy," he tells us in his February 20, 1994, column. One wonders if, now that the Time Warner executives responsible for the *Sports Illustrated Swimsuit Issue* know it is "not even sexy," they might finally stop inflicting their annual orgy of sexual objectification on the public. Unfortunately, Rich does not think so. "Time Warner has too much invested in the message 'Women Are Property' to give up without a fight," he says.[496] See also: **women-as-property model.**

**spreading sex gossip.** One of several offenses ("staring or leering with sexual overtones" is another) officially defined as "sexual harassment" at Amherst-Pelham Regional High School in Massachusetts. "Spreading sex gossip" at this trend-setting educational institution is punishable by "parent conference, apology to victim, detention, suspension, recommendation, or referral to police." To test the limits of the rule against malicious chitchat, *U.S. News &*

*World Report* columnist John Leo called up superintendent of schools Gus Sayer and asked him what would happen if a student told a friend, "I think Marcie and Allen have something going"? "That would qualify as sexual harassment," Sayer assured him. (Leo notes that, by banning sex gossip, Amherst-Pelham Regional High School may have earned the distinction of being the first high school in the United States that "censors or punishes private conversation.")[497]

**SRS.**  See: sexual reassignment surgery.

**standing on one's head.**  North Carolina surrogate mother Julie Johnson ascribes at least partial credit for the success of her turkey-baster conception of John Franklin Wittle—a child she bore for her infertile sister, Janet—to the fact that she was standing on her head when her brother-in-law's sperm was injected into her womb.[498] See also: **baster babies; turkey-baster insemination.**

**standing too close.**  "Standing too close" is one of a long list of "sexually harassing behaviors" that Susan Strauss and Pamela Espeland caution us have been "reported in U.S. high schools."[499] See also: **dancing too close; touching.**

**staring, prolonged.**  See: prolonged staring.

**STDs.**  An acronym for "sexually transmitted diseases."[500] Because of the stigma the dominant culture places on such conditions, sensitivity experts advise us that, whenever practical, we should use the acronym instead of the actual words it represents.

**stickering.**  A slang term for the guerilla technique, pioneered by antirape activists at Brown University, of taping up, or scrawling, lists of men alleged to be sexually abusive on the walls of women's restrooms.[501] See also: **potential rapists.**

**stomach that has no ears, the.**  As Carol J. Adams points out in *The Sexual Politics of Meat,* men not only oppress women; they also oppress animals to get the meat that they insist on eating as a "mirror and representation of patriarchal values." Thus, she argues, it follows that "animals' oppression and women's oppression are linked together," and that women who are forced to ignore the knowledge that they are "consuming dead animals" in order to join a male significant other in a nonvegetarian meal are faced with a horrifying paradox:

> [We] are the consumers *and* the consumed. We are the ones whose stomachs do not listen—having no ears—and we are the ones who seek to be heard from within the stomach that has no ears.

There is only one solution, Adams concludes: "To destabilize patriarchal consumption we must interrupt patriarchal meals of meat."[502] See also: **hamburgers; meat eating.**

**straight.** A colloquial term for "heterosexual." Before using it in the company of gays, lesbians, or bisexuals, however, one should be aware that, as Alan Hamilton writes in his *Sexual Identity and Gender Identity Glossary,* "many members of the sexual identity community object to the implication that one who is not straight is 'bent,' 'adulterated,' 'impure,' or 'dishonest.' " (Note: Hamilton also warns that, because "straight" has "connotations of 'narrow,' 'straight-laced' or 'conservative,' " many "heterosexual-identified people" find it offensive, too.)[503]

**Strauss, Richard.** The music of Richard Strauss and Gustave Mahler, warns "feminist musicologist" Susan McClary of the University of Minnesota, is "filled with themes of male masturbation." Therefore, editorialist Michael Costello advises, concerts or recordings featuring either composer's work should be assiduously avoided by all men and women who believe in gender-justice.[504]

**Richard Strauss,** *a composer whose music is filled with themes of male masturbation.*

**stupid-women jokes.** A report issued by a committee charged with planning "diversity education" for incoming freshmen at the University of Pennsylvania lists the telling of "stupid-women jokes" as an example of sexual harassment.[505] See also: **mopping jokes.**

**success objects.** Men's movement leader John Lee argues that the so-called "privilege" of running the country, granted to American white males, is actually a curse because it has led them to be viewed as "success objects," valued only for the salaries they earn, rather than as individuals. "[Society says] we'll let you run the country," Lee argues, "but in the meantime stop feeling, stop talking and continue swallowing your pain and your hurt and keep dying younger than you need to be dying."[506] Luckily, Lee and his movement offer solutions. For some examples, see: **dolphin, pretending to be a; drum therapy; gorilla, dressing up as a; sweat lodge; talking stick; New Warrior Weekend Adventures.**

*Viacom's Sumner Redstone,*
*a* **success object.**

**suggestive looks.** Looking at a woman suggestively is never an appropriate way for a man to ascertain if she has any sexual interest in him. Indeed, the United Methodist Church has officially categorized "unsolicited suggestive looks" as a form of sexual harassment.[507] See also: **prolonged staring.**

**Super Bowl Sunday.** Citing an Old Dominion University study showing that Super Bowl Sunday was "the biggest day of the year for violence against women," with reports of domestic battery running a full 40 percent above the norm, a group of women's groups issued a press release just before the 1993 Super Bowl game in Pasadena, warning women: "Don't remain at home with him during the game." The media response was immediate and gratifying. The Super Bowl causes "boyfriends, husbands and fathers" to "explode like mad linemen," wrote Michael Collier of the *Oakland Tribune,* "leaving girlfriends, wives and children beaten." *New York Times* columnist Robert Lipsyte suggested the contest should be renamed the "Abuse Bowl," and CBS and the Associated Press officially labeled Super Bowl Sunday the "Day of Dread." (Note: It soon developed that reports that the Old Dominion survey had discovered a link between the Super Bowl and violence against women were erroneous—"That's not what we found at all," remarked a spokesperson for the research team—and spot checks with shelters and hot lines shortly after the game indicated that there had been no increase whatsoever in the number of assaults. When Ken Ringle of *The Washington Post* reported this revisionist information in a page one story, however, he was properly, if somewhat incoherently, chastised. Observed Laura Walker, author of *The Battered Woman:* "[Ringle] decided to use his pen as a sword as a batterer does with his fist.")[508]

**support.** Is it appropriate for a woman to lend support to the man (or men) in her life? Emphatically not, says Andrea Dworkin. "We must stop supporting the men who oppress us," she writes in *Our Blood.* "We must refuse to feed and clothe them; [and] we must refuse to let them take their sustenance from our lives."[509]

**survivor.** The only word appropriate for describing a woman who has experienced a rape; attempted rape; sexual assault; incidence of battery, harassment, or sexual intimidation; or has been made uncomfortable by unwanted sexual behavior, conversation or innuendo—without being killed in the process. See: **victims.**

**Susan B. Anthony Coven #1.** See: **Goddess Movement.**

**sweat lodge.** A Native American purification ritual that has been adopted by the men's movement and, notes writer Lenore Skenazy, "may outlive it." To participate, groups of men strip naked, gather in a pitch-dark tent or hut warmed by fire-heated rocks to temperatures as high as 150 degrees Fahrenheit, rub sage or other spices on one another, and concentrate on recovering from the inability to relate to others that the modern pressure of being **success objects** has thrust upon them. According to former Santa Monica mayor and sweat lodge veteran Jim Conn, participants pray, chant, cry, scream, yell, and gurgle a lot. If you want to be included in a sweat lodge ceremony but can't afford the time or expense to attend one, don't despair: The *Minneapolis Star Tribune* reports you can now order your own "portable backyard sweat hut," complete with a "FREE carrying case and a handbook on the history and health benefits of Sweat Lodge Ceremonies." Two words of warning before you proceed: (1) Take off your jewelry or contact lenses—as Skenazy points out, "they might melt"; and (2) Don't go out of your way to tell a member of the Lakota, Dakota, or Nakota Sioux nations about your plans—they've recently issued a formal "Declaration of War" against "New Agers, the men's movement, the feminist spirituality movement," and other "non-Indian 'wannabes'" who have appropriated their sacred rites.[510] See also: **mythopoetic men's movement; New Warrior Weekend Adventures.**

**tables for two.** Sally Cline, author of *Women, Celibacy and Passion*, condemns "restaurant tables automatically laid for two" as a symbol of "society's onerous insistence on coupledom."[511] See also: **candlelight dinners; couples; couple busting.**

A **table for two,** *a symbol of society's onerous insistence on coupledom.*

**tactile-vestibular activity.** The scientific name for drum therapy. According to Matt Weitz of *The Dallas Morning News*, research by "physiological and neuropsychological" experts has shown that "a set program of tactile-vestibular activity . . . can temporarily alter brain-wave activity, thereby facilitating altered states of consciousness."[512] Bruce Silverman, director of the Sons of Orpheus drumming circle, puts it a bit more simply: "A piccolo will get you there," he says, "but a drum will get you there quicker."[513] See: **drum therapy; Sons of Orpheus.**

**talking stick.** A ceremonial staff, sometimes decorated with feathers or fur, that gives anyone holding it the right to speak and be heard without interruption. The "talking-stick council"—a traditional Native American ritual in which a talking stick is passed from one man to another—is a central feature of many of the **Wild Man weekend gatherings** that have become popular since the publication of Robert Bly's *Iron John* touched off the so-called "mythopoetic" men's movement. According to Joseph Jastrab, a self-described "facilitator of the inevitable" from New Paltz, New York, the talking stick "serves as an invitation and encouragement to speak from the most undefended place in the self," and, as such, it can work wonders for any man who needs help overcoming his natural resistance to sharing intimacy. For best results, Jastrab tells potential talking stick holders, "put yourself in good relation with the animal, plant and mineral people of your place. Invite those who have gone before." It also helps if listeners utter an affirmative "Ho!" (a Native American expression meaning "I understand"[514]) or "Amen!" (with an emphasis on the "men") at appropriate moments during their brothers' speeches (such "hearty grunts," Jastrab notes, are an official exception to the no-interruption rule).[515] *Newsweek*'s Jerry Adler recently pondered the question of whether, as men's movement leader Christopher Harding has asserted, rituals such as the talking stick council can "vastly improve" men's relationships with women.[516] "Aha," Adler imagined women saying, "men are finally learning to talk about their feelings. But they have to hold a *stick* to do it."[517] See: **New Warrior Weekend Adventures; mythopoetic men's movement.**

**tape-recording one's date.** In her book *Back Off!*, Martha J. Langelan suggests that a woman who has reason to suspect she'll be harassed when she is alone with a particular man may want to consider tape-recording all her one-to-one encounters with him.[518] Columnist Asa Baber, for his part, advises his *male* readers to bring electronic recording equipment along whenever they're scheduled to be alone with a woman: The tapes will come in handy, he reasons, if it becomes necessary to fend off false allegations of harassment or rape.[519] Since *both* parties apparently have an interest in taping their time together, there really is no need for secrecy; indeed, openly cooperating on such matters as mike placement and sound levels can significantly increase the quality of the recording.

*Survival strategy #8:* **Tape-recording one's date.**

**teeth licking.**  See: lip licking.

**telephone rape.**  A crime defined by the Society for the Scientific Study of Sex as the act of calling up a woman, telling her that one is a therapist, and requesting that, as part of her prescribed treatment, she perform one or more sex acts and describe them over the phone.[520]

**tey, ter, tem.**  The so-called "human pronouns," first offered in 1972 as gender-neutral improvements upon "she/he," "her/his," and "her/him," respectively.[521] Example: **Tey** *told* **tem tey** *would tie* **ter** *tie for* **tem** *if* **tey** *would tie* **ter** *tie for* **tem**, *too.*

**thealogian.**  A feminist theologian.[522] See: **Christa, Daughter of God; God, our queen and lover; Goddess Movement; Sophia.**

**theological harassment.**  Graydon Snyder, a biblical scholar who teaches at the Chicago Theological Seminary, was officially condemned by his institution's "sexual harassment task force" after a female student complained that his use, during a comparative ethics lesson, of a somewhat improbable story from the Talmud had created a "hostile and offensive academic environment" for her and her classmates. The tale with which Snyder allegedly harassed his students concerned a married man working on the roof of a building who had removed his clothing to counter the heat. A sudden gust of wind blew the man off the roof and he landed on top of a woman who was not his wife (and who also happened to be naked) in such a way that he inadvertently had sexual intercourse with her. In cases such as this, Snyder had explained, Judaic and Christian law differ: Judaism would teach that the "affair" was an accident, not adultery, while Christianity would take the position that "Anyone who so much as looks at a woman has already committed adultery with her in his heart." The Talmudic source of Snyder's story, and the fact that he had been using it in his classes for over thirty years, failed to influence the task force, which placed him on "probation," recommended that he undergo psychotherapy, and issued a letter to the student body pronouncing him guilty of "verbal conduct of a sexual nature." The unrepentant Snyder has countered with a lawsuit.[523]

**THIS INSULTS WOMEN stickers.** Donna Jackson, author of *How to Make the World a Better Place for Women in Five Minutes a Day*, calls on her readers to ruin the effectiveness of advertising that objectifies or trivializes women by pasting a THIS INSULTS WOMEN sticker on every offending billboard they run across.[524] The stickers cost just one dollar (plus postage) for a quantity of twenty, and you can get your supply by calling (203) 455-9621 or writing to:

Donnelly Colt
P.O. Box 188
Hampton, CT 06247

**tickling.** Bernice Sandler of the Center for Women Policy Studies in Washington, D.C., tells the harrowing story of a second-grade girl who was thrown to the ground by a male classmate and tickled against her will. A few days later, the little girl confronted her young tormentor and accused him of sexual harassment. "This happens to be a sexual offense in New York, and in most states," Sandler commented to Ruth Shalit, who wrote about the incident in *The New Republic.* "She labeled the behavior correctly." Sue Sattel, sex-equity specialist for the Minnesota Department of Education, agrees that such sex crimes, even when committed by very young children, must be dealt with promptly and severely. "Serial killers tell interviewers they started sexually harassing at age ten, and got away with it," she says. Sattel's vigilance is paying off: In the 1991–92 school year alone, *The New Republic* reports, over one thousand Minneapolis schoolchildren were suspended or expelled on charges related to sexual harassment.[525]

**touching.** It would be insensitive of a man to touch a woman—and foolhardy for a woman to permit herself to be touched by a man—without first considering the sage advice about touching that Nancy Henley imparts in her book *Body Politics.* "In this male-dominated society," she writes, "touching is one more tool used to keep women in their place, another reminder that women's bodies are free property for everyone's use." If some readers—particularly those anxious to touch their partners—are troubled by Henley's words, they should be comforted by the knowledge that Henley *herself* finds them troublesome, too. "One is appalled to consider," she laments, "that something so human, so natural as touching should be perverted into a symbol of status and power."[526] See also: **social touching; sexual assault.**

**traditional family.**   See: **family, traditional.**

**tree, tying oneself to the top of a.**   Well-known gender reconciliation facilitator Aaron R. Kipnis advises that a man can gain useful insights into how to come to relationships in a "fecund, life-affirming" manner by tying himself to the top of a tree.[527] For more details, see: **masculinity, regreening of.**

**trying to pass as nonvictimized.**   Mary P. Koss of the University of Arizona, who conducted *Ms.* magazine's famous survey on sexual assault, notes that a frequent obstacle rape researchers encounter in their work is victims' stubborn insistence on "trying to pass as nonvictimized." "Research designs that depend for participation on a subject's self-identification as a victim," she writes, fail to take into account "the many women who have sustained harm but may not see the injury as unfair."[528]

**turkey-baster insemination.**   The technique— increasingly popular among procreation- without-sex advocates who wish to avoid the expense and humiliation of dealing with the male-dominated medical community—of fertilizing oneself at home using a turkey baster. One particularly satisfying aspect of turkey-baster insemination, notes single-parent- hood author- ity C. Pies,

The **turkey baster,** *an instrument of woman-controlled conception.*

is that it serves "as a means of redefining a female cooking tool," changing it from an implement designed to "keep her in the kitchen and pregnant" to one of "woman-controlled conception."[529] See also: **baster babies; sperm-egg mixers; standing on one's head.**

**two-leggeds, leaving the world of.** See: four-leggeds, joining the world of.

**two-party sexual system.** Western society's nature-defying insistence that there are only two sexes. As the noted geneticist and intersexual-rights advocate Anne Fausto-Sterling points out, "there are many gradations running from female to male; along that spectrum lie at least five sexes—perhaps even more."[530] See also: **ferms; herms; intersexual; merms.**

# U

**UNCIRC.** A popular acronym for the Uncircumcising Information Resources Center.[531] See: **uncircumcising.**

**uncircumcising.** A technique, perfected by California psychologist Jim Bigelow, in which adhesive tape and, later, a combination of tape and small lead fishing weights, are used to stretch the skin at the shaft of a circumcised male's penis downward until it forms a "re-created" foreskin. Although the complete process may take as long as four years, it entails little or no pain and only minor inconvenience (such as choosing stalls over urinals in public rest rooms, having to remove one's weights before passing through airport metal detectors, and foregoing genital sexual relations except at the times when one is scheduled to change one's tape).[532] Those interested in learning more about Bigelow's technique can do so by consulting his book, *The Joy of Uncircumcising*, which may be obtained by writing:

> UNCIRC (the Uncircumcising Information Resources Center)
> P.O. Box 52138
> Pacific Grove, CA 93950

See also: **BUFF; circumcision survivors; foreskin restoration movement; keratinization; NOHARMM; RECAP; UNCIRC.**

**Uncumber's Day.** A holiday observed July 20 in honor of St. Uncumber, a Portuguese princess who prayed fervently that she might become physically repellent to men in order to avoid having to marry the king of Sicily, to whom her father had promised her hand. Uncumber's prayers were answered when, overnight, she sprouted a full beard and mustache, whereupon her irate father had her crucified. From the cross, the princess announced that all women who invoked her assistance would be freed from male encumbrances; hence, her name and her feast day, which a growing number of gender-fairness activists suggest should be celebrated instead of Valentine's Day (February 14). (Note: An account of the life of St. Uncumber authored by ecclesiastical scholars Sean Kelly and Rosemary Rogers states that the most famous depiction of St. Uncumber—"a bearded figure in regal robes on a cross" at Lucca, Italy—is believed by "some art historians" to be "merely a figure of Christ." "Yet," Kelly and Rogers add, "there is no denying that a minstrel who prayed to her at that very crucifix was rewarded by the Saint with the gift of her silver foot.")[533]

**underwear advertisements.** See: bra advertisements.

**underwear, sexy.** "If what men want is our underwear," Jane Rule suggests in *The Hot-Eyed Moderate,* "let them be welcome to it. It's a great swap for the shirts off their backs which we wear so comfortably."[534]

**uninvited endearment.** A form of sexual harassment specifically condemned by Rolland Dille, president of Moorhead State University in Minnesota. To demonstrate his commitment to stamping out "uninvited endearment," Dille has officially outlawed the use of mistletoe as a holiday decoration anywhere on the Moorhead State campus.[535]

**un-men.** See: antirape activism, male.

**unpaid sex worker.** A sexually correct term for "wife" or "girlfriend." See: sex workers.[536]

**unsolicited suggestive looks.** See: suggestive looks.

**unwelcome invitations.** Cornell University professor Andrea Parrot, author of *Coping with Date Rape and Acquaintance Rape,* specifically classifies "unwelcome invitations" as sexual harassment.[537]

*A blatant example of an* **unwelcome invitation.**

**vagina gratitude.** Australian psycholinguist Dale Spender offers the term "vagina gratitude" as "a good corrective in a society which has only, and falsely, named 'penis envy.'" "The renaming of sexuality in woman-centered, and not necessarily heterosexual terms," she adds, "will certainly make it difficult, if not impossible, for men to retain an image of their own supremacist sexuality."[538] See also: **enclosure; engulfment; envelopment; nutting; positive language; womb envier.**

**vagina-specific fucking.** Andrea Dworkin's elegant phrase for the specific means men use to "enforce" the concept of "gender," which, she reminds us, is merely a "social construct."[539] See also: **essentialism.**

**Valentine's Day.** Pointing to the results of a survey indicating that women in the District of Columbia are twenty-five times more likely than their male partners to contract AIDS through heterosexual contact, Denise Rouse, director of the Washington Women's Council on AIDS, urges that, instead of offering tender sentiments to their sweethearts on Valentine's Day, women should send them cards inscribed with the pro-condom-use ultimatum "No glove, no love."[540] (Note: A growing number of women who feel that even a self-empowering observance of Valentine's Day would represent a surrender to patriarchy are advocating that Uncumber's Day, July 20, be celebrated instead.) See also: **"No glove, no love"; Uncumber's Day.**

**ve, vis, ver.** Non-gender-differentiated pronouns suggested by Varda One, editor of *Everywoman* magazine, as replacements for "she" and "he," "her" and "his," and "her" and "him," respectively.[541] Example: **Ve** *advised* **ver** vis *wish was* vis *command.*

**vegetarianism.** See: **meat-eating; stomach that has no ears, the.**

**Venus of Willendorf.** A 27,000-year-old statue of a nude paleolithic female deity, widely believed to be the oldest sculpture of the human form ever recovered. The Venus of Willendorf is cherished by the Goddess Movement as the Great Mother who "gave birth to all creation out of her bountiful body"; by feminist archaeologists as proof that peaceful matriarchal societies reigned in ancient Europe; and by members of the size-acceptance movement as a role model whose "round and abundant body symbolizes the bulk and stability of the earth."[542] As noted Earth theologian Carol Graywing points out, the fact that the Venus of Willendorf has come down to us through the centuries sans eyes, nose, mouth, and the bottom portion of her legs in no way diminishes the reverence many women feel for her. (She has no feet because she is "not *on* the earth but *of* the earth," Graywing exults. She has no face because she is "not *a* woman, but *all* women.")[543]

A much more formidable obstacle for the Venus to overcome, however, has been the growing movement, spearheaded by Professor Nancy Stumhofer of Penn State University, to banish art works featuring the naked female torso from public view on the grounds that their presence in mixed company "makes females uncomfortable."[544] See also: **Goddess Movement; prepatriarchal cultures; art "masterpieces" featuring nude women.**

*The* **Venus of Willendorf.**

**ver.** See: ve, vis, ver.

**verbal comments about clothing.** See: clothing, verbal comments about.

**verbal rape.** A form of assault characterized by a man's describing, without consent, a sexual act he imagines performing, or desires to perform, with a woman. As Professor Catharine MacKinnon has written, "To say it is to do it, and to do it is to say it."[545] (Before one asks, in an attempt to obey the Antioch Rules, for "explicit consent" to touch or otherwise approach one's partner, it's important to remember that the very act of *requesting permission* to perform a sexual act may in and of itself constitute verbal rape. See: **Antioch Rules.**)

**victims.** Antirape crusader Rus Ervin Funk defines "victims" as "women, children, or men who have died during a rape attack."[546] Because the term "victim" has come, in our society, to imply weakness or a certain "loser" quality, it is not appropriate to describe as a "victim" anyone who actually succeeds in *living* through an incident of rape, attempted rape, sexual assault, sexual coercion, sexual imposition, sexual negligence, or sexual harassment. The only acceptable term for such an individual is **survivor**.

**violation.** Catharine MacKinnon has observed that "violation, conventionally penetration and intercourse, defines the paradigmatic sexual encounter."[547]

**virtual castration.** See: virtual rape.

**virtual gender bending.** See: virtual rape.

**virtual rape.** A term used to describe nonconsensual sex acts committed against fictional characters in the multiplayer computer fantasy role-playing games commonly known as MUDs (an acronym for "multiuser dimensions" or "multiuser dungeons") and MOOs (which stands for "MUDs, object-oriented"). The phrase "virtual rape" leapt to national prominence after a young man at New York University used the Internet to seize control of two female characters in "LambdaMOO," a popular game residing in a computer at the Xerox Palo Alto Research Center, and forced them to satisfy the unusual sexual desires of *his* character, an unsavory clown named Mr. Bungle. One of the two women whose characters had been violated, a doctoral candidate from Seattle, sent out an E-mail bulletin calling for Bungle's "virtual castration" (she later told *Village Voice* correspondent Julian Dibbell that "posttraumatic tears" had been streaming down her face as she wrote those words). Many hours of enraged on-line argument ensued, during which such issues as whether Mr. Bungle's real-life (RL) counterpart should be charged with sexual harassment, or with violating the California statutes against obscene phone calls, were hotly debated. Finally, after much soul-searching, the controllers of the game at Xerox PARC sentenced Bungle to virtual execution, and his owner-controller was denied future access to the game. In the aftermath of "the Bungle Affair," *Voice* writer Dibbell was left to ponder whether a *real* rape had indeed occurred. His conclusion: It had. "Since rape can occur without any physical pain or damage," he found himself reasoning, "then it must be classed as a crime against the mind. [And] the more seriously I took the notion of virtual rape, the less seriously I was able to take the notion of freedom of speech, with its tidy division of the world into the symbolic and the real."[548] See also: **First Amendment; on-line cross dressing**.

**vis.** See: ve, vis, ver.

**visiting a man's apartment.** See: going to a man's apartment.

**walking a woman home.** See: protection rackets.

**water-filled condom tosses.** See: Condom Olympics.

**wearing an obscene hat.** See: headgear, sexually objectionable.

**weddings.** Women, if you feel you *must* get married, you owe it to society—if not to yourself—to eschew a "standard marriage ceremony." This advice is offered by feminist scholar Ann Ferguson, who notes that it's important "not to perpetuate the public symbolic meaning of heterosexism and women as legal possessions of men." "Private 'ceremonies of commitment' or legal contracts are permissible" she adds, "since they don't carry the same patriarchal and heterosexual interpretation."[549]

**well-intentioned compliments.** A landmark court ruling against a San Mateo, California, IRS agent who wrote an unsolicited letter to a female colleague praising her "style and élan" has established the important legal principle that even "well-intentioned compliments" are punishable as sexual harassment under the Civil Rights Act of 1964.[550]

**Wicca.** See: Goddess Movement.

**Wild Man weekend gatherings.** See: New Warrior Weekend Adventures.

**Wild Man within.** According to Robert Bly, it is not an ape (as Douglas Gillette has suggested), a Cro-Magnon man (as Asa Baber asks us to believe), or a mouse or parakeet (as Sherman Alexie has surmised) that lives deep within men's souls, but rather "Iron John," the shaggy, pond-dwelling "Wild Man" who, rescued by Bly from the obscurity of a little-known Grimm Brothers' fairy tale, became the protagonist of the book with which the former National Book Award–winning poet jumpstarted the mythopoetic men's movement. "What I'm proposing," writes Bly, "is that every modern male has, lying at the bottom of his psyche, a large, primitive man covered with hair down to his feet. Making contact with this Wild Man . . . is the process that still hasn't taken place in contemporary culture. . . . Freud, Jung, and Wilhelm Reich are three men who had the courage to go down into the pond and accept what's there. . . . The job of modern males is to follow them down."[551] See also: **mythopoetic men's movement; ape within; Cro-Magnon man within; parakeet within; woman within.**

**Wild Woman within.** Feminist witch Zsuszanna Emese Budapest, founder of the Susan B. Anthony Coven #1, writes of her encoun-

*Macy's, an ideal location for a **Wild Woman**– inspired foraging spree.*

ters with a "natural creature" called the "Wild Woman" whose image dwells inside the psyches of all women. "Wild Woman represents our bodies, our genetic past, our gender and instincts, and our right brain," Budapest writes. "The Wild Woman loves a ritual, the chanting and the humming, the shared breath." And, Budapest tells us, she is also "fond of shopping, because it reminds her of ancient foraging."[552] See also: **woman within**.

**wimmin.** An improvement upon the inherently sexist word "women," coined by the editors of *This Magazine Is For, About, and By Young Wimmin*, who explained in their inaugural issue:

> We have spelt it this way because we are not wo*men* and neither are we fe*male*. . . . You may find it trivial—it's just another part of the deep, very deep, rooted sexist attitudes.[553]

The singular of "wimmin" is **womon**.

**wimyn.** An alternative spelling of **womyn**. According to Theresa Pellow-McCauley, "wimyn" should be used only in the plural, and **womyn** should be used only in the singular.[554] (McCauley's view is a matter of some controversy, however; see: **womyn**.)

**wine.** See: **alcohol; seduction**.

**Witches' Eve.** Andrea Dworkin suggests that Halloween be renamed "Witches' Eve" and recast as a day of mourning for the millions of women who have been burned or otherwise slaughtered as witches since the mid-seventeenth century.[555] See also: **Halloween; Halloween parties**.

**wofem.** A nonsexist spelling of "woman" recommended by Bina Goldfield, creator of *The Efemcipated English Handbook*. Goldfield defines "wofem" as "the female hufem being."[556] See: **efemcipation**.

**woman-controlled conception.** See: **turkey-baster insemination**.

**woman within.** Will Roscoe, author of *The Zuni Man-Woman*, suggests that rather than seeking the "ape within," the "Cro-

Magnon man within," the "spirit animal within," or the "Wild Man within," as various men's movement leaders have recommended, men would do well to "embrace the woman inside us." "Men need to be weaned from other men," he writes, "which is why the whole thrust of the Bly-Keen men's movement to go off somewhere with other men to learn how to be men is scary to me."[557] (Note: The woman within every *man* is not to be confused with the **Wild Woman within** every *woman;* and any man planning to embrace the woman within himself should first consider whether such an embrace might not constitute sexual harassment.)

**womban.** A bitterly ironic spelling of the word "woman," coined by Una Stannard to dramatize the fact that most men consider women to be nothing more than "baby-making machines." Not to be confused with **wombmoon!**[558]

**womb envier.** A term used by "Rita," an attendee at the 1992 convention of the American Association of University Women in Oakland, California, to characterize Smith College music professor Raphael Atlas, who had been invited to the meeting to participate in a panel on "The Perils and Pleasures of Feminist Teaching." Rita—who also branded Atlas a "feminist wannabe" and "a poseur in our midst"—noted vehemently that men had "no place in women-centered spheres." "Let him take his voice into an all-male forum," she demanded. Professor Faye Crosby, moderator of the panel and also a professor at Smith College, at first chided Rita for her attack on her colleague, which she branded "extremely rude." "You are breaking norms by attacking our speaker like that, and that is wrong," she added. However, after a moment's reflection, Crosby—famous for the condom relay races she once hosted at Smith (see: **condom relay races**)—softened. "But, as a feminist," she told the assemblage, "I *believe* in breaking norms."[559] See also: **vagina gratitude**.

**wombmoon.** A celebratory improvement upon the word "woman," coined by the Goddess Movement to honor female lifegiving power and the relationship between celestial rhythms and women's reproductive cycles, while literally (to use Debbie Alicen's felicitous phrase) "removing 'man' from the picture."[560] Not to be confused with **womban!**

**women, young.** See: aging.

**women-as-property model.** The world view that underlies the twin institutions of heterosexual monogamy and male supremacy. As Cheryl Clarke points out, white men have learned to relate to a woman in exactly the same way they relate to a black person: "as property, as a sexual commodity, as a servant, as a source of free or cheap labor, and as an innately inferior being."[561] Example: *It came as something of a surprise to Supreme Court justice Ruth Bader Ginsberg that many men related to her as property, as a sexual commodity, as a servant, as a source of free or cheap labor, and as an innately inferior being.*

**Women's Empowerment in the '90s.** A \$150-a-day, for-women-only gun-handling course taught by "feminist self-defense expert" Paxton Quigley, who argues, in her book *Armed & Female*, that "the arming of American women" is "perhaps the last frontier to be won by women on the road to equality." Undeterred by criticism that the fees she earns as spokesperson for the gunmaker Smith & Wesson might affect her partiality, or by research such as a Kings County, Washington, study showing that guns in the home are forty-three times more likely to kill their owners or their friends and family members than to kill an intruder, Quigley cites as proof that owning a firearm is a woman's best defense against sexual assault the fact that "11 imprisoned rapists" she interviewed for her book assured her that they would not intentionally target an armed female. "If you think it is time to do your share to end the victim status of women," she writes, "and if you can bear to undertake the attendant responsibilities, you should know that finding a gun in the hand of a potential victim is one of the most feared and avoided incidents a felon can imagine—feared and avoided even more than the police."[562] (Note: Readers can also do their share to end the victim status of women by purchasing Quigley's signature line of handgun accessories—leather purses, briefcases, and waist-packs—or her limited-edition "collectible" handgun, designed and marketed in partnership with Smith & Wesson and Lew Horton Distributing.[563])

**women's names, failure to remember.** A report issued by a committee charged with planning "diversity education" for incoming freshmen at the University of Pennsylvania lists "women's names not remembered" as an example of illegal sexual discrimination.[564]

*A blatant example of a* **failure to remember a woman's name.**

**womon.** The singular form of **wimmin**. Debbie Alicen, who deserves much of the credit for the popularity these terms enjoy today, explained their appeal in an article she wrote for the magazine *Trivia:* "I deny the necessity and/or the desirability of [the connection of woman and man] and use the spellings womon/wimmin to remove man from the picture."[565]

**womyn.** *The Random House Webster's College Dictionary* cites "womyn" as a plural noun, and defines it as an alternative spelling for "women" "used to avoid the suggestion of sexism perceived in the sequence *m-e-n*."[566] Linguistic expert Theresa Pellow-McCauley, on the other hand, insists that "womyn" is a *singular* noun, and notes that the correct *plural* form of the word is **wimyn**.[567]

**wormboy.** Margaret Edwards writes passionately in *Working Woman* magazine about a disturbing trend in the evolution of the New Man: The more he accepts the fact that he must not "enslave or dominate" a woman, the less anxious he seems to be to "create a longstanding or passionate bond" with her. This tendency (which, it can be argued, is yet another manifestation of the "backlash" against feminism first documented by Susan Faludi) has so angered journalist Deborah Laake that she has invented a new term—"wormboy"—for men who shrink from marriage, from having children, and even from making "the simplest assertion," such as deciding where they'd like to go for the weekend. Wormboys prefer to ask women out for a drink rather than for dinner, Laake notes, "because it implies so much less commitment on their part," and they're even "unashamed" of letting women pick up the check.[568] How to avoid being rejected as a "wormboy" without scaring off the women who have read Robin Warshaw's stern warning that, to avoid being raped, "you [should] run, not walk, from . . . any man who refuses to let you share any of the expenses on a date and gets angry when you offer to pay"[569] is one of the great unanswered challenges confronting men today. See: **dates, paying for.**

**writing (as an antifeminist act).** Before setting one's opinions—even impeccably sexually correct ones—down on paper, prospective authors should be aware that a women's studies seminar at Swarthmore College recently condemned Naomi Wolf's book *The Beauty Myth* on the grounds that the very act of writing is "exclusionary to women who cannot read."[570]

**Y chromosome.** "The y (male) gene is an incomplete x (female) gene, that is, [it] has an incomplete set of chromosomes," explains Valerie Solanas in a slightly muddled, but nonetheless revealing, passage explaining the scientific underpinnings of her celebrated *SCUM Manifesto.* (Actually, if patriarchal biologists are to be believed, it's the Y *chromosome* that has an incomplete set of *genes.*) "In other words," Solanas continues, "the male is an incomplete female, a walking abortion, aborted at the gene stage. To be male is to be deficient, emotionally limited; maleness is a deficiency disease and males are emotional cripples."[571] See also: **androcide; SCUM; human creatures with a Y chromosome.**

**" 'Yes' means 'no'!"** University of Southern California Law Center professor Susan Estrich, who managed Governor Michael Dukakis's presidential campaign in 1988, notes that, because "women in today's society are powerless relative to men, viewing a 'yes' as a sign of true consent is misguided."[572] Those seeking to avoid arrest or disciplinary action under the Antioch College Sexual Offense Policy should be forewarned. See also: **Antioch Rules; consensual sex, male-initiated; consent, sexual; intercourse, male-initiated; " 'Maybe' means 'no'!"; " 'No' means 'no'!"**

# SOURCE NOTES

1. Parrot, Andrea, PhD, and Bechhofer, Laurie, *Acquaintance Rape: The Hidden Crime*, New York: John Wiley & Sons, 1991, page 12; and Taylor, John, "Are You Politically Correct?," *New York*, January 21, 1991, page 38.

2. Guttman, Stephanie, "Date Rape on Campus," *Playboy*, October 1990, page 50.

3. Cooper, Kenneth C., "The Six Levels of Sexual Harassment," anthologized in A. Pablo Iannone, *Contemporary Moral Controversies in Business*, New York: Oxford University Press, 1989, page 190, cited in Wall, Edmund, "The Definition of Sexual Harassment," anthologized in Wall, Edmund, *Sexual Harassment*, Buffalo, N.Y.: Prometheus Books, 1992, page 70.

4. Wolf, Naomi, *Fire with Fire,* New York: Random House, 1993, page 195.

5. "Definitions," handout published by the Smith College Office of Student Affairs, 1990.

6. Wolf, Naomi, *The Beauty Myth,* New York: William Morrow and Co., 1991, page 14.

7. Burkhart, Barry R., and Fromuth, Mary Ellen, "Individual Psychological and Social Psychological Understandings of Sexual Coercion," anthologized in Grauerholz, Elizabeth, and Koralewski, Mary A., *Sexual Coercion: A Sourcebook on Its Nature, Causes, and Prevention,* Lexington, Mass.: Lexington Books/D.C. Heath and Co., 1991, page 85.

8. McDowell, Josh, *It Can Happen to You: What You Need to Know About Preventing and Recovering from Date Rape,* Dallas: Word Publishing, 1991, page 34.

9. Handout, Department of Rhetoric, University of California at Berkeley, 1991; and Kramarae, Cheris, and Treichler, Paula A., *A Feminist Dictionary,* Boston: Pandora Press, 1985, page 154.

10. Solanas, Valerie, *The SCUM Manifesto,* London: Olympia Press, 1971, page 43.

11. Ferguson, Ann, "Androgyny as an Ideal for Human Development," anthologized in Rothenberg, Paula S., *Racism and Sexism,* New York: St. Martin's Press, 1988, pages 362–71.

12. Ferguson, Ann, *Blood at the Root: Motherhood, Sexuality and Male Dominance,* London: Pandora Press, 1989, page 231.

13. Blumenfield, Dr. Michael, "Psychiatry Today" column, Gannett News Service, June 15, 1994.

14. Brumberg, Joan Jacobs, *Fasting Girls: The Emergence of Anorexia Nervosa as a Modern Disease,* Cambridge, Mass.: Harvard University Press, 1988, pages 19–20.

15. Wolf, Naomi, *The Beauty Myth,* New York: William Morrow and Co., 1991, pages 180–82.

16. Dunn, Thomas, Division of Vital Statistics at the National Center for Health Statistics, quoted by Sommers, Christina Hoff, in *Who Stole Feminism?,* New York: Simon & Schuster, 1994, page 12.

17. Gross, Jane, "Combating Rape on Campus in a Class on Sexual Consent," *The New York Times,* September 25, 1993, pages 1, 9; and Crichton, Sarah, "Sexual Correctness: Has It Gone Too Far?," *Newsweek,* October 25, 1993, page 54.

18. "Different Strokes," *The New Yorker,* November 29, 1993, page 10.

19. Funk, Rus Ervin, *Stopping Rape: A Challenge for Men,* Philadelphia: New Society Publishers, 1993, pages 5, 31.

20. Gillette, Douglas, "Men and Intimacy," anthologized in Harding, Christopher, *Wingspan: Inside the Men's Movement,* New York: St. Martin's Press, 1992, pages 58–59.

21. Viner, Katharine, "To P or Not to P," *The Guardian,* July 7, 1992, page 37.

22. Strauss, Susan, with Espeland, Pamela, *Sexual Harassment and Teens: A Program for Positive Change,* Minneapolis: Free Spirit Publishing Co., 1992, page 8.

23. Leo, John, "PC Follies: The Year in Review," *U.S. News & World Report,* January 27, 1992, page 22.

24. Igou, Woody, "Emission Standards Eased!," *In These Times,* March 7, 1994, page 6.

25. Faludi, Susan, *Backlash: The Undeclared War Against American Women,* New York: Crown, 1991, pages xviii, xxii.

26. "The Year in Style '93," *The Atlanta Journal and Constitution*, January 2, 1994, section L, page 3.

27. Foster, R. Daniel, "Palm Latitudes: L.A. Speak," *Los Angeles Times Magazine*, August 1, 1993, page 10; and Wikler, Daniel, and Wikler, Norma J., "Turkey-Baster Babies: The Demedicalization of Artificial Insemination," *The Milbank Quarterly*, March 22, 1991, pages 5ff.

28. Wolf, Naomi, *The Beauty Myth*, New York: William Morrow and Co., 1991, pages 12, 16–18.

29. Ibid., pages 12, 17–18.

30. Costello, Michael, "New Feminist Findings Show What a Louse I Am," *Lewiston Morning Tribune*, December 28, 1991, page 10A.

31. Stoltenberg, John, *Refusing to Be a Man: Essays on Sex and Justice*, New York: Meridian, 1990, pages 5, 185.

32. Budapest, Zsuzsanna E., *The Goddess in the Office: A Personal Energy Guide for the Spiritual Warrior at Work*, San Francisco: HarperSanFrancisco, 1993, page 43.

33. Urry, Meg, interview broadcast on CNN Headline News, June 14, 1993, 9:55 P.M. EST, cited in Sommers, Christina Hoff, *Who Stole Feminism?*, New York: Simon & Schuster, 1994, pages 72, 282.

34. Santoriello, Karen, remarks cited in the minutes of the Human Relations Forum discussion "Pornography on Campus," University of Massachusetts, Amherst, May 15, 1984, quoted in Hentoff, Nat, "The Gospel According to Catharine MacKinnon," *Free Speech for Me—But Not for Thee*, New York: HarperCollins, 1993, page 336.

35. Daly, Mary, *Gyn/Ecology*, Boston: Beacon Press, 1978, pages 10, 59; and Frye, Marilyn, *The Politics of Reality: Essays in Feminist Theory*, Trumansburg, N.Y.: The Crossing Press, 1983, page 100.

36. Hamilton, Alan, *Sexual Identity and Gender Identity Glossary*, Open Software Foundation, prepublication copy, distributed online via the Internet, December 19, 1992.

37. McDowell, Josh, *It Can Happen to You: What You Need to Know About Preventing and Recovering from Date Rape*, Dallas: Word Publishing, 1991, page 34.

38. Strauss, Susan, with Espeland, Pamela, *Sexual Harassment and Teens: A Program for Positive Change*, Minneapolis: Free Spirit Publishing Co., 1992, page 8.

39. Muelenhard, Charlene N., PhD, and Schrag, Jennifer L., "Nonviolent Sexual Coercion," anthologized in Parrot, Andrea, and Bechhofer, Laurie, *Acquaintance Rape: The Hidden Crime,* page 122.

40. "Sexual Harassment College Policy," *Official Survival Handbook,* Yellow Springs, Ohio: Antioch College Student Government, 1993–94, page 12.

41. Parrot, Andrea, PhD, *Coping with Date Rape and Acquaintance Rape,* New York: Rosen Publishing Group, 1993, page 24.

42. "New Words for Webster" and "Penile Protection," letters section, *Time,* February 14, 1994, page 10.

43. Ibid.

44. Shalit, Ruth, "Romper Room," *New Republic,* March 29, 1993, pages 13ff.

45. "Free Expression at Work," editorial, *St. Petersburg Times,* November 10, 1991, page 2D; and Leo, John, "An Empty Ruling on Harassment," *U.S. News & World Report,* November 29, 1993, page 20.

46. Funk, Rus Ervin, *Stopping Rape: A Challenge for Men,* Philadelphia: New Society Publishers, 1993, page 33.

47. "alt. feminism" news group, excerpt from message downloaded from Internet, February 23, 1994.

48. Roiphe, Katie, *The Morning After: Sex, Fear, and Feminism on Campus,* Boston: Little, Brown and Co., 1993, pages 123–24.

49. "alt. feminism" news group, excerpt from message downloaded from Internet, February 23, 1994.

50. Ayoob, Massad, "The Armed Women's Aptitude Test," *Women & Guns,* December 1991, page 38, quoted in Wolf, Naomi, *Fire with Fire,* New York: Random House, 1993, page 218.

51. MacKinnon, Catharine A., *Toward a Feminist Theory of the State,* Cambridge, Mass.: Harvard University Press, 1989, page 176.

52. Cited by Kaminer, Wendy, in "Feminists Against the First Amendment," *Atlantic Monthly,* November 1992, page 115.

53. Leo, John, "A Political Correctness Roundup," *U.S. News & World Report,* June 22, 1992, page 31.

54. "The Trouble with Big-Eyed Owls," editorial, *The Atlanta Journal and Constitution,* October 2, 1993, page A16; and "Weekend Report

News Briefs," *The Atlanta Journal and Constitution*, February 13, 1994, page D2.

55. Hamilton, Alan, *Sexual Identity and Gender Identity Glossary*, Open Software Foundation, prepublication copy, distributed online via the Internet, December 19, 1992.

56. Gross, Jane, "Combating Rape on Campus in a Class on Sexual Consent," *The New York Times*, September 25, 1993, page 9.

57. Hicks, Cherrill, "They Took My Foreskin, and I Want It Back," *The Independent*, August 3, 1993, page 11.

58. Blumenfield, Dr. Michael, "Psychiatry Today" column, Gannett News Service, June 15, 1994.

59. Iazzetto, Demetria, PhD, "What's Happening with Women and Body Image?," *The Network News*, National Women's Health Network, May 1992, page 1.

60. Taylor, John, "Are You Politically Correct?," *New York*, January 21, 1991, page 38.

61. Zalk, Sue Rosenberg, "Men in the Academy: A Psychological Profile of Harassment," anthologized in Rothenberg, Paula S., *Racism and Sexism: An Integrated Study*, New York: St. Martin's Press, 1988, page 150.

62. Asmus, Kristen, "Blaming the Dress," *Colorado Daily*, October 27–29, 1989, page 13, quoted in D'Souza, Dinesh, *Illiberal Education: The Politics of Race and Sex on Campus*, New York: Free Press, 1991, page 11.

63. Segal, Lynne, book review of *Women, Celibacy and Passion*, *New Statesman & Society*, March 19, 1993, pages 37ff.

64. Smith, Joan, "When No Means Never," *The Independent*, April 11, 1993, page 37.

65. Burchill, Julie, quoted in Porlock, Harvey, "On the Critical List," *Sunday Times*, London, March 14, 1993.

66. Katz, Montana, and Vieland, Veronica, *Get Smart: What You Should Know (but Won't Learn in Class) About Sexual Harassment and Sex Discrimination*, New York: The Feminist Press at the City University of New York, pages 14–16, 31–33.

67. "Responsibility. It's Your Choice," advertisement in *The Village Voice*, March 1, 1994, page 7.

68. Sowers, Leslie, "Going Native: Just a Trend, Heartfelt Seeking—or Cultural Theft?," *The Houston Chronicle,* September 12, 1993, "Lifestyle" section, page 1.

69. Henley, Nancy, *Body Politics: Power, Sex and Nonverbal Communication,* New York: Touchstone Books, Simon & Schuster, 1986, page 64.

70. Woodward, Kenneth L., "Feminism and the Churches," *Newsweek,* February 13, 1989, page 58.

71. Leo, John, "PC Follies: The Year in Review," *U.S. News & World Report,* January 27, 1992, page 22.

72. Hicks, Cherrill, "They Took My Foreskin, and I Want It Back," *The Independent,* August 3, 1993, page 11.

73. Dreyfous, Leslie, "Surgery Can 'Uncirc' Men," *Calgary Herald,* May 31, 1993, page B1.

74. Strauss, Susan, with Espeland, Pamela, *Sexual Harassment and Teens: A Program for Positive Change,* Minneapolis: Free Spirit Publishing Co., 1992, page 8.

75. Pei, Mario, *Double-Speak in America,* New York: Hawthorn Books, 1973, page 56.

76. Kramarae, Cheris, and Treichler, Paula A., *A Feminist Dictionary,* Boston: Pandora Press, 1985, page 99.

77. Kors, Alan Charles, "Harassment Policies in the University," anthologized in Wall, Edmund, *Sexual Harassment: Confrontations and Decisions,* Buffalo, N.Y.: Prometheus Books, 1992, page 46.

78. "Sexual Violence," *The Barnard/Columbia Women's Handbook 1992,* chapter 8, downloaded from Internet, January 26, 1994.

79. Dworkin, Andrea, quoted in Leo, John, "The Words of the Culture War," *U.S. News & World Report,* October 28, 1991, page 31.

80. Hamill, Pete, "Woman on the Verge of a Legal Breakdown," *Playboy,* January 1993, pages 138ff.

81. Sandler, Bernice, article included in "An Ecological Perspective to Understanding Sexual Harassment," a multipart foreword to Paludi, Michele A., ed., *Ivory Power: Sexual Harassment on Campus,* Albany: State University of New York Press, 1990, page xvii.

82. Clarke, Cheryl, "Lesbianism: An Act of Resistance," anthologized in Moraga, Cherríe, and Anzaldúa. Gloria, *This Bridge Called My Back:*

*Writings by Radical Women of Color,* New York: Kitchen Table: Women of Color Press, 1983, page 130.

83. Rich, Adrienne, "Compulsory Heterosexuality and Lesbian Existence," *Signs,* 5:4, 1980, page 647, quoted in: Kramarae, Cheris, and Treichler, Paula A., *A Feminist Dictionary,* Boston: Pandora Press, 1985, pages 115–16.

84. Jeffreys, Sheila, *Anticlimax,* London: Women's Press, 1990, page 295.

85. Beard, Henry, and Cerf, Christopher, *The Official Politically Correct Dictionary and Handbook,* updated edition, New York: Villard Books, 1993, page 95.

86. Barker, Karlyn, "A New Kind of Store for Personal Security," *The Washington Post,* December 11, 1991, page D3.

87. Ibid.; and Recer, Paul, "Rubber Latex Triggering Allergic Reactions, Doctor Says," Associated Press, December 8, 1993, P.M. cycle.

88. Bolus, Josephine, "Teaching Teens About Condoms," *RN,* March 1994, pages 44ff.

89. Katz, Jesse, "A Story of Love in the San Gabriel Valley," *Los Angeles Times,* February 14, 1990, part E, page 3C.

90. Sommers, Christina Hoff, *Who Stole Feminism?,* New York: Simon & Schuster, 1994, page 37.

91. Langelan, Martha J., "The Confrontation Survey," *Back Off!,* New York: Fireside/Simon & Schuster, 1993, pages 336–39.

92. MacKinnon, Catharine A., *Toward a Feminist Theory of the State,* Cambridge, Mass.: Harvard University Press, 1989, page 178.

93. Kors, Alan Charles, "Harassment Policies in the University," anthologized in Wall, Edmund, *Sexual Harassment: Confrontations and Decisions,* Buffalo, N.Y.: Prometheus Books, 1992, page 45.

94. Shulruff, Lawrence I., "In Sex Case, Focus Is on Multiple Personalities," *The New York Times,* August 10, 1990, page B10; Lovett, Brian, "Woman with 46 Personalities Testifies at Her Rape Trial," Reuters News Service, November 8, 1990; and Ball, Ian, "Man Guilty of '46 Selves' Rape," the *Daily Telegraph,* November 10, 1990.

95. Menand, Louis, "The War of All Against All," *The New Yorker,* March 14, 1994, page 75.

96. Langelan, Martha J., *Back Off!,* New York: Fireside/Simon & Schuster, 1993, page 249.

97. Baker, Helen, "Cosmetics and Economic Pressure," anthologized in Hansen, Joseph, and Reed, Evelyn, *Cosmetics, Fashions, and the Exploitation of Women*, New York: Pathfinder Press, 1986, page 39.

98. Shilts, Randy, "Conduct Unbecoming: The Women Who Don't Fit In," *San Francisco Chronicle*, April 27, 1993, page B3.

99. Hellman, Peter, "Crying Rape: The Politics of Date Rape on Campus," *New York*, March 8, 1993, page 37.

100. Solanas, Valerie, *The SCUM Manifesto*, London: Olympia Press, 1971, page 43.

101. Leeds Revolutionary Feminist Group, "Political Lesbian" paper, 1979, quoted by Sheila Jeffreys in *Anticlimax*, London: Women's Press, 1990, page 292.

102. "*Harper's* Index," *Harper's*, June 1993.

103. Baber, Asa, "Call of the Wild," anthologized in Harding, Christopher, ed., *Wingspan: Inside the Men's Movement*, New York: St. Martin's Press, 1992, page 9.

104. Brownmiller, Susan, *Against Our Will: Men, Women and Rape*, New York: Simon & Schuster, 1975, pages 14–15.

105. Garchik, Leah, "Personals," *San Francisco Chronicle*, December 14, 1989, page A10; and Klein, Jeffrey S., "Sexual Harassment Can Be Costly," *Los Angeles Times*, December 21, 1989, page E13.

106. Parrot, Andrea, and Bechhofer, Laurie, *Acquaintance Rape: The Hidden Crime*, New York: John Wiley & Sons, 1991, pages 12–13.

107. Langelan, Martha J., *Back Off!*, New York: Fireside/Simon & Schuster, 1993, page 249.

108. Warshaw, Robin, *I Never Called It Rape: The* Ms. *Report on Recognizing, Fighting and Surviving Date and Acquaintance Rape*, New York: HarperPerennial, 1988, pages 152, 156.

109. Dworkin, Andrea, *Our Blood: Prophecies and Discourses on Sexual Politics*, New York: Harper & Row, 1976, page 43.

110. Segal, Lynne, book review of *Women, Celibacy and Passion*, *New Statesman & Society*, March 19, 1993, pages 37ff.

111. Gilbert, Neil, "The Phantom Epidemic of Sexual Assault," *The Public Interest*, spring 1991, excerpted in *CQ Researcher*, February 26, 1993, page 185; Warshaw, Robin, *I Never Called It Rape: The* Ms. *Report on*

*Recognizing, Fighting and Surviving Date and Acquaintance Rape,* New York: HarperPerennial, 1988, pages 11–13; Collison, Michele N.-K., "A Berkeley Scholar Clashes with Feminists Over Validity of Their Research on Date Rape," *The Chronicle of Higher Education,* February 26, 1992, page A35; Kahn, Alice, " 'Date Rape' Studies Called Exaggerated," *San Francisco Chronicle,* May 31, 1991, Page A1; Hendrix, Kathleen, "Professor Raises Furor by Claiming Date Rape Statistics Are Inflated," *Los Angeles Times,* July 9, 1991, page E1; Faludi, Susan, "Whose Hype?," *Newsweek,* October 25, 1993, page 61; and Kuehl, Sheila, "Skeptic Needs Taste of Reality Along with Lessons About Law," *Los Angeles Daily Journal,* September 5, 1991, quoted in Sommers, Christina Hoff, *Who Stole Feminism?,* New York: Simon & Schuster, 1994, page 222.

112. Gordon, Sue, "Oral Examination," *The Guardian,* February 19, 1992, page 35.

113. Kaukas, Dick, "Say What?," *Louisville Courier-Journal,* May 22, 1993, page 31S.

114. Crichton, Sarah, "Sexual Correctness: Has It Gone Too Far?," *Newsweek,* October 25, 1993, page 55.

115. Jeffreys, Sheila, *Anticlimax,* London: Women's Press, 1990, page 299.

116. Hopfensperger, Jean, "Elementary Instruction: Board Expected to OK Sexual Harassment Curriculum," *Minneapolis Star Tribune,* October 9, 1993, page 1A.

117. Kramarae, Cheris, and Treichler, Paula A., *A Feminist Dictionary,* Boston: Pandora Press, 1985, page 328.

118. Beard, Henry, and Cerf, Christopher, *The Official Politically Correct Dictionary and Handbook,* updated edition, New York: Villard Books, 1993, page 18.

119. Tevlin, Jon, "Of Hawks and Men: A Weekend in the Male Wilderness," *Utne Reader,* November–December 1989, page 50, quoted in Faludi, Susan, *Backlash: The Undeclared War Against American Women,* New York: Crown, 1991, page 309.

120. "*Harper's* Index," *Harper's,* June 1993.

121. Brown, Mick, "Man, This Is Really Wild," *Sunday Telegraph,* September 27, 1992, page 109.

122. D'Souza, Dinesh, *Illiberal Education: The Politics of Race and Sex on Campus,* New York: Free Press, 1991, page 214.

123. Ibid., pages 197–99.

124. Frye, Marilyn, "Oppression," anthologized in Rothenberg, Paula S., *Racism and Sexism: An Integrated Study,* New York: St. Martin's Press, 1988, page 41.

125. MacKinnon, Catharine A., quoted in Smith, Dinitia, "Love Is Strange," *New York,* March 22, 1993, page 43.

126. Crichton, Sarah, "Sexual Correctness: Has It Gone Too Far?," *Newsweek,* October 25, 1993, page 54.

127. Kahn, Alice, "Do Real Men Feel the Beat?," *San Francisco Chronicle,* November 20, 1991, page B3.

128. Weitz, Matt, "Beats of Different Drummers," *The Dallas Morning News,* September 5, 1993, page 1F.

129. Alexie, Sherman, "White Men Can't Drum," *San Francisco Chronicle,* October 18, 1992, page 7/Z1.

130. Brown, Laura S., "Essential Lies: A Dystopian View of the Mythopoetic Men's Movement," anthologized in Hagan, Kay Leigh, *Women Respond to the Men's Movement,* San Francisco: Pandora/HarperSanFrancisco, 1992, page 96.

131. Kaminer, Wendy, "Feminists Against the First Amendment," *Atlantic Monthly,* November 1992, page 112.

132. Dworkin, Andrea, quoted in Wilkerson, Isabel, "Foes of Pornography and Bigotry Join Forces," *The New York Times,* March 12, 1993, page 16.

133. Goldfield, Bina, *The Efemcipated English Handbook,* New York: Westover Press, 1983, pages 5, 87.

134. Mehrhof, Barbara, cited in Spender, Dale, *Man Made Language,* London: Pandora Press, 1980, page 178.

135. Harney, Patricia A., MA, and Muehlenhard, Charlene L., PhD, "Factors that Increase the Likelihood of Victimization," anthologized in Parrot, Andrea, PhD, and Bechhofer, Laurie, *Acquaintance Rape: The Hidden Crime,* New York: John Wiley & Sons, 1991, page 164.

136. Baker, Robert, " 'Pricks' and 'Chicks': A Plea for 'Persons,' " anthologized in Rothenberg, Paula S., *Racism and Sexism: An Integrated Study,* New York: St. Martin's Press, 1988, pages 280–94.

137. Steinem, Gloria, "What If *Freud* Were *Phyllis*?," *Moving Beyond Words,* New York: Simon & Schuster, 1994, page 49.

138. *Random House Webster's College Dictionary,* New York: Random House, 1991, page 449.

139. *Girls and Boys Getting Along: Teaching Sexual Harassment Prevention in the Elementary Classroom,* St. Paul, Minn.: Minnesota Department of Education, 1993, page 28.

140. Dworkin, Andrea, "Renouncing Sexual Equality," *Our Blood: Prophecies and Discourses on Sexual Politics,* New York: Harper & Row, 1976, page 12.

141. Sommers, Christina Hoff, *Who Stole Feminism?,* New York: Simon & Schuster, 1994, pages 51, 224–25.

142. Flint, Anthony, "New Breed of Feminist Challenges Old Guard," *The Boston Globe,* May 29, 1994, page 1.

143. Carton, Barbara, "A Rebel in the Sisterhood," *The Boston Globe,* June 16, 1994, page 69.

144. Bartky, Sandra Lee, *Femininity and Domination: Studies in the Phenomenology of Oppression,* New York: Routledge, 1990, page 50, cited in Sommers, Christina Hoff, *Who Stole Feminism?,* New York: Simon & Schuster, 1994, page 22.

145. Flint, Anthony, "New Breed of Feminist Challenges Old Guard," *The Boston Globe,* May 29, 1994, page 1.

146. McElvaine, Robert S., "Perspective on Language: What Ever Happened to S-X?," *Los Angeles Times,* July 22, 1993, page B7.

147. Butler, Judith, *Gender Trouble: Feminism and the Subversion of Identity,* New York: Routledge, Chapman and Hall, 1990, pages ix, 1–6, 148–49.

148. Piccoli, Sean, "It Came from Outer Space," *The Washington Times,* April 27, 1992, page D2.

149. "Sexual Violence," *The Barnard/Columbia Women's Handbook 1992,* chapter 8, downloaded from Internet, January 26, 1994.

150. MacKinnon, Catharine A., *Toward a Feminist Theory of the State,* Cambridge, Mass.: Harvard University Press, 1989, page 115.

151. Noble, Vicki, "A Helping Hand from the Guys," anthologized in Hagan, Kay Leigh, *Women Respond to the Men's Movement,* San Francisco: Pandora/HarperSanFrancisco, 1992, page 105.

152. Hansen, Joseph, and Reed, Evelyn, *Cosmetics, Fashions, and the Exploitation of Women,* New York: Pathfinder Press, 1986, pages 65–66.

153. Zalk, Sue Rosenberg, "Men in the Academy: A Psychological Profile of Harassment," anthologized in Paludi, Michele A., *Ivory Power: Sexual Harassment on Campus,* Albany: State University of New York Press, 1990, page 150.

154. See, Carolyn, "Angry Women and Brutal Men," *The New York Times Book Review,* December 28, 1980, page 4.

155. Daly, Mary, *Websters' First New Intergalactic Wickedary of the English Language,* Boston: Beacon Press, 1987, page 198.

156. Ibid., page 214.

157. Goldfield, Bina, *The Efemcipated English Handbook,* New York: Westover Press, 1983, page 94.

158. Hamilton, Alan, *Sexual Identity and Gender Identity Glossary,* Open Software Foundation, prepublication copy, distributed online via the Internet, December 19, 1992.

159. Fausto-Sterling, Anne, "How Many Sexes Are There?," *The New York Times,* March 12, 1993, page A29.

160. Kimball, Roger, *Tenured Radicals,* New York: HarperPerennial, 1991, page 68.

161. Wolfe, Alan, "Dirt and Democracy: Feminists, Liberals and the War on Pornography," *The New Republic,* February 19, 1990, pages 27ff.

162. Yee, Laura, "Now, a 'Safer Sex Kit,' " Cleveland *Plain Dealer,* May 18, 1993, "Health and Science" section, page 7C.

163. Stoltenberg, John, "Confronting Pornography as a Civil-Rights Issue," *Refusing to Be a Man: Essays on Sex and Justice,* New York: Meridian, 1990, pages 169–70.

164. Kramarae, Cheris, and Treichler, Paula A., *A Feminist Dictionary,* Boston: Pandora Press, 1985, page 165.

165. McShane, Claudette, *Warning! Dating May Be Hazardous to Your Health!,* Racine, Wis.: Mother Courage Press, 1988, page 45.

166. Stein, Nan, "Secrets in Public: Sexual Harassment in Public (and Private) Schools," working paper number 256, Wellesley, Mass.: Wellesley College Center for Research on Women, 1993, page 4, quoted in: Sommers, Christina Hoff, *Who Stole Feminism?,* New York: Simon & Schuster, 1994, page 46.

167. Dworkin, Andrea, "The Night and Danger," *Letters from a War Zone,* London: Secker and Warburg, 1988, page 14.

168. Viner, Katharine, "To P or Not to P," *The Guardian,* July 7, 1992, page 37.

169. "UMCP Sexual Harassment Policy," University of Maryland at College Park, College Park, Md., downloaded from Internet, February 7, 1994.

170. Wilkins, Stacey, "A little courtesy please! Waiters are people, too," *Nation's Restaurant News,* February 1, 1993, page 24.

171. "The Heterosexual Fix," *Scarlet Women,* 1981, issue 13, page 5, quoted in: Kramarae, Cheris, and Treichler, Paula A., *A Feminist Dictionary,* Boston: Pandora Press, 1985.

172. Koedt, Anne; Levine, Ellen; and Rapone, Anita; *Radical Feminism,* New York: Quadrangle Books/New York Times, 1973, page 201, quoted in Kramarae, Cheris, and Treichler, Paula A., *A Feminist Dictionary,* Boston: Pandora Press, 1985, page 166.

173. "Different Strokes," *The New Yorker,* November 29, 1993, pages 9–10.

174. Cooper, Kenneth C., "The Six Levels of Sexual Harassment," anthologized in A. Pablo Iannone, *Contemporary Moral Controversies in Business,* New York: Oxford University Press, 1989, page 190, cited in Wall, Edmund, "The Definition of Sexual Harassment," anthologized in Wall, Edmund, *Sexual Harassment,* Buffalo, N.Y.: Prometheus Books, 1992, page 72.

175. Hicks, Cherrill, "They Took My Foreskin, and I Want It Back," *The Independent,* August 3, 1993, page 11; and Condon, Garret, "Circumcision Revision," *The Hartford Courant,* January 20, 1994, page E1.

176. Tevlin, Jon, "Of Hawks and Men: A Weekend in the Male Wilderness," *Utne Reader,* November–December, 1989, page 50, quoted in Faludi, Susan, *Backlash: The Undeclared War Against American Women,* New York: Crown, 1991, page 309.

177. Shilts, Randy, "Conduct Unbecoming: The Women Who Don't Fit In," *San Francisco Chronicle,* April 27, 1993, page B3.

178. Seigenthaler, John, "Politically Correct Speech: An Oxymoron," *Editor & Publisher,* March 6, 1993, page 48.

179. Funk, Rus Ervin, *Stopping Rape: A Challenge for Men,* Philadelphia: New Society Publishers, 1993, page 8.

180. Bolus, Josephine, "Teaching Teens About Condoms," *RN,* March 1994, pages 44ff.

181. Zalk, Sue Rosenberg, "Men in the Academy: A Psychological Profile of Harassment," anthologized in Rothenberg, Paula S., *Racism and Sexism: An Integrated Study,* New York: St. Martin's Press, 1988, page 24.

182. Hentoff, Nat, "Fear and Deliverance at the University of Nebraska," *The Village Voice,* January 18, 1994, page 22.

183. Dworkin, Andrea, quoted in Stoltenberg, John, *Refusing to Be a Man: Essays on Sex and Justice,* New York: Meridian, 1990, page 88.

184. Henley, Nancy M., *Body Politics: Power, Sex and Nonverbal Communication,* New York: Touchstone Books, Simon & Schuster, 1986, pages 63–65.

185. Prince, Virginia, "Sex, Gender, and Semantics," *Journal of Sex Research 21,* 1985, pages 92–96, cited in Frank, Francine Wattman, and Treichler, Paula A., *Language, Gender, and Professional Writing,* New York: Modern Language Association of America, 1989, page 10.

186. Fausto-Sterling, Anne, "How Many Sexes Are There?," *The New York Times,* March 12, 1993, page A29.

187. Hamilton, Alan, *Sexual Identity and Gender Identity Glossary,* Open Software Foundation, prepublication copy, distributed online via the Internet, December 19, 1992.

188. Ibid.

189. Stein, Nan, "Secrets in Public: Sexual Harassment in Public (and Private) Schools," working paper number 256, Wellesley, Mass.: Wellesley College Center for Research on Women, 1993, page 4, quoted in: Sommers, Christina Hoff, *Who Stole Feminism?,* New York: Simon & Schuster, 1994, page 46.

190. Franklin, P.; Moglin, J.; Zatling-Boring, P.; and Angress, R.; "Sexual and Gender Harassment in the Academy," New York: Modern Language Association, cited in Grossman, Marc; Scott, Carole Ann; Kindermann, Joni; Matula, Susan; Oswald, Julie; Dovan, Judi; and Mulcahy, Donna, "Myths and Realities: Sexual Harassment on Campus," anthologized in Paludi, Michele A., *Ivory Power: Sexual Harassment on Campus,* Albany: State University of New York Press, 1990, page 3.

191. Hamilton, Alan, *Sexual Identity and Gender Identity Glossary,* Open Software Foundation, prepublication copy, distributed online via the Internet, December 19, 1992.

192. Brod, Harry, "The Mythopoetic Men's Movement: A Political Critique," anthologized in Harding, Christopher, ed., *Wingspan: Inside the Men's Movement,* New York: St. Martin's Press, 1992, page 236.

193. Clarke, Cheryl, "Lesbianism: An Act of Resistance," anthologized in Moraga, Cherríe, and Anzaldúa, Gloria, *This Bridge Called My Back: Writings by Radical Women of Color,* New York: Kitchen Table: Women of Color Press, 1983, page 131.

194. Harding, Christopher, ed., *Wingspan: Inside the Men's Movement*, New York: St. Martin's Press, 1992, page 262.

195. Hamilton, Alan, *Sexual Identity and Gender Identity Glossary*, Open Software Foundation, prepublication copy, distributed online via the Internet, December 19, 1992.

196. Smith, Joan, "When No Means Never," *The Independent*, April 11, 1993, page 37.

197. Cline, Sally, *Women, Celibacy and Passion*, quoted in Wolf, Naomi, *Fire with Fire*, New York: Random House, 1993, page 183.

198. Moggach, Deborah, book review of *Women, Celibacy and Passion* by Sally Cline, *Sunday Times*, London, March 7, 1993.

199. Henley, Nancy, *Body Politics: Power, Sex and Nonverbal Communication*, New York: Touchstone Books, Simon & Schuster, 1986, page 110.

200. Katz, Jesse, "A Story of Love in the San Gabriel Valley," *Los Angeles Times*, February 14, 1990, part E, page 3C.

201. Leo, John, "PC Is Still Alive," *The San Diego Union-Tribune*, January 26, 1994, page B7.

202. Budapest, Zsuzsanna E., *The Goddess in the Office: A Personal Energy Guide for the Spiritual Warrior at Work*, San Francisco: HarperSanFrancisco, 1993, page 148.

203. Todd, Douglas, "Divinely Female," *Vancouver Sun*, January 2, 1993, page C13; Lacher, Irene, "She Worship: Return of the Great Goddess," *Los Angeles Times*, September 19, 1990, page E1; Budapest, Zsuzsanna E., *The Goddess in the Office: A Personal Energy Guide for the Spiritual Warrior at Work*, San Francisco: HarperSanFrancisco, 1993; and Lattin, Don, "Breaking the Silence," *San Francisco Chronicle*, April 14, 1991, Sunday review section, page 3.

204. Pritchard, Carol, *Avoiding Rape On and Off Campus*, cited in "The Feminist Definition of Rape," *Sunday Times*, London: October 31, 1993, "Features" section.

205. "A New Offence," the *Daily Telegraph*, October 30, 1993, page 17; and "Probation for Rape Claim Woman," *The Independent*, November 24, 1993, page 6.

206. Faludi, Susan, *Backlash: The Undeclared War Against American Women*, New York: Crown, 1991, page 307.

207. Schrof, Joannie M., "Feminism's Daughters," *U.S. News & World Report,* September 27, 1993, page 69; and "On Special Night, Men Get Lesson on Fear of Rape," *The New York Times,* March 24, 1991, pages 45–46.

208. Starhawk, "A Men's Movement I Can Trust," anthologized in Hagan, Kay Leigh, *Women Respond to the Men's Movement,* San Francisco: Pandora/HarperCollins, 1992, page 31.

209. Heimel, Cynthia, "Brotherhood Could Maybe Be Powerful," *The Village Voice,* June 11, 1991, page 47.

210. McNutt, Karen, "Perpetuating the Victim Status of Women," *Women & Guns,* December 1991, page 7. Quoted in: Wolf, Naomi, *Fire with Fire,* New York: Random House, 1993, page 218.

211. Ferguson, Ann, *Blood at the Root: Motherhood, Sexuality and Male Dominance,* London: Pandora Press, 1989, page 231.

212. Ferguson, Ann, "Androgyny as an Ideal for Human Development," anthologized in Rothenberg, Paula S., *Racism and Sexism: An Integrated Study,* New York: St. Martin's Press, 1988, pages 362–71.

213. Dworkin, Andrea, *Our Blood: Prophecies and Discourses on Sexual Politics,* New York: Harper & Row, 1976, pages 16, 19.

214. Ibid., pages 16, 21.

215. *Newsweek,* December 24, 1990, page 51.

216. Leo, John, "A Political Correctness Roundup," *U.S. News & World Report,* June 22, 1992, page 29.

217. Weitz, Matt, "Beats of Different Drummers," *The Dallas Morning News,* September 5, 1993, page 1F.

218. Henley, Nancy, *Body Politics: Power, Sex and Nonverbal Communication,* New York: Touchstone Books, Simon & Schuster, 1986, page 110.

219. Clarkson, Carla A., "Harassment in the Hallways," Gannett News Service, July 19, 1993.

220. Strauss, Susan, with Espeland, Pamela, *Sexual Harassment and Teens: A Program for Positive Change,* Minneapolis: Free Spirit Publishing Co., 1992, page 8.

221. Adler, Jerry, "Drums, Sweat and Tears" and "Heeding the Call of the Drums," *Newsweek,* June 24, 1991, pages 46, 52; and Queenan, Joe, "Is This a Man's World?," *Chief Executive,* November 1992, page 10.

222. Fausto-Sterling, Anne, "How Many Sexes Are There?," *The New York Times,* March 12, 1993, page A29.

223. Hamilton, Alan, *Sexual Identity and Gender Identity Glossary*, Open Software Foundation, prepublication copy, distributed online via the Internet, December 19, 1992.

224. "Definitions," a handout published by the Smith College Office of Student Affairs, 1990.

225. Spender, Dale, *Man Made Language*, London: Pandora Press, 1980, pages 176–77.

226. Clarke, Cheryl, "Lesbianism: An Act of Resistance," anthologized in Moraga, Cherríe, and Anzaldúa, Gloria, *This Bridge Called My Back: Writings by Radical Women of Color*, New York: Kitchen Table: Women of Color Press, 1983, page 130.

227. Dworkin, Andrea, *Women Hating*, New York: E. P. Dutton, 1974, page 184.

228. Firestone, Shulamith, *The Dialectic of Sex*, New York: William Morrow, 1970, chapter 6, paraphrased by Ferguson, Ann, in "Androgyny as an Ideal for Human Development," anthologized in Rothenberg, Paula S., *Racism and Sexism: An Integrated Study*, New York: St. Martin's Press, 1988, pages 367, 370.

229. Gaines, Judith, "Ads Are Bullish on Bare Men," *Orlando Sentinel*, September 19, 1993, page F1.

230. Jastrab, Joseph, "Every Man's Story, Every Man's Truth," anthologized in Harding, Christopher, ed., *Wingspan: Inside the Men's Movement*, New York: St. Martin's Press, 1992, page 220.

231. Alexie, Sherman, "White Men Can't Drum," *San Francisco Chronicle*, October 18, 1992, page 7/Z1.

232. Hamilton, Alan, *Sexual Identity and Gender Identity Glossary*, Open Software Foundation, prepublication copy, distributed online via the Internet, December 19, 1992.

233. Mohr, Richard D., *Gays/Justice: A Study of Ethics, Society and the Law*, New York: Columbia University Press, 1988, cited in Frank, Francine Wattman, and Treichler, Paula A., *Language, Gender, and Professional Writing*, New York: Modern Language Association of America, 1989, page 17.

234. Cortissoz, Marie, "ACLU May Challenge Student's Punishment Over Word 'Faggot,' " Gannett News Service, December 7, 1993; and "PC Is No Laughing Matter," *The Washington Times*, June 5, 1993, page C2.

235. Kaufman, Gloria, and Blakely, Mary Kay, *Pulling Our Own Strings*, Bloomington: Indiana University Press, 1980, page 175, quoted in Kra-

marae, Cheris, and Treichler, Paula A., *A Feminist Dictionary,* Boston: Pandora Press, 1985, page 196.

236. Howard, Mona, speech at "Feminists at Fawcett" meeting, quoted in Kramarae, Cheris, and Treichler, Paula A., *A Feminist Dictionary,* Boston: Pandora Press, 1985, page 196.

237. Paul, Ellen Frankel, "Bared Buttocks and Federal Cases," anthologized in Wall, Edmund, *Sexual Harassment: Confrontations and Decisions,* Buffalo, N.Y.: Prometheus Books, 1992, pages 155–56; "Talking Dirty," editorial, *The New Republic,* November 4, 1991, page 7; and Leo, John, "An Empty Ruling on Harassment," *U.S. News & World Report,* November 29, 1993, page 20.

238. Budapest, Zsuzsanna E., *The Goddess in the Office: A Personal Energy Guide for the Spiritual Warrior at Work,* San Francisco: HarperSanFrancisco, 1993, page 40.

239. Hamill, Pete, "Woman on the Verge of a Legal Breakdown," *Playboy,* January 1993, pages 138ff.

240. Ferguson, Ann, *Blood at the Root: Motherhood, Sexuality and Male Dominance,* London: Pandora Press, 1989, page 217.

241. Stoltenberg, John, *Refusing to Be a Man: Essays on Sex and Justice,* New York: Meridian, 1990, pages 5, 185.

242. Ibid., page 61.

243. Brown, Laura S., "Essential Lies: A Dystopian Vision of the Mythopoetic Men's Movement," anthologized in Hagan, Kay Leigh, *Women Respond to the Men's Movement,* San Francisco: Pandora/HarperSanFrancisco, 1992, page 95.

244. Stoltenberg, John, *Refusing to Be a Man: Essays on Sex and Justice,* New York: Meridian, 1990, page 69.

245. Barickman, Richard; Korn, Sam; Sandler, Bernice; Gold, Yael; Ormerod, Alayne; and Weitzman, Lauren M., "An Ecological Perspective to Understanding Sexual Harassment," anthologized in Paludi, Michele A., *Ivory Power: Sexual Harassment on Campus,* Albany: State University of New York Press, 1990, page xvii.

246. Dworkin, Andrea, quoted in *Newsweek,* October 25, 1993, page 54.

247. Falk, William B., "That Alien Feeling," *Newsday,* April 12, 1993, section 2, page 44.

248. Stoltenberg, John, *Refusing to Be a Man: Essays on Sex and Justice,* New York: Meridian, 1990, front endpaper.

249. Taylor, John, "Are You Politically Correct?," *New York,* January 21, 1991, page 38.

250. Snyder, Dia, quoted in Beard, Henry, and Cerf, Christopher, *The Official Politically Correct Dictionary and Handbook,* updated edition, New York: Villard Books, 1993, page 37.

251. "Definitions," handout published by the Smith College Office of Student Affairs, 1990.

252. Sommers, Christina Hoff, *Who Stole Feminism?,* New York: Simon & Schuster, 1994, page 116.

253. Dworkin, Andrea, *Intercourse,* New York: Free Press, 1987, page 138.

254. Baker, Robert, " 'Pricks' and 'Chicks': A Plea for 'Persons,' " anthologized in Rothenberg, Paula S., *Racism and Sexism: An Integrated Study,* New York: St. Martin's Press, 1988, pages 280–94.

255. See, Carolyn, "Angry Women and Brutal Men," *The New York Times Book Review,* December 28, 1980, page 4.

256. Bartky, Sandra Lee, *Femininity and Domination: Studies in the Phenomenology of Oppression,* New York: Routledge, 1990, pages 75, 80, cited in Sommers, Christina Hoff, *Who Stole Feminism?,* New York: Simon & Schuster, 1994, pages 230–31.

257. Fausto-Sterling, Anne, "How Many Sexes Are There?," *The New York Times,* March 12, 1993, page A29.

258. Funk, Rus Ervin, *Stopping Rape: A Challenge for Men,* Philadelphia: New Society Publishers, 1993, page 32.

259. The American Gender Society, internal memo, December 6, 1992.

260. The American Gender Society, internal memo, December 7, 1992.

261. Crichton, Sarah, "Sexual Correctness: Has It Gone Too Far?," *Newsweek,* October 25, 1993, page 55.

262. Hicks, Cherrill, "They Took My Foreskin, and I Want It Back," *The Independent,* August 3, 1993, page 11.

263. Waugh, Auberon, "Whither the Newly Empowered American Female," *The Spectator,* February 27, 1993, page 8.

264. Funk, Rus Ervin, *Stopping Rape: A Challenge for Men,* Philadelphia: New Society Publishers, 1993, page 8.

265. Mack, Dana, "What the Sex Educators Teach," *Commentary,* August 1993, page 33; and Bolus, Josephine, "Teaching Teens About Condoms," *RN,* March 1994, pages 44ff.

266. Rovner, Sandy, "Study Finds Higher Latex Allergy Rate," *The Washington Post,* June 7, 1994; and Recer, Paul, "Rubber Latex Triggering Allergic Reactions, Doctor Says," Associated Press, December 8, 1993, P.M. cycle.

267. Hamilton, Alan, *Sexual Identity and Gender Identity Glossary,* Open Software Foundation, prepublication copy, distributed online via the Internet, December 19, 1992.

268. Mast, Kent, quoted in Cooper, Marc, "Chastity 101," *The Village Voice,* June 7, 1994, page 34.

269. Morgan, Robin, "Theory and Practice: Pornography and Rape," *The Word of a Woman,* New York: W. W. Norton, 1993, pages 83.

270. Kuehl, Sheila, "Skeptic Needs Taste of Reality Along with Lessons About Law," *Los Angeles Daily Journal,* September 5, 1991, quoted in Sommers, Christina Hoff, *Who Stole Feminism?,* New York: Simon & Schuster, 1994, page 222.

271. Parrot, Andrea, PhD, *Coping with Date Rape and Acquaintance Rape,* New York: Rosen Publishing Group, 1993, page 12.

272. Rule, Jane, *The Hot-Eyed Moderate,* Tallahassee, Fla.: Naiad Press, 1985, cited in Silva, Rosemary, *Lesbian Quotations,* Boston: Alyson Publications, 1993, page 152.

273. "UMCP Sexual Harassment Policy," University of Maryland at College Park, College Park, Md., downloaded from Internet February 7, 1994.

274. Wolf, Sharyn, *Guerilla Dating Tactics,* New York: Plume Books, 1993, page 286.

275. Moggach, Deborah, book review of *Women, Celibacy and Passion* by Sally Cline, *Sunday Times,* London, March 7, 1993.

276. Kipnis, Aaron R., PhD, "The Blessings of the Green Man," Harding, Christopher, ed., *Wingspan: Inside the Men's Movement,* New York: St. Martin's Press, 1992, pages 161–65.

277. "Definitions," a handout published by the Smith College Office of Student Affairs, 1990.

278. Based on the description of "lookism" supplied in "Definitions," a handout published by the Smith College Office of Student Affairs, 1990.

279. Dworkin, Andrea, *Our Blood: Prophecies and Discourses on Sexual Politics,* New York: Harper & Row, 1976, page 105.

280. "Talking Dirty," editorial, *The New Republic*, November 4, 1991, page 7.

281. Jones, Maggie, "Gunmakers Target Women," *Working Woman*, July 1993, page 10.

282. Heimel, Cynthia, "Brotherhood Could Maybe Be Powerful," *The Village Voice*, June 11, 1991, page 47.

283. Costello, Michael, "New Feminist Findings Show What a Louse I Am," *Lewiston Morning Tribune*, December 28, 1991, page 10A.

284. Muelenhard, Charlene N., PhD, and Schrag, Jennifer L., "Nonviolent Sexual Coercion," anthologized in Parrot, Andrea, and Bechhofer, Laurie, *Acquaintance Rape: The Hidden Crime*, New York: John Wiley & Sons, 1991, page 122.

285. "Sexual Harassment College Policy," *Official Survival Handbook*, Yellow Springs, Ohio: Antioch College Student Government, 1993–94, page 12.

286. Parrot, Andrea, PhD, *Coping with Date Rape and Acquaintance Rape*, New York: Rosen Publishing Group, 1993, page 24.

287. Ayoob, Massad, "The Armed Woman's Attitude Test," *Women & Guns*, December 1991, page 38.

288. Greaves, Steve, "Letters to the Editor," *Yoga Journal*, September–October 1991, page 16, quoted in Noble, Vicki, "A Helping Hand from the Guys," anthologized in Hagan, Kay Leigh, *Women Respond to the Men's Movement*, San Francisco: Pandora/HarperSanFrancisco, 1992, pages 102–3.

289. MacKinnon, Catharine A., *Only Words*, Cambridge, Mass.: Harvard University Press, 1993, page 24.

290. Frye, Marilyn, *The Politics of Reality: Essays in Feminist Theory*, Trumansburg, N.Y.: Crossing Press, 1983, pages 98–100.

291. Stoltenberg, John, *Refusing to Be a Man: Essays on Sex and Justice*, New York: Meridian, 1990, pages 5, 185.

292. Sommers, Christina Hoff, *Who Stole Feminism?*, New York: Simon & Schuster, 1994, page 116.

293. Cline, Sally, *Women, Celibacy and Passion*, quoted in Wolf, Naomi, *Fire with Fire*, New York: Random House, 1993, page 183.

294. Lorde, Audre, "The Master's Tools Will Never Dismantle the Master's House," anthologized in Moraga, Cherríe, and Anzaldúa. Gloria, *This*

*Bridge Called My Back: Writings by Radical Women of Color,* New York: Kitchen Table: Women of Color Press, 1983, page 98.

295. Dworkin, Andrea, *Our Blood: Prophecies and Discourses on Sexual Politics,* New York: Harper & Row, 1976, page 27.

296. Spender, Dale, *Women of Ideas and What Men Have Done to Them,* London: Routledge and Kegan Paul, 1982, page 341.

297. Harding, Christopher, ed., *Wingspan: Inside the Men's Movement,* New York: St. Martin's Press, 1992, page 161.

298. Kipnis, Aaron R., PhD, "The Blessings of the Green Man," anthologized in Harding, Christopher, ed., *Wingspan: Inside the Men's Movement,* New York: St. Martin's Press, 1992, pages 161–65.

299. Smith, Joan, "When No Means Never," *The Independent,* April 11, 1993, page 37.

300. Kaminer, Wendy, "Feminists Against the First Amendment," *Atlantic Monthly,* November 1992, page 116.

301. Jackson, Donna, "Rape Awareness List for Nice Guys," *How to Make the World a Better Place for Women in Five Minutes a Day,* New York: Hyperion, 1992, page 60.

302. Adams, Carol J., *The Sexual Politics of Meat: A Feminist-Vegetarian Critical Theory,* New York: Continuum Publishing Co., 1990, pages 13, 18.

303. Cooper, Kenneth C., "The Six Levels of Sexual Harassment," anthologized in A. Pablo Iannone, *Contemporary Moral Controversies in Business,* New York: Oxford University Press, 1989, page 190, cited in Wall, Edmund, "The Definition of Sexual Harassment," anthologized in Wall, Edmund, *Sexual Harassment,* Buffalo, N.Y.: Prometheus Books, 1992, page 71.

304. Ritchie, Bruce, "School Board Approves AIDS Teaching Resolution," United Press International, Alabama regional news item, June 11, 1987, A.M. cycle.

305. Murphy, Kim, "Scientologists Achieve 'Peace' by Settling Suits," *Los Angeles Times,* December 17, 1986, Part 1, page 3; and United Press International, California regional news item, May 8, 1984. Ms. Hubbard defended her use of the term "mental rape" by stating, under oath, in a Los Angeles courtroom: "Someone comes in and ravishes your personal belongings. Here I am having to be in court, I mean really, to get them back. I mean that is outrageous."

306. Patrick, Gregory G., MD, "The Mental Anguish of Being Sued," *The Washington Post,* November 8, 1988, page Z8.

307. Fausto-Sterling, Anne, "How Many Sexes Are There?," *The New York Times,* March 12, 1993, page A29.

308. Leo, John, "Looking Back at a PC Extravaganza," *U.S. News & World Report,* January 31, 1994, page 20.

309. Daly, Mary, *Gyn/Ecology,* Boston: Beacon Press, 1978, page 239.

310. Daly, Mary, *Websters' First New Intergalactic Wickedary of the English Language,* Boston: Beacon Press, 1987, page 212.

311. "Current Quotations," Associated Press, December 13, 1989.

312. Hamilton, Alan, *Sexual Identity and Gender Identity Glossary,* Open Software Foundation, prepublication copy, distributed online via the Internet, December 19, 1992.

313. Dworkin, Andrea, *Women Hating,* New York: E. P. Dutton, 1974, page 185.

314. Leo, John, "What Qualifies as Sexual Harassment?," *U.S. News & World Report,* August 13, 1990, page 17.

315. Heimel, Cynthia, "Brotherhood Could Maybe Be Powerful," *The Village Voice,* June 11, 1991, page 47.

316. Waugh, Auberon, "Whither the Newly Empowered American Female," *The Spectator,* February 27, 1993, page 8.

317. Based on a report by Janice Castro in *Time,* April 20, 1992, page 21.

318. Asmus, Kristen, "Blaming the Dress," *Colorado Daily,* October 27–29, 1989, page 13, quoted in D'Souza, Dinesh, *Illiberal Education: The Politics of Race and Sex on Campus,* New York: Free Press, 1991, page 11.

319. Harding, Christopher, "What's All This About a Men's Movement," introduction to his anthology *Wingspan: Inside the Men's Movement,* New York: St. Martin's Press, 1992, page xiii.

320. Ibid., page xiii.

321. Brown, Laura S., "Essential Lies: A Dystopian View of the Mythopoetic Men's Movement," anthologized in Hagan, Kay Leigh, *Women Respond to the Men's Movement,* San Francisco: Pandora/HarperSanFrancisco, 1992, page 96.

322. Daly, Mary, *Gyn/Ecology,* Boston: Beacon Press, 1978, pages 10, 59.

323. McShane, Claudette, *Warning! Dating May Be Hazardous to Your Health!,* Racine, Wis.: Mother Courage Press, 1988, page 111.

324. "Slow Times at Amherst High," *Harper's,* April 1991, page 32.

325. O'Connor, Colleen, "A New Volley in an Age-Old Battle," *The Dallas Morning News,* September 1, 1993, page 1C.

326. Wolfe, Alan, "Dirt and Democracy: Feminists, Liberals and the War on Pornography," *The New Republic,* February 19, 1990, pages 27ff.

327. Harding, Sandra, *The Science Question in Feminism,* Ithaca, N.Y.: Cornell University Press, 1986, page 113, quoted in Sommers, Christina Hoff, *Who Stole Feminism?,* New York: Simon & Schuster, 1994, page 66.

328. Stanton, Doug, "Inward, Ho!," *Esquire,* October 1991, pages 113–22.

329. Lenhard, Elizabeth, "AIDS Prevention: Targeting Women of Color," *The Atlanta Journal and Constitution,* December 7, 1993, page F1.

330. Condon, Garret, "Circumcision Revision," *The Hartford Courant,* January 20, 1994, page E1.

331. Muehlenhard, Charlene N., PhD, and Hollabaugh, Lisa, *Journal of Personality and Social Psychology,* volume 54, pages 872–79, cited in Bozzi, Vincent, *Psychology Today,* March 1989, page 62.

332. Bozzi, Vincent, *Psychology Today,* March 1989, page 62.

333. Funk, Rus Ervin, *Stopping Rape: A Challenge for Men,* Philadelphia: New Society Publishers, 1993, page 27.

334. Kors, Alan Charles, "Harassment Policies in the University," anthologized in Wall, Edmund, *Sexual Harassment: Confrontations and Decisions,* Buffalo, N.Y.: Prometheus Books, 1992, page 45.

335. Lennert, Midge, and Willson, Norma, *A Woman's New World Dictionary,* 1973, page 9, quoted in Kramarae, Cheris, and Treichler, Paula A., *A Feminist Dictionary,* Boston: Pandora Press, 1985, page 308.

336. Dworkin, Andrea, *Right-Wing Women: The Politics of Domesticated Females,* London: Women's Press, 1983, page 84.

337. Dworkin, Andrea, *Intercourse,* New York: Free Press, 1987, pages 139–40.

338. Katz, Diane, "Unlikely Alliance Targets Pornographers," Gannett News Service, April 4, 1992.

339. Bright, Susie, "The Prime of Miss Catharine MacKinnon," *In These Times,* March 7, 1994, page 39.

340. Gilbert, Neil, "Examining the Facts: Advocacy Research Overstates the Incidence of Date and Acquaintance Rape," cited in Gelles, Richard,

and Loseke, Donileen, eds., *Current Controversies in Family Violence*, Newbury Park, Calif.: Sage Publications, 1993, pages 120–32.

341. McDowell, Josh, *It Can Happen to You: What You Need to Know About Preventing and Recovering from Date Rape*, Dallas: Word Publishing, 1991, page 32.

342. "Modem Butterfly," *The Village Voice*, March 25, 1994.

343. Adler, Jerry, "Drums, Sweat and Tears," *Newsweek*, June 24, 1991, page 51.

344. gossett, hattie, "Sex at a Certain Age," *Essence*, July 1993, page 65.

345. Cline, Sally, *Women, Celibacy and Passion*, quoted in Wolf, Naomi, *Fire with Fire*, New York: Random House, 1993, page 183.

346. Funk, Rus Ervin, *Stopping Rape: A Challenge for Men*, Philadelphia: New Society Publishers, 1993, page 8.

347. Fields, Suzanne, "Would St. Valentine Only Lose His Head Today?," *The Atlanta Journal and Constitution*, February 14, 1994, page A8.

348. "Brave New Word of Bonking Burbulence," *The Guardian*, August 19, 1993, page 11.

349. Chiles, Nick, "Focus on Abstinence: Sex, No Sex?," *Newsday*, May 13, 1993, page 15.

350. Evans, Rachel W., letter to *Ms.*, May 1978, page 15, cited in Kramarae, Cheris, and Treichler, Paula A., *A Feminist Dictionary*, Boston: Pandora Press, 1985, page 317.

351. The American Gender Society, internal memo, May 23, 1994.

352. Alexie, Sherman, "White Men Can't Drum," *San Francisco Chronicle*, October 18, 1992, page 7/Z1.

353. Frye, Marilyn, *The Politics of Reality: Essays in Feminist Theory*, Trumansburg, N.Y.: Crossing Press, 1983, pages 103–4.

354. Tuttle, Lisa, *Encyclopedia of Feminism*, Essex: Longman, 1986, page 342.

355. Dworkin, Andrea, *Our Blood: Prophecies and Discourses on Sexual Politics*, New York: Harper & Row, 1976, page 20.

356. Leo, John, "Looking Back at a PC Extravaganza," *U.S. News & World Report*, January 31, 1994, pages 19–20.

357. Parrot, Andrea, PhD, *Coping with Date Rape and Acquaintance Rape*, New York: Rosen Publishing Group, 1993, page 51.

358. Kramarae, Cheris, and Treichler, Paula A., *A Feminist Dictionary*, Boston: Pandora Press, 1985, page 328.

359. Funk, Rus Ervin, *Stopping Rape: A Challenge for Men,* Philadelphia: New Society Publishers, 1993, page 32.

360. "Penile Protection," letters section, *Time,* February 14, 1994, page 10.

361. Shalit, Ruth, "Romper Room," *New Republic,* March 29, 1993, pages 13ff.

362. Leo, John, "Madison Avenue's Gender War," *U.S. News & World Report,* October 25, 1993, page 25.

363. Urban, Jerry, "Man Files Lawsuit Against Continental for Sexual Harassment," *The Houston Chronicle,* February 5, 1994, page A28.

364. Kramarae, Cheris, and Treichler, Paula A., *A Feminist Dictionary,* Boston: Pandora Press, 1985, page 329.

365. Rule, Jane, *The Hot-Eyed Moderate,* Tallahassee, Fla.: Naiad Press, 1985, cited in Silva, Rosemary, *Lesbian Quotations,* Boston: Alyson Publications, 1993, page 152.

366. Allan, Keith, and Burridge, Kate, *Euphemism and Dysphemism,* New York: Oxford University Press, 1991, page 190.

367. Mack, Dana, "What the Sex Educators Teach," *Commentary,* August 1993, page 33; and Yee, Laura, "Now, a 'Safer Sex Kit,'" Cleveland *Plain Dealer,* May 18, 1993, "Health and Science" section, page 7C.

368. Cooper, Marc, "Chastity 101," *The Village Voice,* June 7, 1994, pages 1, 32.

369. Monagle, Katie, "Are Animals Equal?," *Scholastic Update,* April 16, 1993, page 19.

370. Leo, John, "A Political Correctness Roundup," *U.S. News & World Report,* June 22, 1992, page 29.

371. Daly, Mary, *Websters' First New Intergalactic Wickedary of the English Language,* Boston: Beacon Press, 1987, page 216.

372. The American Gender Society.

373. "Free Expression at Work," editorial, *St. Petersburg Times,* November 10, 1991, page 2D; and Leo, John, "An Empty Ruling on Harassment," *U.S. News & World Report,* November 29, 1993, page 20.

374. Yastrow, Joe, quoted by Novak, Lindsey, and Spier, Lauren, in "Workplace Solutions," *Chicago Tribune,* December 5, 1993, "Jobs" section, page 1.

375. Editors of *Time* magazine, "Squeals, Oinks and Grunts," commentary on readers' letters transmitted via *America Online,* February 27, 1994.

376. Budapest, Zsuzsanna E., *The Goddess in the Office: A Personal Energy Guide for the Spiritual Warrior at Work*, San Francisco: HarperSan-Francisco, 1993, page 42.

377. Jordan, Mary, "A Short Course on Courting," *The Washington Post*, February 14, 1994, page A1.

378. Wilson, Andrew, "Who's Afraid of the Face in the Mirror?," *The Guardian*, June 20, 1994, page T10.

379. Allan, Keith, and Burridge, Kate, *Euphemism and Dysphemism*, New York: Oxford University Press, 1991, page 190.

380. Giles, Jeff, with Holmes, Stanley, "There's a Time for Talk, and a Time for Action," *Newsweek*, March 7, 1994, page 55.

381. Tuttle, Lisa, *Encyclopedia of Feminism*, Essex: Longman, 1986, page 256.

382. Leo, John, "Looking Back at a PC Extravaganza," *U.S. News & World Report*, January 31, 1994, pages 19–20.

383. The American Gender Society.

384. Hackney, Sheldon, quoted by Storch, Charles, in "NEH Chairman Seeks New Era of Dialogue," *Chicago Tribune*, November 10, 1993, Zone C, page 3; and Davidson, Nicholas, "Making a Difference: Psychology and the Construction of Gender," *National Review*, August 20, 1990, pages 42ff.

385. Hentoff, Nat, "Fear and Deliverance at the University of Nebraska," *The Village Voice*, January 18, 1994, page 22.

386. Petersen, James R., "Catharine MacKinnon: Again," *Playboy*, August 1992, pp. 37ff.

387. Wolf, Naomi, *Fire with Fire*, New York: Random House, 1993, pages 53, 191, 236, and 320.

388. Walters, Suzanna, message posted to the Women's Studies Network bulletin board on the Internet, February 2, 1994, quoted in Sommers, Christina Hoff, *Who Stole Feminism?*, New York: Simon & Schuster, 1994, page 245.

389. Zalk, Sue Rosenberg, "Men in the Academy: A Psychological Profile of Harassment," anthologized in Paludi, Michele A., *Ivory Power: Sexual Harassment on Campus*, Albany: State University of New York Press, 1990, page 164.

390. Based on the term "marital slave" as used by Lorde, Audre, in "The Master's Tools Will Never Dismantle the Master's House," antholo-

gized in Moraga, Cherríe, and Anzaldúa, Gloria, *This Bridge Called My Back: Writings by Radical Women of Color,* New York: Kitchen Table: Women of Color Press, 1983, page 98.

391. Hamilton, Alan, *Sexual Identity and Gender Identity Glossary,* Open Software Foundation, prepublication copy, distributed online via the Internet, December 19, 1992.

392. Ahlgren, Calvin, "Goddess Movement Balancing Sexes' Power," *San Francisco Chronicle,* November 18, 1990, "Sunday Datebook" section, page 25.

393. Butler, Judith, *Gender Trouble: Feminism and the Subversion of Identity,* New York: Routledge, Chapman and Hall, 1990, page 36.

394. Haraway, Donna, quoted on the back cover of Butler, Judith, *Gender Trouble: Feminism and the Subversion of Identity,* New York: Routledge, Chapman and Hall, 1990.

395. Roiphe, Katie, *The Morning After: Sex, Fear, and Feminism on Campus,* Boston: Little, Brown and Co., 1993, pages 130, 135.

396. Leo, John, *U.S. News & World Report,* January 22, 1992, page 16.

397. Spender, Dale, *Women of Ideas and What Men Have Done to Them,* London: Routledge and Kegan Paul, 1982, page 341, quoted in Kramarae, Cheris, and Treichler, Paula A., *A Feminist Dictionary,* Boston: Pandora Press, 1985, page 362.

398. McClintock, Anne, "Safe Sluts," *The Village Voice,* August 20, 1991, page 26.

399. *The Quarterly Review of Doublespeak,* a publication of the National Council of Teachers of English, Urbana, Ill., October 1991, page 4.

400. *The Toronto Sun,* September 6, 1991, quoted in *The Quarterly Review of Doublespeak,* a publication of the National Council of Teachers of English, Urbana, Ill., April 1992, page 9.

401. Lutz, William, *Doublespeak,* New York: Harper Perennial, 1989, page 227.

402. Henley, Nancy M., *Body Politics: Power, Sex and Nonverbal Communication,* New York: Touchstone Books, Simon & Schuster, 1986, pages 63–64.

403. Ferguson, Andrew, "America's New Man," *The American Spectator,* January 1992, page 27.

404. "UMCP Sexual Harassment Policy," University of Maryland at College Park, College Park, Md., downloaded from Internet, February 7, 1994.

405. Daly, Mary, *Pure Lust*, Boston: Beacon Press, 1984, page 14, quoted in Kramarae, Cheris, and Treichler, Paula A., *A Feminist Dictionary*, Boston: Pandora Press, 1985, page 365.

406. "UMCP Sexual Harassment Policy," University of Maryland at College Park, College Park, Md., downloaded from Internet, February 7, 1994.

407. Kors, Alan Charles, "Harassment Policies in the University," anthologized in Wall, Edmund, *Sexual Harassment: Confrontations and Decisions*, Buffalo, N.Y.: Prometheus Books, 1992, pages 45–46.

408. Sommers, Christina Hoff, "Sister Soldiers: Live from a Women's Studies Conference," *The New Republic*, October 5, 1992, page 29ff.

409. Paul, Ellen Frankel, "Bared Buttocks and Federal Cases," anthologized in Wall, Edmund, *Sexual Harassment: Confrontations and Decisions*, Buffalo, N.Y.: Prometheus Books, 1992, page 154.

410. Tevlin, Jon, "Of Hawks and Men: A Weekend in the Male Wilderness," *Utne Reader*, November–December 1989, page 50, quoted in Faludi, Susan, *Backlash: The Undeclared War Against American Women*, New York: Crown, 1991, page 309.

411. MacKinnon, Catharine A., *Toward a Feminist Theory of the State*, Cambridge, Mass.: Harvard University Press, 1989, page 178.

412. Brownmiller, Susan, *Against Our Will: Men, Women and Rape*, New York: Simon & Schuster, 1975, page 15.

413. MacKinnon, Catharine A., *Feminism Unmodified*, Cambridge, Mass.: Harvard University Press, 1982, page 82, cited in Roiphe, Katie, *The Morning After: Sex, Fear, and Feminism on Campus*, Boston: Little, Brown and Co., 1993, page 70.

414. Gibbs, Nancy, "When Is It Rape?," *Time*, June 3, 1991, pages 48ff.

415. Ibid.

416. Asmus, Kristen, "Blaming the Dress," *Colorado Daily*, October 27–29, 1989, page 13, quoted in D'Souza, Dinesh, *Illiberal Education: The Politics of Race and Sex on Campus*, New York: Free Press, 1991, page 11.

417. Funk, Rus Ervin, *Stopping Rape: A Challenge for Men*, Philadelphia: New Society Publishers, 1993, page 27.

418. Ibid., page 28.

419. Stoltenberg, John, "Rapist Ethics," *Refusing to Be a Man: Essays on Sex and Justice,* New York: Meridian, 1990, page 19.

420. Harney, Patricia A., MA, and Muehlenhard, Charlene L., PhD, "Factors that Increase the Likelihood of Victimization," anthologized in Parrot, Andrea, PhD, and Bechhofer, Laurie, *Acquaintance Rape: The Hidden Crime,* New York: John Wiley & Sons, 1991, page 164.

421. Funk, Rus Ervin, *Stopping Rape: A Challenge for Men,* Philadelphia: New Society Publishers, 1993, page 27.

422. Taylor, John, "Are You Politically Correct?," *New York,* January 21, 1991, page 38.

423. Kaminer, Wendy, "Feminists Against the First Amendment," *Atlantic Monthly,* November 1992, page 116.

424. Hendrix, Kathleen, "Professor Raises Furor by Claiming Date Rape Statistics Are Inflated," *Los Angeles Times,* July 9, 1991, page E1; and Kahn, Alice, " 'Date Rape' Studies Called Exaggerated," *San Francisco Chronicle,* May 31, 1991, Page A1.

425. Oricchio, Michael, "Only in California . . . ," *Calgary Herald,* October 13, 1991, page A2.

426. Zalk, Sue Rosenberg, "Men in the Academy: A Psychological Profile of Harassment," anthologized in Rothenberg, Paula S., *Racism and Sexism: An Integrated Study,* New York: St. Martin's Press, 1988, page 153.

427. O'Connor, Colleen, "Women's Self-Defense: Big Business," *The Dallas Morning News,* October 24, 1993, page 4F.

428. Stanton, Doug, "Inward, Ho!," *Esquire,* October 1991, page 120.

429. Hopfensperger, Jean, "Elementary Instruction: Board Expected to OK Sexual Harassment Curriculum," *Minneapolis Star Tribune,* October 9, 1993, page 1A.

430. Rauch, Jonathan, *Kindly Inquisitors: The New Attacks on Free Thought,* Chicago: University of Chicago Press, cited in Kakutani, Michiko, "Books of the Times," *The New York Times,* April 23, 1993, page C30.

431. Leo, John, "The Politics of Feelings," *U.S. News & World Report,* March 23, 1992, page 28.

432. Ibid.

433. MacKinnon, Catharine A., quoted in "The Feminist Definition of Rape," *Sunday Times,* London: October 31, 1993, "Features" section.

434. Funk, Rus Ervin, *Stopping Rape: A Challenge for Men,* Philadelphia: New Society Publishers, 1993, page 9.

435. *What You Should Know About Sexual Harassment,* Princeton, N.J.: SHARE, cited in Roiphe, Katie, *The Morning After: Sex, Fear, and Feminism on Campus,* Boston: Little, Brown and Co., 1993, page 87.

436. Dworkin, Andrea, "The Night and Danger," *Letters from a War Zone,* London: Secker and Warburg, 1988, page 14.

437. Harwood, Anthony, "Head Bans 'Hetro' Romeo and Juliet," London *Daily Mirror,* January 20, 1994, News section, page 13.

438. Schorow, Stephanie, "Acceptance on Campus Can Depend on Whether One Is 'Politically Correct,' " Associated Press, March 25, 1991, A.M. cycle.

439. Sommers, Christina Hoff, *Who Stole Feminism?,* New York: Simon & Schuster, 1994, pages 204–5.

440. Geitner, Paul, "How Much Is Too Much for Anti-AIDS Ads?," Associated Press newswire item, December 18, 1989.

441. Ibid.; and Cephas, Valerie, "Responsibility 101," *Newsday,* June 10, 1992, page 75.

442. Ventura, Michael, "Notes on Three Erections," anthologized in Harding, Christopher, ed., *Wingspan: Inside the Men's Movement,* New York: St. Martin's Press, 1992, pages 43–51.

443. Daly, Mary, *Websters' First New Intergalactic Wickedary of the English Language,* Boston: Beacon Press, 1987, page xv.

444. Sommers, Christina Hoff, *Who Stole Feminism?,* New York: Simon & Schuster, 1994, page 66.

445. Taylor, John, "Are You Politically Correct?," *New York,* January 21, 1991, pages 32–40; and Sommers, Christina Hoff, *Who Stole Feminism?,* New York: Simon & Schuster, 1994, page 66.

446. Costello, Michael, "New Feminist Findings Show What a Louse I Am," *Lewiston Morning Tribune,* December 28, 1991, page 10A.

447. Ibid.

448. Masters, Kim, article in *Vanity Fair,* November 1993, page 170, quoted in Sommers, Christina Hoff, *Who Stole Feminism?,* New York: Simon & Schuster, 1994, page 45.

449. Solanas, Valerie, *The SCUM Manifesto,* London: Olympia Press, 1971.

450. Cooper, Marc, "Chastity 101," *The Village Voice,* June 7, 1994, page 31.

451. Dworkin, Andrea, *Letters from a War Zone,* Chicago: Lawrence Hill Books, 1993, page 119.

452. Asmus, Kristen, "Blaming the Dress," *Colorado Daily,* October 27–29, 1989, page 13, quoted in D'Souza, Dinesh, *Illiberal Education: The Politics of Race and Sex on Campus,* New York: Free Press, 1991, page 11.

453. Morgan, Robin, "Theory and Practice: Pornography and Rape," anthologized in Lederer, Laura, ed., *Take Back the Night,* New York: William Morrow & Co., 1980, page 136.

454. Prince, Virginia, "Sex, Gender, and Semantics," *Journal of Sex Research 21,* 1985, pages 92–96, cited in: Frank, Francine Wattman, and Treichler, Paula A., *Language, Gender, and Professional Writing,* New York: Modern Language Association of America, 1989, page 10.

455. Dworkin, Andrea, *Our Blood: Prophecies and Discourses on Sexual Politics,* New York: Harper & Row, 1976, page 43.

456. "Definitions," handout published by the Smith College Office of Student Affairs, 1990.

457. Frank, Francine Wattman, and Treichler, Paula A., *Language, Gender, and Professional Writing,* New York: Modern Language Association of America, 1989, page 17.

458. Thompson, Becky, quoted in D'Souza, Dinesh, *Illiberal Education: The Politics of Race and Sex on Campus,* New York: Free Press, 1991, page 8.

459. Danquah, Meri Nana-Ama, "Hanging Up on Phone Sex," *The Washington Post,* June 13, 1993, page C1.

460. Morgan, Robin, "I Read the News Today, Oh Girl," *Ms.,* May–June 1992, page 1.

461. Funk, Rus Ervin, *Stopping Rape: A Challenge for Men,* Philadelphia: New Society Publishers, 1993, page 9.

462. Metch, Margie, quoted in Gutman, Stephanie, "Date Rape: Does Anyone Really Know What It Is?," *Playboy,* October, 1990, pages 48ff.

463. Noble, Vicki, "A Helping Hand from the Guys," anthologized in Hagan, Kay Leigh, *Women Respond to the Men's Movement,* San Francisco: Pandora/HarperSanFrancisco, 1992, pages 102–3.

464. "Report of the New Jersey Supreme Court Committee on Sexual Harassment," *New Jersey Law Journal,* April 1994, "Notices to the Bar" section, page 2.

465. "Our Times: Sexual Politics," *Life*, April 1992, page 18.

466. Muelenhard, Charlene N., PhD, and Schrag, Jennifer L., "Nonviolent Sexual Coercion," anthologized in Parrot, Andrea, and Bechhofer, Laurie, *Acquaintance Rape: The Hidden Crime*, page 122.

467. "Sexual Harassment College Policy," *Official Survival Handbook*, Yellow Springs, Ohio: Antioch College Student Government, 1993–94, page 12.

468. Beauvoir, Simone de, interview with Alice Schwartzer, *Marie-Claire*, October 1976, page 152, translated by Elaine Marks. Quoted in Kramarae, Cheris, and Treichler, Paula A., *A Feminist Dictionary*, Boston: Pandora Press, 1985, page 414.

469. *What You Should Know About Sexual Harassment*, Princeton, N.J.: SHARE, cited in Roiphe, Katie, *The Morning After: Sex, Fear, and Feminism on Campus*, Boston: Little, Brown and Co., 1993, page 87.

470. Funk, Rus Ervin, *Stopping Rape: A Challenge for Men*, Philadelphia: New Society Publishers, 1993, page 9.

471. "Sexual Harassment College Policy," *Official Survival Handbook*, Yellow Springs, Ohio: Antioch College Student Government, 1993–94, page 15.

472. McDowell, Josh, *It Can Happen to You: What You Need to Know About Preventing and Recovering from Date Rape*, Dallas: Word Publishing, 1991, page 36.

473. "Free Expression at Work," editorial, *St. Petersburg Times*, November 10, 1991, page 2D.

474. Hamilton, Alan, *Sexual Identity and Gender Identity Glossary*, Open Software Foundation, prepublication copy, distributed online via the Internet, December 19, 1992.

475. Harvard-Radcliffe Undergraduate Council, "Response to the Report of the Date Rape Task Force," Cambridge, Mass.: Harvard University, May 6, 1992, cited by American Gender Society consultant Adam Smith in a special report, February 15, 1994.

476. Vest, Jason, "The School That's Put Sex to the Test: At Antioch, a Passionate Reaction to Consent Code," *The Washington Post*, December 3, 1993, page G1.

477. May, Larry, and Hughes, John C., "Is Sexual Harassment Coercive?," anthologized in Wall, Edmund, *Sexual Harassment: Confrontations and Decisions*, Buffalo, N.Y.: Prometheus Books, 1992, page 65.

478. Hamilton, Alan, *Sexual Identity and Gender Identity Glossary,* Open Software Foundation, prepublication copy, distributed online via the Internet, December 19, 1992.

479. Moore, Suzanne, "Sexual Discourse," *The Guardian,* October 5, 1993, page 11.

480. Taylor, John, "Men on Trial," *New York,* December 16, 1991, page 34.

481. Banville, John, *The Irish Times,* January 31, 1994, page 12.

482. Dworkin, Andrea, quoted in Stoltenberg, John, "Pornography and Male Supremacy," *Refusing to Be a Man: Essays on Sex and Justice,* New York: Meridian, 1990, page 148.

483. Safire, William, "Meet My Whatsit," *The New York Times Magazine,* November 9, 1986, page 10.

484. Iazzetto, Demetria, PhD, "What's Happening with Women and Body Image?," *The Network News,* a publication of the National Women's Health Network, May 1992, page 1.

485. "Definitions," handout published by the Smith College Office of Student Affairs, 1990.

486. Wong, Wylie, " 'Fat Feminists' Make a Splash at Crowning of Seafair Queen," *The Seattle Times,* July 28, 1993, page B1.

487. Snider, Jerry, "The Zuni Man-Woman: Native America's Third Gender: An Interview with Will Roscoe," *Magical Blend,* January, 1992, page 42, quoted in Noble, Vicki, "A Helping Hand from the Guys," anthologized in Hagan, Kay Leigh, *Women Respond to the Men's Movement,* San Francisco: Pandora/HarperSanFrancisco, 1992, page 103.

488. Strauss, Susan, with Espeland, Pamela, *Sexual Harassment and Teens: A Program for Positive Change,* Minneapolis: Free Spirit Publishing Co., 1992, page 8.

489. Cooper, Kenneth C., "The Six Levels of Sexual Harassment," anthologized in A. Pablo Iannone, *Contemporary Moral Controversies in Business,* New York: Oxford University Press, 1989, page 190, cited in Wall, Edmund, "The Definition of Sexual Harassment," anthologized in Wall, Edmund, *Sexual Harassment,* Buffalo, N.Y.: Prometheus Books, 1992, page 71.

490. Morris, Stephanie, letter to the editor, *The New York Times,* January 19, 1994, page A20; Biagi, Paul, quoted in "Rift Along Sexual Lines After Bobbitt Verdict," *The New York Times,* January 23, 1994, page 20.

491. Parrot, Andrea, PhD, *Coping with Date Rape and Acquaintance Rape,* New York: Rosen Publishing Group, 1993, page 24.

492. Silverman, Bruce, "Descent Into Drum Time with the Sons of Orpheus," anthologized in Harding, Christopher, ed., *Wingspan: Inside the Men's Movement,* New York: St. Martin's Press, 1992, page 215.

493. Adler, Jerry, "Heeding the Call of the Drums," *Newsweek,* June 24, 1991, page 52.

494. Steinfels, Peter, "Female Concept of God Is Shaking Protestants," *The New York Times,* May 14, 1994, page 8.

495. "Gay Babies," *Heterodoxy,* January 1994, page 1.

496. Rich, Frank, "The Girl Next Door," *The New York Times,* February 20, 1994, section 4, page 13.

497. Leo, John, "What Qualifies as Sexual Harassment?," *U.S. News & World Report,* August 13, 1990, page 17; and "Slow Times at Amherst High," *Harper's,* April 1991, page 32.

498. Skinner, John, "Basting the Baby," *The Vancouver Sun,* May 15, 1993, page B1.

499. Strauss, Susan, with Espeland, Pamela, *Sexual Harassment and Teens: A Program for Positive Change,* Minneapolis: Free Spirit Publishing Co., 1992, page 8.

500. Bolus, Josephine, "Teaching Teens About Condoms," *RN,* March 1994, pages 44ff.

501. Hellman, Peter, "Crying Rape: The Politics of Date Rape on Campus," *New York,* March 8, 1993, page 36; and Crichton, Sarah, "Sexual Correctness: Has It Gone Too Far?," *Newsweek,* October 25, 1993, page 52.

502. Adams, Carol J., *The Sexual Politics of Meat: A Feminist-Vegetarian Critical Theory,* New York: Continuum Publishing Co., 1990, pages 13, 187–88.

503. Hamilton, Alan, *Sexual Identity and Gender Identity Glossary,* Open Software Foundation, prepublication copy, distributed online via the Internet, December 19, 1992.

504. Costello, Michael, "New Feminist Findings Show What a Louse I Am," *Lewiston Morning Tribune,* December 28, 1991, page 10A.

505. Kors, Alan Charles, "Harassment Policies in the University," anthologized in Wall, Edmund, *Sexual Harassment: Confrontations and Decisions,* Buffalo, N.Y.: Prometheus Books, 1992, page 45.

506. Adler, Jerry, "Drums, Sweat and Tears," *Newsweek,* June 24, 1991, page 51.

507. Paul, Ellen Frankel, "Bared Buttocks and Federal Cases," anthologized in Wall, Edmund, *Sexual Harassment: Confrontations and Decisions,* Buffalo, N.Y.: Prometheus Books, 1992, page 153.

508. Ringle, Ken, "Wife-Beating Claims Called Out of Bounds," *The Washington Post,* January 31, 1993, page A1; Cobb, Jean, "A Super Bowl–Battered Women Link?" *American Journalism Review,* May 1993, page 35; "Football's Day of Dread," *Wall Street Journal,* February 5, 1993, page A10; and Walker, Laura, quoted by Bob Hohler of *The Boston Globe* in an interview with Christina Hoff Sommers; all cited in Sommers, Christina Hoff, *Who Stole Feminism?,* New York: Simon & Schuster, 1994, pages 189–92.

509. Dworkin, Andrea, *Our Blood: Prophecies and Discourses on Sexual Politics,* New York: Harper & Row, 1976, page 20.

510. Haederle, Michael, "Homage or Ripoff?," *Minneapolis Star Tribune,* May 11, 1994, Page 1E; Skenazy, Lenore, "Dump the Toxic Parents and Get Centered on the New Age," *Calgary Herald,* December 12, 1993, page B7; and Sowers, Leslie, "Going Native: Just a Trend, Heartfelt Seeking—or Cultural Theft?," *The Houston Chronicle,* September 12, 1993, "Lifestyle" section, page 1.

511. Cline, Sally, *Women, Passion and Celibacy* (originally published in the U.K. under the title *Women, Celibacy and Passion*), New York: Carol Southern Books, 1993, page 7.

512. Weitz, Matt, "Beats of Different Drummers," *The Dallas Morning News,* September 5, 1993, page 1F.

513. Adler, Jerry, "Heeding the Call of the Drums," *Newsweek,* June 24, 1991, page 52.

514. Stanton, Doug, "Inward, Ho!," *Esquire,* October 1991, page 118.

515. Jastrab, Joseph, "Every Man's Story, Every Man's Truth," anthologized in Harding, Christopher, ed., *Wingspan: Inside the Men's Movement,* New York: St. Martin's Press, 1992, page 220.

516. Harding, Christopher, ed., *Wingspan: Inside the Men's Movement,* New York: St. Martin's Press, 1992, page xxi.

517. Adler, Jerry, "Drums, Sweat and Tears," *Newsweek,* June 24, 1991, page 49.

518. Langelan, Martha J., *Back Off!,* New York: Fireside/Simon & Schuster, 1993, page 348.

519. Baber, Asa, "The 1991 Low-Risk Dating Kit," *Playboy*, April 1991, page 34.

520. "Conference on Latest Sex Research Slated," New Jersey regional news, United Press International, April 14, 1982.

521. Miller, Casey, and Swift, Kate, "What About New Human Pronouns?," *Current*, number 138, pages 43–48, cited by Baron, Dennis, *Grammar and Gender*, New Haven: Yale University Press, 1986, pages 206–12.

522. Sommers, Christina Hoff, *Who Stole Feminism?*, New York: Simon & Schuster, 1994, page 50.

523. Ellicott, Susan, "Talmud Sex Lesson Ends in the Courts," *Sunday Times*, London: May 15, 1994, "Overseas News" Section.

524. Coady, Elizabeth, "Can You Spare Five Minutes a Day? Book Says It'll Help Promote Equality," *The Atlanta Journal and Constitution*, October 22, 1992, page 5.

525. Shalit, Ruth, "Romper Room," *The New Republic*, March 29, 1993, pages 13ff.

526. Henley, Nancy, *Body Politics: Power, Sex and Nonverbal Communication*, New York: Touchstone Books, Simon & Schuster, 1986, page 123.

527. Kipnis, Aaron R., PhD, "The Blessings of the Green Man," anthologized in Harding, Christopher, ed., *Wingspan: Inside the Men's Movement*, New York: St. Martin's Press, 1992, pages 161–65.

528. Koss, Mary P., "Changed Lives: The Psychological Impact of Sexual Harassment," anthologized in Paludi, Michele A., *Ivory Power: Sexual Harassment on Campus*, Albany: State University of New York Press, 1990, page 75.

529. Wikler, Daniel, and Wikler, Norma J., "Turkey-Baster Babies: The Demedicalization of Artificial Insemination," *The Milbank Quarterly*, March 22, 1991, pages 5ff.

530. Fausto-Sterling, Anne, "How Many Sexes Are There?," *The New York Times*, March 12, 1993, page A29.

531. Hicks, Cherrill, "They Took My Foreskin, and I Want It Back," *The Independent*, August 3, 1993, page 11.

532. Ibid.

533. Kelly, Sean, and Rogers, Rosemary, *Saints Preserve Us!*, New York: Random House, 1993, page 276.

534. Rule, Jane, *The Hot-Eyed Moderate,* Tallahassee, Fla.: Naiad Press, 1985, cited in Silva, Rosemary, *Lesbian Quotations,* Boston: Alyson Publications, 1993, page 152.

535. "Current Quotations," Associated Press, December 13, 1989.

536. Based on views expressed by Dale Spender in *Women of Ideas and What Men Have Done to Them,* London: Routledge and Kegan Paul, 1982, page 341, cited in Kramarae, Cheris, and Treichler, Paula A., *A Feminist Dictionary,* Boston: Pandora Press, 1985, page 362.

537. Parrot, Andrea, PhD, *Coping with Date Rape and Acquaintance Rape,* New York: Rosen Publishing Group, 1993, page 13.

538. Spender, Dale, *Man Made Language,* London: Pandora Press, 1980, page 182.

539. Dworkin, Andrea, quoted in Hamill, Pete, "Woman on the Verge of a Legal Breakdown," *Playboy,* January 1993, pages 138ff.

540. Elvin, John, "Inside the Beltway," *The Washington Times,* February 13, 1990, page A6.

541. Baron, Dennis, *Grammar and Gender,* New Haven: Yale University Press, 1986, page 206.

542. Blair, Nancy, quoted in Corrigan, Patricia, "Tiny Goddess Serves as Large Role Model," *St. Louis Post-Dispatch,* April 10, 1993, page 3C.

543. Graywing, Carol, quoted in Ruttan, Susan, "Female God Empowering," *Calgary Herald,* July 4, 1992, page C13.

544. Hentoff, Nat, "Sexual Harassment by Francisco Goya," *The Washington Post,* December 27, 1991, page A21.

545. MacKinnon, Catharine A., *Only Words,* Cambridge, Mass.: Harvard University Press, 1993, quoted by Hentoff, Nat, in "The Public Rape of Catharine MacKinnon," *The Village Voice,* January 4, 1994, page 16.

546. Funk, Rus Ervin, *Stopping Rape: A Challenge for Men,* Philadelphia: New Society Publishers, 1993, page 8.

547. MacKinnon, Catharine A., quoted in Bennett, Catherine, "Portrait: A Prophet and Porn," *The Guardian,* May 27, 1994, page T20.

548. Dibbell, Julian, "A Rape in Cyberspace," *The Village Voice,* December 12, 1993.

549. Ferguson, Ann, "A Transitional Female Sexual Morality," anthologized in *Feminist Frameworks: Alternative Theoretical Accounts of the Rela-*

*tions Between Women and Men,* New York: McGraw Hill, 1993, page 503.

550. "Talking Dirty," editorial, *The New Republic,* November 4, 1991, page 7.

551. Bly, Robert, quoted in Harding, Christopher, ed., *Wingspan: Inside the Men's Movement,* New York: St. Martin's Press, 1992, page 9.

552. Budapest, Zsuzsanna E., *The Goddess in the Office: A Personal Energy Guide for the Spiritual Warrior at Work,* San Francisco: HarperSanFrancisco, 1993, pages 1–2.

553. Kramarae, Cheris, and Treichler, Paula A., *A Feminist Dictionary,* Boston: Pandora Press, 1985, page 487.

554. Pellow-McCauley, Theresa, *The Peacemaker,* number 32, January 1979, pages 2–3, cited in Baron, Dennis, *Grammar and Gender,* New Haven: Yale University Press, 1986, page 206.

555. Dworkin, Andrea, *Our Blood: Prophecies and Discourses on Sexual Politics,* New York: Harper & Row, 1976, page 21.

556. Goldfield, Bina, *The Efemcipated English Handbook,* New York: Westover Press, 1983, page 119.

557. Snider, Jerry, "The Zuni Man-Woman: Native America's Third Gender: An Interview with Will Roscoe," *Magical Blend,* January, 1992, page 42, quoted in Noble, Vicki, "A Helping Hand from the Guys," anthologized in Hagan, Kay Leigh, *Women Respond to the Men's Movement,* San Francisco: Pandora/HarperSanFrancisco, 1992, page 103.

558. Baron, Dennis, *Grammar and Gender,* New Haven: Yale University Press, 1986, page 188.

559. Sommers, Christina Hoff, *Who Stole Feminism?,* New York: Simon & Schuster, 1994, page 37.

560. Alicen, Debbie, "Intertextuality: The Language of Lesbian Relationships," *Trivia,* fall 1983, page 6, as cited in Kramarae, Cheris, and Treichler, Paula A., *A Feminist Dictionary,* Boston: Pandora Press, 1985, page 505.

561. Clarke, Cheryl, "Lesbianism: An Act of Resistance," anthologized in Moraga, Cherríe, and Anzaldúa, Gloria, *This Bridge Called My Back: Writings by Radical Women of Color,* New York: Kitchen Table: Women of Color Press, 1983, page 131.

562. Quigley, Paxton, *Armed & Female,* New York: St. Martin's Paperbacks, 1990, pages xx, 46, and 47; and "A Call to Arms," *People,* January 10, 1994, pages 60ff.

563. O'Connor, Colleen, "Women's Self-Defense: Big Business," *The Dallas Morning News,* October 24, 1993, page 4F.

564. Kors, Alan Charles, "Harassment Policies in the University," anthologized in Wall, Edmund, *Sexual Harassment: Confrontations and Decisions,* Buffalo, N.Y.: Prometheus Books, 1992, page 45.

565. Alicen, Debbie, "Intertextuality: The Language of Lesbian Relationships," *Trivia,* fall 1983, page 6, quoted in Kramarae, Cheris, and Treichler, Paula A., *A Feminist Dictionary,* Boston: Pandora Press, 1985, page 505.

566. *Random House Webster's College Dictionary,* New York: Random House, 1991, page 1532.

567. Pellow-McCauley, Theresa, *The Peacemaker,* number 32, January 1979, pages 2–3, cited in Baron, Dennis, *Grammar and Gender,* New Haven: Yale University Press, 1986, page 206.

568. Edwards, Margaret, "But Does the New Woman Really Want the New Man?," *Working Woman,* May 1985, pages 54ff.; Laake, Deborah, "Wormboys," article in *The Washington City Paper,* cited in Edwards, ibid.; and Ehrenreich, Barbara, "A Feminists' View of the New Man," *The New York Times,* May 20, 1984, section 6, page 36.

569. Warshaw, Robin, *I Never Called It Rape: The* Ms. *Report on Recognizing, Fighting and Surviving Date and Acquaintance Rape,* New York: HarperPerennial, 1988, page 156.

570. Wolf, Naomi, *Fire with Fire,* New York: Random House, 1993, page 116.

571. Solanas, Valerie, *The SCUM Manifesto,* London: Olympia Press, 1971, page 4.

572. Estrich, Susan, *Real Rape,* Cambridge, Mass.: Harvard University Press, 1987, page 102, quoted by Roiphe, Katie, in *The Morning After: Sex, Fear, and Feminism on Campus,* Boston: Little, Brown and Co., 1993, page 60.

# ACKNOWLEDGMENTS

The compilation of a book designed to codify and redefine the sexual behavior of a whole generation is no small task, and, if we have been up to it, it is because of the contributions of many people—friends, colleagues, scholars, researchers, and authors whose works paved the way for ours.

Above all, we wish to thank the American Gender Society, who made its Annandale-on-Hudson headquarters a second home for us during the course of our work, and the members of its generous and highly skilled Special Projects Task Force—Gina Baroni, Holly Baroni, Ann Burgund, Astrid Cravens, Gwyneth Jones Cravens, Susan Crespi, Helen Escobar, Bill Effros, Tad Floridis, and Cheryl Moch. We're grateful, too, to the Society's international network of consultants, who were there for us whenever we needed them. Jane Aaron, Skip Blumberg, David Kaestle, Adam Smith, and Dia Snyder were particularly helpful, as was Dr. Norman B. Stiles, director of the American Gender Society's Center for Research on Self-Deprecating Humor.

Groundbreaking work by Jerry Adler, Sarah Crichton, Andrew Ferguson, Nancy Gibbs, Kay Leigh Hagan, Alan Hamilton, Christopher Harding, Nat Hentoff, John Leo, Katie Roiphe, Doug Stanton, and John Taylor informed our research, and we offer them our gratitude. We also wish to thank the Modern Language Association, whose identification of "malicious humor directed against feminists" as a particularly pernicious form of harassment saved us from more than one embarassing error.

Not only did the extraordinary scholarship and insight of linguists Cheris Kramarae and Paula A. Treichler, authors of *A Feminist Dictionary,* prove invaluable, but their innovative use of the dictionary format also inspired many of our editorial decisions. The brilliant research conducted by Christina Hoff Sommers of Clark University—much of which is summarized in her book *Who Stole Feminism?*—has also greatly enriched our project.

*The Official Sexually Correct Dictionary and Dating Guide* would have no reason for being, of course, were it not for the remarkable group of educators, philosophers, legal scholars, cultural engineers, and political and sexual theorists who dreamed up and helped popularize the concepts described in its pages. In a very real sense, this is their dictionary, and words are inadequate to express our feelings about all they have contributed, not just to our book, but to society. They are far too numerous to credit individually here (their names are listed in the Source Notes immediately preceding these acknowledgments), but we would be remiss if we failed to pay special tribute to a few who, perhaps, continue to receive less than their fair share of public recognition: the Womyn of Antioch; the sex equity specialists of the Minnesota Department of Education; Bina Goldfield, editor of *The Efemcipated English Handbook;* and Carol J. Adams, author of *The Sexual Politics of Meat.*

We'd like to express our gratitude to Lauren Attinello and Russ Heath, who created many of the fine illustrations that accompany the entries in our dictionary; and to Jordan Schaps and Tohru Nakamura, the art director and photographer responsible for the cover of our U.S. edition.

We are especially grateful for the invaluable help, advice, and friendship extended to us by David Rosenthal, our editor and publisher in the United States, and by Val Hudson, who, almost single-handedly, made our U.K. edition a reality. Very special appreciation is also due Ed Victor, our agent; Robert Bull, our designer; and everyone at Random House, Villard Books, HarperCollins, and Ed Victor, Ltd., who contributed their hard work and encouragement to this enterprise. In particular, we'd like to thank Diane Reverand, Jacqueline Deval, Patricia Abdale, Richard Aquan, Gail Blackwell, Filomena Boniello, Susan DiSesa, Joe Elms, Harry Evans, Deborah Foley, Mary Hahn Hendon, Sophie Hicks, Gerry Hollingsworth, Mitchell Ivers, Heather Kilpatrick, Antonia Kingsland, Phil Lewis, Jennifer Lynes, Kate Parrish, Beth Pearson, Maggie Phillips, Rosanna Pugh, Marcia Lane Purcell, Jamie Sims, Chris Stamey, Walter Weintz, Karen Whitlock, and Janet Wygal.

And finally, our most heartfelt apologies go out to all those whom we may have offended by the very act of setting words down on paper. Had we learned, before signing irrevocable publishing contracts, that a Swarthmore College women's studies seminar had condemned Naomi Wolf for committing a similar act of authorship on the grounds that her behavior was "exclusionary to women who cannot read," we would almost surely have abandoned our project.

# ILLUSTRATION CREDITS

**Antioch College Community Government:** page 62

**AP/Wide World:** pages 3, 17, 25, 27, 41, 50, 53, 66, 75 (top), 77, 82, 83, 87, 93, 104, 119, 121, 126, 128, 137, 139, 150, 159, 164, 182

**Lauren Attinello:** pages 7, 16, 28, 42, 58, 101, 108, 147, 167, 172

**Chastity, U.S.A.:** pages 11, 21

**Dover Publications:** pages 8, 19, 75 (bottom), 76, 81, 99 (top and bottom)

**Russ Heath:** pages 51, 52, 74, 133, 169

**Russ Heath and Susan Crespi:** pages 24, 32, 59, 63, 117, 127, 138, 141, 149, 153, 176, 186

**New York Public Library Picture Collection:** pages 13, 22, 33, 40 (bottom), 96, 103 (top and bottom), 110, 156, 163, 178

**Philadelphia Museum of Art:** page 9

*Random House Dictionary:* page 34

**Edwina Sandys:** page 23

**Alan Shaffer:** page 146

# ABOUT THE AUTHORS

HENRY BEARD was a cofounder and one of the original editors of the *National Lampoon* during its heyday in the 1970s, and he would certainly apologize for that publication's relentless sexism and gross gender insensitivity if the very act of apologizing were not itself a blatant example of the mother-dishonoring male guilt so rightly condemned by feminist author Starhawk. He went on to parlay his mythic celebration of female negation (love) of the sea, the slopes, the links, the land, the table, and the rod and reel into a bestselling series of satirical dictionaries (*Sailing, Skiing, Golfing, Gardening, Cooking,* and *Fishing*) of which there are currently over two million copies in print. His career as a writer of humorous books subsequently received a significant boost when he was fortunate enough to be able to get in touch, in rapid succession, with a number of potent—and from a commercial standpoint, highly exploitable—mythopoetic archetypes dwelling within his psyche, including the Pig Within (*Miss Piggy's Guide to Life*); the Cat Within (*French for Cats, Advanced French for Exceptional Cats,* and *Poetry for Cats*); the Wolf that Suckled Romulus and Remus Within (*Latin for All Occasions,* and *Latin for Even More Occasions*); and Irons, Woods, and Putter John (*The Official Exceptions to the Rules of Golf, Mulligan's Laws,* and the forthcoming *Leslie Nielsen's Stupid Little Golf Book,* written with the deeply insensitive star of the *Naked Gun* movies). Beard is the coauthor, with Christopher Cerf, of *The Official Politically Correct Dictionary and Handbook,* a revolutionary volume to which he attributes his newfound awareness of the critical importance of issues that he has heretofore felt were little more than easy targets for cheap, but financially rewarding, satire.

•

Despite a lifetime spent as a human being who happens to be penised (an accident of birth which, according to Brandeis University professor Becky Thompson, makes him a sexist "whether intentionally or not"), CHRISTOPHER CERF hopes that his coauthorship with Henry Beard of *The Official Sexually Correct Dictionary and Dating Guide* and its bestselling predecessor, *The Official Politically Correct Dictionary and Handbook,* will convince readers to forgive him for his lifelong membership in the Genital Power Elite. Such forgiveness will require his critics to overlook many missteps: Cerf's multiple Grammy- and Emmy-winning musical contributions to the television program *Sesame Street,* which, despite well-meaning attempts to be multicultural and wholesome, offends essayist Katha Pollitt because several of its principal characters are portrayed by male puppeteers; his willingness to accept the unabashedly sexist title of "chairman" of the Modern Library; his collaboration with fellow recovering circumcision survivor Victor Navasky on *The Experts Speak,* a "compendium of authoritative disinformation" that seeks, in the guise of lighthearted humor, to validate concepts, such as "truth" and "rationality," that men have used for centuries to oppress women; his conception and coeditorship of *Not the New York Times,* a satiric celebration of the last great American newspaper to stop refusing to allow the honorific "Ms." to appear on its pages; and his coauthorship, with Henry Beard, Sarah Durkee, and Sean Kelly, of *The Book of Sequels,* which—like many of his other works—was written in English, a language discredited by Patricia A. Harney and Charlene L. Muelenhard for its role in creating a "rape-conducive environment."

## ABOUT THE AMERICAN GENDER SOCIETY

THE AMERICAN GENDER SOCIETY was founded by residents of Annandale-on-Hudson, New York, who, while attending a pro-counter-hegemonic-speech consciousness-raising session held there in 1993 by the American Hyphen Society, heard about University of Massachusetts philosopher Ann Ferguson's dream of a future paradise in which "it would no longer matter what biological sex individuals had," and decided to set about making it a reality. The Society's membership has vowed not to rest until the curse of essentialism—the stubborn belief in the "fictive" categories "man" and "woman"—has been eliminated from the planet and the word "Gender" in their organization's title has been rendered meaningless. In the meantime, the Society has committed itself to such impressive interim goals as the banning from public display of art "masterpieces" featuring nude women; the institution of July 20 as an official holiday celebrating St. Uncumber (who prayed that she might become physically repellant in order to avoid having to marry the King of Sicily); the establishment of hand drumming as the communications medium of choice for individuals on dates; and the placement on the walls of every home and school of a "Pet Your Dog . . . Not Your Date" poster (a mission that, unfortunately, has put them at odds with the animal rights movement). The American Gender Society's official poem is T. S. Eliot's "The Hollow Men," which also serves as the source of its inspiring motto:

> *This is the way the world ends*
> *Not with a bang but a whimper.*